Waiting

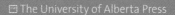

The University of Alberta Press

RONA ALTROWS
& JULIE SEDIVY
Editors

Waiting

An Anthology of Essays

Published by

The University of Alberta Press
Ring House 2
Edmonton, Alberta, Canada   T6G 2E1
www.uap.ualberta.ca

LIBRARY AND ARCHIVES CANADA
CATALOGUING IN PUBLICATION

Waiting (Edmonton, Alta.)
     Waiting : an anthology of essays /
Rona Altrows & Julie Sedivy, editors.

(Robert Kroetsch series)
Issued in print and electronic formats.
ISBN 978–1–77212–383–8 (softcover).—
ISBN 978–1–77212–418–7 (EPUB).—
ISBN 978–1–77212–419–4 (Kindle).—
ISBN 978–1–77212–420–0 (PDF)

     1. Canadian essays (English)—
21st century. 2. Waiting (Philosophy).
I. Altrows, Rona, 1948–, editor II. Sedivy,
Julie, editor III. Title. IV. Series:
Robert Kroetsch series

PS8373.1.W35 2018   C814'.608
C2018–902563–8

First edition, second printing, 2018.
First printed and bound in Canada by
Houghton Boston Printers, Saskatoon,
Saskatchewan.
Copyediting and proofreading by
Meaghan Craven.

A volume in the Robert Kroetsch Series.

The University of Alberta Press is
committed to protecting our natural
environment. As part of our efforts,
this book is printed on Enviro Paper: it
contains 100% post-consumer recycled
fibres and is acid- and chlorine-free.

The University of Alberta Press gratefully
acknowledges the support received for its
publishing program from the Government
of Canada, the Canada Council for the
Arts, and the Government of Alberta
through the Alberta Media Fund.

For Lucy and Grace, my beacons of hope.

   —RA

For Ian, who was—and always is—worth the wait.

   —JS

___ Contents

Moment

Soul

Irretrievable

Guts

⎯ Preface Rona Altrows & Julie Sedivy

We do it in the crib, at the airport, at the graduation ceremony, in hospice. At every stage of life, and in umpteen circumstances, we find ourselves waiting. Waiting is common to all ethnicities, all social and economic conditions. Even in our hyper-efficient age, when we are taught that every moment should be filled with the productivity of *doing*, we wait. At every turn, the flow of our lives is interrupted by forces outside our control. But these periods of suspended time are far from empty; what happens within them reveals and shapes us. Waiting may feel like pain or pleasure, may bring us agonizing apprehension or joyful expectancy or both. It may last for a brief but intense moment, or stretch out over lifetimes. We may wait alone, or collectively. In some languages, the word for waiting is also the word for hope.

In this anthology of personal essays, thirty-two writers present their own encounters with waiting and share their lived experiences of this universal human phenomenon. The book is divided into six parts: *Burgeoning*, *Scope*, *Moment*, *Soul*, *Irretrievable*, and *Guts*.

In *Burgeoning*, writers explore how travelling the path from childhood innocence to adult experience involves much standing still, whether it's the frozen dread of a child waiting for adult events she can't control, the bristling impatience of a teen waiting to seize the reins of her life, or the transformation of a young man into an artist as he reflects on the creativity that dwells in suspended time. Growing and waiting, so inextricably woven together, continue throughout life, as we discover from a retired teacher who continues to learn from his long-ago students.

In *Scope*, writers grapple with the sometimes wide cultural, historic, and geographic reach of waiting. Individuals' experiences of waiting are embedded within broader communities and cultures, intertwined with language, art, and politics. In these essays, waiting is a serious business and cannot be accomplished quickly or resolved with certainty.

In *Moment*, writers dive into the kind of waiting rooted in the here and now—on the threshold of spring, in the minutes before a grim diagnosis, in pregnancy, before an interview, at the tailor shop to pick up alterations.

The essays in *Soul* focus on waiting as it relates to the self. A child in care yearns for family love and a sense of belonging, a writer with disabilities embraces slowness and finds his voice, an insomniac separates her private and professional personae to reflect on her life. Deep frustrations of waiting, surprising pleasures of waiting, discovery of what the wait has been for and how it can be moved through—all find a place in *Soul*.

Irretrievable takes us to places of waiting and deep loss, as writers recount their feelings about the last days of a mother, the recent death of a father, the theft of a woman's sexual agency, a traumatic rescue attempt by a daughter, the funeral of a less-than-perfect ex-husband.

In *Guts*, we learn of acts of bravery. A writer living with chronic illness becomes a seasoned waiting-room denizen. A victimized person is surprised to learn the identity of her deliverer. A daughter supports her mother through chronic illness with careful listening, uncensored conversation, shared laughter. A terminally ill teenager uses her short remaining time to contribute art, humour, and love. A worrier confronts her phobias. An army spouse, herself a veteran, awaits her beloved's upcoming dangerous deployment.

Waiting, like breathing, gives rhythmic structure to our lives. Like breathing, it is rarely written about. The writers of these essays are Zen masters who turn our attention to the details of the human experiences that take place in the in-out, in-out, in-out moments of waiting.

── Acknowledgements

THE IDEA FOR THIS BOOK struck me while I waited for a train. My family agreed that I was on to something and have never flagged in their support of the project. I am grateful to them. In Julie Sedivy I found an editing partner with commitment, competence, compassion, and a great big brain. It has been a delight to work with her. Thank you, Julie.

—*Rona*

⋮ A hunk of joyous gratitude goes to Rona Altrows for sparking the idea for this anthology and inviting me to join her in fanning its flames. It's been a deep pleasure and privilege to work with someone of her intelligence, wit, precision, and humanity. Ian Graham, as always, granted me unlimited access to his loving support for this project, simply because I found it worth pursuing. Cafe Fresco in Calgary provided the coffee, food, sunlight, and warm human contact needed to complete my share of the work.

—*Julie*

⋮ We are both grateful to the University of Alberta Press— in particular, Peter Midgley, Cathie Crooks, Mary Lou Roy, and Monika Igali. Thank you to Meaghan Craven for a thorough, thoughtful copyedit. Thank you to Alan Brownoff for the great design and to Alex Pinna for the stunning cover image. Huge thanks to our contributors, who have made *Waiting* the rich and varied anthology it is. And thank you to all who submitted, even those whose work is not included in the book.

Burgeoning

1 — Bill of Fare

SUSAN OLDING

Appetizers
Pimento-stuffed olives
Celery with cream cheese
Julienned carrots chilled in ice water
Angels on horseback
Pigs in blankets

Your career begins early, before your head even clears the
kitchen counter. The crystal dish your mother places in your
hands feels much heavier than you expect. Pressing it to your
chest, you look down at your red patent party shoes, nervous
you might skid on the kitchen's vinyl tile or trip on the lip of the
living-room carpet. Music greets you, music and smoke; clinking
ice cubes and the smells of mingled perfumes. The women's
faces glow. Their dresses rustle like the plumage of exotic birds.
Like birds, the women coo and sing at your offerings, pecking
and cooing while watching you with bright eyes. Someday you
would like to join their dazzling flock. But for now, you observe
them observing you. Passing your plate of savouries, you pause
in front of one guest, whose jewel-encrusted bracelets jingle
when she reaches for a morsel of sausage tucked in a blanket of
pastry. She takes a bite and turns to her companion with shining
lips. Your mouth waters. Your tongue craves the pastry's buttery

caress. You are so hungry. Will anyone offer you a taste? Will anyone notice if you serve yourself? You stand, hip-high, amid the throng of grown-ups. Waiting.

Soup
Cream of mushroom
Chicken noodle
Vegetable beef

Mostly, for your part-time job in the old folks' home, you crouch over a cavernous sink to scrub industrial-sized pots or stand within plumes of dank steam at the service counter, where you dish out Salisbury steak, watery beans, and instant mashed potatoes. But every seventh shift, your boss assigns a special task, such as pushing a snack cart to the residents' rooms or pouring out tea and coffee at their lakeside tables. The residents are eccentric. They shout or whisper their orders and sneer or slip shiny quarters into your palms. Some entertain their families every weekend; others never greet a single visitor. Some play cards in the great room; others do their best to ignore their neighbours. All old people look alike at first—there's no arguing about that. But over time you come to know most of them. Mrs. Mary Harrison is your favourite. Haughty and imperious, one day she shows up at breakfast naked except for her mink and pearls.

You serve them soup, they ask for crackers. *Where are my Saltines? If you please, I'd like a packet of those oyster crackers.* How they lick their lips, craving the salt they are not supposed to eat. Salt, and its evil sidekick, sugar. The snack cart overflows with that stuff. Nothing homemade, nothing "healthy" there—all Rowntree's chocolate and Peek Freans biscuits, and you're not supposed to give those to anyone who's diabetic or on a diet plan. You carry a list of all their names. You are under strictest orders. But this is the generation that survived the

4

Great Depression, not to mention several wars and many years of rationing. They will not go gentle into that dark night. Deaf or no, they hear the rattle of your metal cart even before it exits the elevator; focused, despite their failing vision, they scan their shelves and shuffle through their drawers, searching for trinkets they might use to bribe you. *Just a taste, my dear, just a taste won't hurt*, they say, in tones as wheedling as any toddler's. Waiting all their lives for this small indulgence that the fates deny them.

Salad Bar
Iceberg lettuce
Shredded carrot
Shredded red cabbage
Chopped tomato
Chopped cucumber
Sliced green pepper
Tinned chickpeas
Tinned black olives
Bacon bits
French, Thousand Island, oil and vinegar,
    or blue cheese dressing

At the pizza chain where you go to work at age eighteen, the kitchen is a long narrow corridor, one side lined with ovens and the other a counter for prepping dough and salads. Under the dim yellow lights of a cramped staff bathroom, you change into The Uniform. The Uniform is not a getup that you, or anyone else, would ever wish to wear in public. It starts with a dress, whose puff-sleeved bodice is constructed of a crunchy, white-dotted Swiss that soon stains yellow under the armpits and gapes whenever you bend, the better to show your nonexistent cleavage. The bodice is sewn to a gathered gingham skirt in red or blue that would make even the thinnest girl look broad in the hips. On top of the dress you add a matching gingham apron, tied at the waist; a black velvet choker, like an Edwardian lady's; and a cap.

Cap. That bland and innocent word does nothing to conjure this ruffled, white monstrosity; it's a frilly, poisonous pillowslip that, throughout your shift, drifts lower on your forehead. What is the purpose of this thing? Again and again you push it back into place, again and again it slides towards your nose, wreaking havoc with your hairstyle and leaving you frazzled, frowsy, and pissed off. Still, at least you don't have to pay for it—unlike your shoes, which the restaurant doesn't provide. Yours come from K-Mart—white vinyl slip-ons that you picked up cheap but come to hate for the way they attract and hang onto smells, no matter how often you spray them with Lysol.

Out front, you take your station at an antique hutch and wait for the rush to begin. You roll the knives and forks into paper napkins, count the number of side plates, fill the salt and pepper shakers. In your pocket, you carry the waiter's timeworn tools—an order pad and pencil. Personal computers have not arrived yet; the world is still waiting. You have to do the math yourself.

The name of this place is Mother's. Famous for its family meals, its towering stainless-steel pizza stands, its big pitchers of pop, and its silent black-and-white films that loop continuously on large-size screens, it is also known for its reclaimed furniture, including tables made from ancient sewing machines—tables that rudely scrape the knees of anyone taller than four feet who is foolish enough to try to sit at one. Most people come here for the pizza and the inexpensive beer. The draft is served in heavy glass tankards. You pull them, chilled, from a special fridge and place them strategically on cork-lined trays. These you balance above your head as you dodge unruly children and swerve between the tightly angled tables. Friday nights can be crazy here. Parents and noisy kids; nervous couples on first dates; big, boisterous groups. Guys show up in clusters of eight or ten, already three sheets to the wind, determined to make a pass or pass out in the attempt.

On this particular Friday, your section fills up fast with exactly the kind of rowdy crowd you dread. They lumber in, laughing and catcalling and ogling, then sprawl at one of the larger tables, demanding beer. One guy sneaks a peek up your skirt and gloats when he gets a glimpse of thigh. Another grabs a draft from your tray, almost upending you in the process. Worst is the one who wants to untie your apron. Glazed eyes, red face, slurred words— something isn't right with him. He's not just teasing. He's not just fooling around. He can't take a hint or even a no. He paws at the gingham strings, laughs when you slap his hand away. *Trophy, trophy, trophy!* For all you care, he can have the damned apron, but you're not taking it off here, and you hate his drunken sense of entitlement.

These guys. Treat you like some kind of toy. Think because you're hired to serve them they can do and say whatever they want. Just once, you'd like to answer rudeness with rudeness. Just once, you'd like to get the last word. No. Scrap that. Forget words. They're useless. Right now, you'd like to stab that jerk with a fork.

Up on the screen, Charlie Chaplin plays the Little Tramp. Here on the floor, there's not an empty seat in the place, not a spot to stand at the pizza pickup counter. You scrape leftover crusts into a garbage bin. It's going to be a long night. But at least this group won't stay forever. Thank goodness for the one guy who looks like he has a little sense. *Enough, enough, give her a break*, he says, pulling his friend's hand back, trying to get him to focus on something different. *Let's get some dessert*, he says. *Coffee. Tea.*

Tea. Damn. Those metal pots with their poorly designed spouts, always dripping and spilling and sloshing. There's no predicting where scalding water from one of those things might splash. The saucer, the vinyl tablecloth, the floor, your foot... almost anywhere except the cup.

Wait: to watch with hostile intent.

Hot water can be a weapon.

Who would object? Who would suspect? Everybody knows the direction of those drips is uncontrollable.

The trophy hunter wears jeans. Their heavy fabric will offer just enough but not too much protection.

"Hey!" He jumps. "You spilled on me!"

"I'm *so* sorry." Your eyes make Os; your mouth is a round of spicy pepperoni.

"Nice move," says the quiet one as they pay the bill and beat a hasty exit. Clearing the table later, you find an extra dollar under his plate.

On break you load your salad with black olives, red cabbage, and plenty of blue cheese dressing. Bitter tastes to act as a homeopathic remedy. *It's okay*, you tell yourself, *it's really okay.* You won't be working in this place for long. You're just waiting until it's time for you to kick off those stinky shoes and toss that stupid cap and untie those apron strings forever.

Fish
Oysters on the half shell
Jamaican conch chowder
Steamed mussels
Prawns in batter
Seafood platter

The oyster bar is a cut above. Near the city's waterfront, it is the upstairs, more casual sibling of a fancy seafood restaurant. Here, you wear black shoes, black pants, and a crisp white shirt. Here, you serve columnists and publishers and actors and producers. No gingham, no frilly caps, no crowds of drunken louts. Which is not to say you're safe from all harassment. For starters, take your boss. His name is Jake. He's tall, curly-haired, London-born.

He invites his buddies to join him at the bar. After closing, they drink brandy and smoke Cuban cigars while he comments in Cockney slang on the shape of his servers' asses.

Yours, apparently, is just a touch too wide for Jake's taste. But some of your customers disagree. At any rate, they seem eager to flirt despite your flaws. *Susan*, says one man, peering lasciviously at your nametag through progressive lenses. He turns to his female companion. Both wear wedding rings. *Don't you think that is a beautiful name*, he says. She looks you up and down—a long look. Long, and sharp as a razor clam. *A bit common for my taste*, she says.

To succeed in your duties, you learn to let this and similar insults wash over you like a tide. And after all, it isn't so difficult. Because customers come and go. Your co-workers are the constant. Together they enclose you in a protective shell of camaraderie. Victor and Grant and Mark, fellow servers, back you up when your section overfills and teach you the waiters' tricks and shortcuts. Maggie and, yes, *Sue*, who happen to be a couple, oversee the bar. They know when to tell someone their drink is on the house; they know when it's time to cut somebody off; often they can sniff out those customers who'll try to sneak down the stairway and out the main door without paying.

Even so, this happens. It happens quite a lot. The design of the bar makes it tempting. The bathrooms are downstairs, near the main door. People do have to pee when they drink beer and wine; you can't exactly stop them. And sometimes, when it's busy, instead of returning right away, they stay gone for a longer than usual time. In the midst of the weekend crush, it can take you a while to notice that something's fishy.

Night after night you find yourself clattering out to the street in your clogs. Night after night you race after sheepish or defiant patrons. *Wait, wait, you forgot something*, you shout. For you're the one who suffers when this happens—not Jake, not the restaurant, not the corporation. You pay the bill if they get away, and with all the seafood and wine on these tabs, you certainly can't afford it.

One night, everybody boils. Maggie has to eject two drunks in a row. Three of Victor's tables and one of Mark's try to sneak out without properly settling. And Jake rags on everybody, switching and cancelling shifts without explanation, barking at Grant when he ventures to complain. After close, you cash out, all of you feeling misused.

Who needs this?

What if we all just quit?

You mean all of us at once?

They're never going to treat us any better.

Maggie and I have already made a list of places to apply.

We could quit and not even tell them.

Next weekend, Jake can deal with it all. On his own, the bastard.

Things are moving fast. The rest of them have totalled all their bills; they're sorting their tips. And you, always the slowest to cash out, you're still counting.

Are you with us? Are you coming?

This job pays your rent and tuition. You have no idea if you'll find a better one, or even another one.

They're buttoning their coats. They're heading towards the stairs. You leap to your feet, waving and shouting as if they're yet another group of errant customers.

Wait up!

Meat and Fowl

Pâté maison avec cornichons

Tarte de chèvre

Salade verte

Bacalao

L'entrecôte

Confit de canard

The Basque-inflected restaurant on Baldwin Street serves tapas, wine, and meals. You carry a corkscrew in your apron pocket. The customers do not grope you; your boss does not leer. Like Jake, Alan is English-born, but his accent is less Cockney than Cambridge. Calm and controlled, he never raises his voice at the chef or messes with the schedule. He understands you are a beginner—of course he does—but he assures you they can train you, if you're willing to make a commitment. *Will you work here for at least a year, preferably longer?* He is looking for someone who will stay. *How soon can you start? Friday would be fine; tomorrow would be better. Bien! You will take over for Cassandre, who leaves next week for an extended holiday to visit her family in France.*

Years of reading your mother's *Gourmet* magazines have given you some second-hand knowledge about food. A Book-of-the-Month Club *Encyclopaedia of Wine* has taught you to recognize the names of various grapes. You purchase a new white shirt. You invest in an excellent corkscrew. You memorize the menu. And after your shifts, you sit down with the others to enjoy a delicious *plat du jour* and a tumbler of red or white. Later, you cross the street and mount the steps to your new walk-up apartment. It is the perfect job, *n'est-ce pas?*

En fait, it is not. For here, you don't fit in. And the harder you try, the more you feel like *une poule qui a trouvé un couteau.* A headless chicken. The other servers hail from France. A decade older than you, they work here full-time to support their families, while you are only working part-time to pay your way through school. Still, that's no call for them to treat you like some kind of *enfant stupide.* It shouldn't license them to laugh at your accent or tease you when you trip on the basement stairs. They tell you the flan is all finished then mysteriously find some for their own customers. When the chef backs up on busy nights, they steal your orders for their tables and *c'est dommage* if you complain. Dominique is the worst, with her assessing eyes and her mouth perpetually pursed in that distinctive French pout. "*Ah, quelle vache*—clumsy cow—*elle ne sait rien faire*," you overhear her mutter. Sure enough, you start spilling the soup and forgetting the coffee under her exacting stare.

Hélas, you are so vulnerable, such an awful innocent. It almost makes sense to you when your boss pulls you aside one night at the end of your shift to fire you. *Bien sûr*, you understand. He simply can't afford to keep someone as clumsy and ignorant as you. *Tu n'es pas au courant*. You make more work for the other staff. You lower the overall tone of his fine establishment. Yet somehow this fails to add up, because your tips are as high as Dominique's, and several of the regulars have started to ask if they can sit in your section.

The next day as you return home from class, who should you see walking towards the restaurant but Cassandre. She wears a white shirt, a black skirt, and a furtive expression. *Bonjour*, you say. *I didn't know you were expected back in Canada so soon.*

Weeks pass. You watch out your window. Dominique and Cassandre and your old boss come and blithely go. They never display the slightest hint of embarrassment. Your firing was illegal. Alan never said there was a problem. He never gave you any kind of warning. So why are you the one who hesitates to leave home in case you should run into him? Why are you the one who feels ashamed? It's months before you muster the courage to write a letter, months before you ask Alan for the severance he owes you along with your vacation pay. A different person would march across the street, stare him in the eye, and demand to be paid *tout de suite!* But you, *pauvre petite*, you can't. Instead, you write, rewrite, write again, send by registered mail. And wait. And wait. And wait.

Desserts
Soufflé au fromage
Coquille St. Jacques

Bavette frites
Tarte au citron
Crème caramel
Gâteau au chocolat

In theory, you are a socialist. Not for nothing did you study the *Theses on Feuerbach* last semester. The point, you understand, is not to interpret the world but to change it. But with a chef screeching obscenities and shoving scalding plates into your hands, customers returning their wine just for the sake of impressing their dates, your co-workers smoking on the back steps when they should be overseeing their own tables, and the pool of tips that you divide at the end of the night shrinking smaller and ever smaller, this is alienated labour. The restaurant serves decent bistro fare and better sweets. It stands not far from Honest Ed's and the self-same family owns it. Honest? Maybe. The manager told you when he hired you that when a team works well, splitting tips works out, and you would love with all your heart to believe this. But it's been months now. Your work shoes are getting worn down at the heels. You have never once earned what you earned in your previous jobs over the course of a month, and you need to buy a winter coat. You are getting awfully tired of waiting for your just desserts.

Beverages
Cosmopolitan
Cuba Libre
Long Island Iced Tea
Piña Colada
Heineken
Tuborg
Chardonnay
Pinot Grigio

I've got a blonde here, the interviewer says to his in-house phone. *About five-four. Experienced.* He tells you to buy yourself a white bathing suit and hands you the rest of the uniform—a pair of floral harem pants, slit up the sides but sufficiently voluminous to disguise your too-wide ass. You will wear this getup at the poolside bar of the upscale Four Seasons Hotel. Even your mother is impressed.

This is the first unionized job you have ever had. When you peel open your first paycheque, you let out a long sigh. For once, it's going to be easy to make your rent. Shifts are regular, and you never work later than eight in the evening. The customers are rich and many of them are famous, and they're liberal with their tips. Some are movie stars. Some are producers. A few are writers. They never harass you or treat you like a servant. They never tell you that your name is common. They never leave without paying. Sometimes they ask you what you are studying, talk to you about politics or plays or books. You bring them burgers and beer, or colourful cocktails festooned with strawberries and lime slices and pineapple. Sunny afternoons on that patio rarely even feel like work.

That summer, you plan your wedding. Walking home along Bloor Street's Golden Mile, you peer into glittering windows. You're making more money than you've ever made at a waitressing job before, but it isn't enough. You can't afford a real trousseau. No stylish wedding gown for you; you'll be wearing your mother's. You won't have an engagement ring. You can't afford a honeymoon. Yet you pick out china at Ashley's, register at Birks, think about the ideal table service. You ask for a cocktail shaker, a soufflé dish, a vegetable steamer, an oval platter, a good teapot, a soup tureen, and crystal serving dishes. You have no idea, really, why you suddenly crave these things, why suddenly they seem so important and even necessary, when in the past, any greedy impulses of yours found their focus in your growing collection of books. All you know is that you fear going unequipped into this new state of life. You feel as if you need some kind of armour. It seems so easy for your customers, signing for fifty dollars of drinks without blinking an eye, ordering more for their friends, coming in day after day and signing their room numbers with a flourish. You can't imagine such ease, such largesse. Someday, you hope, instead of scrimping and saving and worrying about your future, you'll be able to do the same. You can hardly wait.

Nightcap

For years after your final service job, you dream about waiting tables. Sometimes, in these dreams, you're at the pool, but sometimes you're back at the pizza place or running down the stairs at the oyster bar. The kitchen is slow, and the customers complain; they tell the manager you're useless and rude. Tables are turning over every five minutes and there's not a way in the world you can keep up. Somebody pinches your butt. The fire alarm goes off while you're standing directly under the bell. You forget a customer's order and he starts screaming at you. You get to the restaurant and discover that you are supposed to work a double shift, but you have a paper due. Your uniform is filthy and wrinkled. The schedule's been changed, and your boss is on the phone demanding to know where you are. You pick up another server's orders by mistake and the chef throws a pan at you. You've forgotten to charge for half the meal and now you'll be responsible. You get to your section and realize that you don't recognize a single person there and you have no idea what any of them ordered. You can't make the bills add up. When you cash out, you are hundreds of dollars short and you will have to pay.

When do those dreams about waiting begin to fade? When do you cease to be always alert, always on guard, always dancing attendance? When do you stop expecting others to pay you back for every favour? When do you begin to imagine a way of being in the world that involves walking forward with deliberation instead of rushing around in senseless circles? When do you give up on the idea that your only purpose in life is to satisfy other people's desires? When do you stop to consider the meaning of your own?

Take-Away
Charm
Watchfulness
Resourcefulness
Sense of adventure
Distrust of authority
Ideological impurity
Big dreams
Bad dreams

Serves you right.

2 __ Saturday

ANNE LÉVESQUE

ON WEEKDAYS we were a happy family.

When my father came home from work I liked to sit beside him on the back step chatting about my day while he emptied his boots of wood chips and peeled off his heavy wool socks. My mother cooked roast pork and *patates jaunes* and *bouilli de légumes*. A different dessert every night. My brother and I watched television and played with our baby sister. We all went to bed early.

Things were different on Saturday. On Saturday my mother plotted, schemed, and watched out. One strategy was to have us accompany our father when he went out after lunch. This must have worked at some time, I don't know.

From the alley, my brother and I watched my father back the car out of the garage. The building had once been the town's first church. It still held a whiff of sanctity with its hardwood floor and black ampoules of fire extinguisher in sconces on the walls. The communion wine had been replaced by the sherry my father stashed in the firewood closet; the altar, by his workbench; the pews, by his tools, fishing gear, and car—a two-tone blue Meteor, then a hot-red Mercury. A vinyl-topped Pontiac the colour of cold butter. My sister remembers her first ride in the Pontiac. A few miles outside of town, just before a good straight stretch on the Trans-Canada, my father turned to her and said: "Lie down." Her cheek against the new smell of the dark gold carpeting, she closed her eyes while he pushed the accelerator all the way down. Because a man needed to know just how fast his car could go.

On Saturday afternoons, however, my father never drove fast, or far. He went to the hardware store, the chainsaw dealership, the beer store (my favourite, because he let me sit on the case of empties and I could see *everything*), and sometimes, to the town dump. We knew it was over when he let us off at the corner of our street. I was always a little sad walking home. I knew that we had failed in our mission.

On the rare occasions that he drove us right into the garage, there was usually a last stop. I remember the dusty, pot-holed parking lot, as wide and beige as the afternoon, the railway tracks, the smell of hot upholstery. My brother and I could have easily walked home—it wasn't far—but we didn't.

My father left us waiting like that in a strange town once. It was strange to us, but he had worked there and knew many people. That day we lost heart. A man walking by saw us crying and went in to tell my father. He appeared a few minutes later holding two bags of potato chips. He chided us, but gently, for being so foolish. Then he left again.

But on most Saturday afternoons we were home with our mother and he was gone. As the day wore on, I remember listening for the car in the alley, the clang of the metal garage door, his steps in the porch.

This is what I remember: Bugs Bunny and Wile E. Coyote. The tension. *The Barber of Seville*. The tension. My mother at the counter, preparing supper. The tension. *Hockey Night in Canada*. The tension. My brother and I put out a false brittle cheerfulness then, like the sun on a cold winter day. We made up clever inventive games. We were good as gold.

And then we heard it. It surged through the walls of the old church into the alley and yard, the houses of our neighbours, all the rooms in our house. It was my father, gunning the car's engine before he turned off the ignition. As if he wanted to make sure that everyone knew he was coming home drunk.

3 — Waiting for Now

STEVEN ROSS SMITH

Four Stories

1. Watching

In 1967 my Advertising Writing instructor Len McColl played us a recording of a BBC broadcast of *Waiting for Godot* in a classroom at Ryerson University in Toronto. (It was then called Ryerson Polytechnic Institute.) I was a young, naive media student whose critical and creative brain was just beginning to wake up.

En attendant Godot—(*Waiting for Godot*)—was written in French by Samuel Beckett in 1948 and 49 and premiered in the Théâtre de Babylone in Paris on January 5, 1953. Beckett then wrote the English translation, and in 1961 the BBC staged and filmed an English version and aired it on June 26. A half-dozen years after that, I sat on a hard chair in my Ryerson classroom, watching the BBC film. The play mesmerized me. I could even say—in the jargon of the day—it blew my mind. Today, looking back almost fifty years through my rear-view mirror, I can't relive the moment in its fullness, so I can't say why the play had such a visceral effect on me. Perhaps it was its spareness, or that it distilled aspects of humankind and human life (represented by its two main characters Vladimir [Didi] and Estragon [Gogo]) that I'd not yet considered—feelings of hopelessness, the inability to articulate, incomprehensible forces, power, singular moments containing the arc of a lifespan. I had never seen anything like this creation of Beckett's—the way a small cast of actors, speaking an unadorned and repeated vocabulary on an almost bare stage, could—with astounding acting, a remarkable script, effective lighting, stark design, and the close-ups that a camera allows—transmit such power. The play was at once mundane and eloquent, bizarre and realistic, funny and dismal. The pulse that went through me as I watched, and as the film ended—with the characters static, unable to move, waiting—was so strong that I still recall it, though I struggle to feel all the sensations it triggered. And I reach now to find words to express what I remember. I do know that this near two-hour experience changed my life—my way of thinking, of looking at society, of being.

Viewing that production of *Waiting for Godot* was a formative moment that awakened in me the desire to become an artist, to use my creative power to express something, though at the time I didn't know what that something was; it made me want to write, though I couldn't articulate these low rumblings at the time. Yet, it was then that I decided not to wait for life to happen to me. I decided to do.

It was at that moment too that I became a kind of rebel in thought—a critical thinker, a social being who came to dwell, often at the edge, of just about every cluster (institutional, social, organizational) I inhabited.

Today I'm sitting in my study, staring at the pine wall, yet beyond, reflecting on that classroom, that moment almost five decades ago—an impossible, impassable gap, perhaps. I stare and wait—yes, I wait—for the moment to appear on my mind's screen with as much intensity as possible, to recall what it felt like in my body, in my mind, that moment that was such an eye-opener, a soul-stirrer, a creativity can-opener. Though the moment resonates, today I am aware of other awakenings around that same time and within the same institution, and of later effects.

2. Hovering

In my final year at Ryerson, in late 1967 or early 1968, our History of Music instructor, Al Sauro, played two compositions by American composer Steve Reich—"It's Gonna Rain" (composed, 1965) and "Come Out" (1966). Again, my mind was...you know what I'm saying. These tape-recorder-generated compositions created a new kind of music based on the spoken word—a single speaker—and manipulation of the audio-taped recording to play the voice against itself. The pieces feature repetition and delay, sonic patterns unfolding and evolving. The composer has described the structure of these pieces: "You have one tape loop going and another identical loop slipping slightly behind the first one, and what you really have is a unison canon or round where the rhythmic interval between the first and second voices is variable and constantly changing." In those first hearings I found the pieces unpredictable and surprising and startlingly engaging. (They still are, despite many listenings over the years.) The effect is of hovering in the expanding temporal intervals, then being propelled along by a wave of continuing present with new ripples being constantly added. There is a tension here, the self stretched between moving and waiting.

As I think about it now, listening to music may be the antithesis of waiting. To give any piece of music full attention on first and even repeated listenings, I must dwell in the present, as the past scurries away and the next moment has not arrived. In the present moment can dwell surprise, exultation, and perhaps ecstasy. This is, I think, the reason I want to listen to complex music, even innovative popular music, because when I give myself to it, I dwell thoroughly in the present moment.

In deep and focused listening, I am not looking backward or ahead but am in the single sonic instant. I am not waiting.

But now, let me contradict myself with a musical adventure and further awakening from that same epic time.

3. Processing

I attended the iconic performance of *Reunion* conceived by the influential, radical, and controversial composer John Cage. This performance, in the Ryerson Theatre on March 5, 1968, was based on a chess game played live between Cage and Marcel Duchamp. Though it was a Cage conception, the sonic creation was a collaborative composition. I had forgotten, but know now, through a bit of research, that the other composers were David Behrman, Gordon Mumma, David Tudor, and Lowell Cross. I recall seeing a cluster of cables running from the bottom of the chessboard. That chessboard, wired with photoresistors and contact mics, was created by Cross, who was at that time a graduate student and research associate in the Electronic Music Studios at the University of Toronto.

I settled into my seat near the middle of the theatre, drawn by the artistic stars and unsure of what was to occur. Without fanfare (or even introductions, as I recall, or have forgotten), the game began. In fact, two games were played; the first was quite short, and the second remained unfinished. As the games progressed, the moves of the chessmen on the board activated and blended random parts of four electronic music compositions and distributed them to eight speakers, set at compass points surrounding the audience. The chess aficionados on stage—Cage, Duchamp, and Alexina Duchamp, Marcel's wife—drank wine (a 1964 Château Kirwan, apparently) and smoked—Duchamp puffed cigars, and Mrs. Duchamp and Cage smoked cigarettes. The rest of us could not smoke.

The electronic sounds that evolved seemed random and patternless, totally unpredictable, ranging between surprising and boring. Yet I sat, listened, experienced, and waited—waited without knowing what I was waiting for. It was an experience in patience, attention, and abandonment of expectation. There was no message or melody, no anthemic or lyrical flourish, no discernible movement toward a finish—just dynamic shifts and dazzling, seemingly unrelated sounds. It was a challenge to simply "be [t]here now." As I recall, I was transported at moments, dazed at others, scurry-minded sometimes, mystified, and certainly after a couple of hours or so began to wonder where I was (where we were) temporally or structurally—still at the beginning, in the middle, or near the end, in a theatre or outer space. The performance began at 8:30 p.m. and the game and its live-generated music continued until about 1:00 a.m. in the presence of a waning audience. By the end there were, reportedly, less than ten persons in the audience, one of whom, Lowell Cross reports, shouted, "Encore!" I can't remember if I was still there or not...though I seem to recall that "Encore." Or is that a manufactured memory? Whatever duration I managed, I'd been engaged in, at different times, listening, yawning, wondering, forgetting, drifting, twitching, slumping, hovering, and yes, waiting. But for what?

In this performance I experienced an intense matrix of responses, some active, some passive, not unlike Estragon and Vladimir, awaiting a "Godot" moment. Waiting is a form of not living in the present, but rather in the future. It is a giving of attention to what might come, and hence is an out-of-moment consciousness (or unconsciousness?). It is expectant, not present. It is not active.

And yet, this experience of waiting left its mark; to this day, I remain interested in indeterminacy in artistic practice, my own and that of others.

By the way, this was Marcel Duchamp's last public performance. He passed on October 2, 1968.

4. Waving

John Cage would turn up one more time in my life, fourteen years later. In January 1982, Cage was in Toronto for the performance of *Roaratorio*, at Convocation Hall, University of Toronto. The concept and composition featured imported Irish musicians

playing traditional instruments live, with Cage reading frag-
mented passages from *Finnegan's Wake* accompanied by
electronic warbles, buzzes, hums, and crescendos; this entire
sonic collage was delivered in surround sound. By thrilling
circumstance, I was assigned the role of personal chauffeur
for Mr. Cage and his partner, dancer and choreographer Merce
Cunningham. After the wonderful concert, I drove them back
to their hotel, the Park Plaza at Bloor and Avenue Road. It was
winter, snowy, and I was driving a borrowed Pontiac Firebird,
two-door, with all-season tires. I pulled into the hotel driveway,
stopped in front of the big glass doors, leapt out, scurried around
to open the door, and pushed the front seat forward, for the
gentlemen to exit. They clambered out. At this time, Cage was
seventy and Cunningham sixty-three. I was thirty-seven. We
shook hands and waved, and I jumped back into the driver's seat.
Being the cordial men they were, they paused inside the doors
to wait for my departure, and we waved once again as I shifted
into drive. The tires spun, and the car did not move. I was stuck
in a small snow bank. John and Merce peered through the glass
doors. I waved again to liberate these artistic elders from their
waiting. But they did not leave. Instead they pressed open the
doors and came back outside and offered to give me a push. I
had a moment of terror, worried that such exertion might be the
end of them. I protested; they insisted; I acquiesced. They leaned,
heaved, and my wheels grabbed pavement and I pulled forward.
I shouted "thanks," we waved again, and I drove away with a
big exhale. If they had not been gracious enough to wait for my
departure before heading to their room none of this would have
happened and I would not have had this wonderful experience
and memory. I've been waiting since then—thirty-four years—
to tell this story. I'm now the age Mr. Cage was then and realize
that I could push a car if I had to, hoping that my tender back,
surgeried shoulder, and angio'd artery would survive.

5. Now

To bring these stories forward, into the present, I've had to visit my past. Some things are worth waiting for. I'm writing these words, continuing to live out the decision I made in 1967 to express myself in words. These words have had to wait for their exposure. And though I write these moments from the past in moments today, which pass as I type, they are for your eyes in the future, the now of your reading that you did not know you were awaiting.

Meanwhile Vladimir and Estragon remain—sitting, pacing, or standing stock still in their stark habitation—unwitting and perhaps witless, unaware they are trapped by their own inaction, just as Samuel Beckett placed them, waiting for that mysterious and illusive figure, Godot, to whom they've given the power of a god, but who is not God, but is their own misguided attention, their excuse, their energy, and their existence gone static.

4 —— The Escape EDYTHE ANSTEY HANEN

WE ARE TRAPPED in a world of grimy windows, dusty blackboards, the heat of summer, and closed doors. Droning voices of discontent float from somewhere in the back of the room, hazy, unformed balloons of sound. A boy gets up from his desk and shoves one of the windows up. Thin, lank hair the colour of rusted metal. Greasy. Freckles sprayed across his nose. Last year he signed everyone's high-school annual *Numb Bum* after getting the strap in front of the whole class. His one great moment of unflinching pride.

Blue sky and the promise of that other world waiting just beyond our reach. The white sand beaches of Spanish Banks; Neil Sedaka on the radio, singing, "I love, I love, I love my little calendar girl"; the moon over a summer sea. We are all restless in the stale atmosphere of dust and chalk and boredom in these last weeks of high school. From somewhere in the back, the shuffle of feet, slap of notebooks, slam of books. The edges of this picture begin to soften, spread out like honey leaking from a honey jar. Sweet. Difficult to move in, like the summer heat that slowly seeps in through the dirty glass.

A note is passed from girl to girl. The boys begin to sense a conspiracy, a betrayal of sorts. Hands jerk out to confiscate the folded white piece of scribbler paper. A laugh. Loud, this time.

The teacher is a heavy man who always wears vests and polished shoes. He is sweating in the heat, pushing his shiny damp hair off his forehead. He senses rebellion, a low murmuring of discontent. But he is helpless before this room full of teenage energy, barely subdued laughter, a world of plans and calculations beyond his wildest imagination. He makes no attempt at control but takes a stab at convincing us that he truly does know what we're all up to.

"I smell banana oil," he says, turning his nose toward the stained ceiling, as though the source of his discovery could be found there, hovering above us all. It is what he always says when he catches one of us girls polishing our fingernails in class. He looks straight at me. "Is that you?" No. Never me. Though he knows it often is me, he never goes further than that. He is timid, overweight, uncertain of anything in his life, a man too afraid to even attempt to penetrate our secret, unforgiving world.

He has lunch every day with Mr. Rainsley, our science teacher. Hair shining with brilliantine. A waistcoat with a gold watch on a chain. Straight-as-a-die side part. The word "gay" in relation to sexuality has not been invented yet, but we gossip voraciously about what those two might do together.

The tide of voices rises. Another window is shoved open, slammed into the top of the frame. The teacher wipes one long, starched, white sleeve across his damp forehead. He wishes he had some solid ground to stand on, but he doesn't. He knows it. We know it. I sit and wait in my seat as we all do, wait for the next explosion of sound, for the next eruption that will carry us all on the wave that by now has grown too big for any of us to tame.

A nudge in the ribs and I turn around. The note has reached me. I wait until the teacher turns his back and rummages in his desk drawer for his mints. They are the only thing that will give him any sense of normalcy now. I open the note that has come from one of the girls who sits at the back of the room. *Let's all meet at noon*, the note says. *The* Coral Sea *is in town and the city is crawling with sailors.* I grin and look back at all the girls who have already seen the note and who are smirking and nudging one another. The boys are guffawing, huge braying laughs that are supposed to tell us they know what we're up to. Of course, they don't. Like the teacher, they are powerless.

By noon, all the girls but two have agreed to leave school and take the bus downtown to the Port of Vancouver to meet sailors from the *Coral Sea.* Never have we finagled such a coup. We are a solid front of female energy, unbridled dreams, reach-for-the-sky expectations. The classroom breathes and expands with the trapped chaos of our daring plans, vibrates with the unspoken words we all want to shout, trembles with the promise of outright delicious rebellion.

The teacher's shoulders fall, his hair hangs over his dripping forehead like a swatch of wet fabric. Even his suit looks shiny, sweaty from the heat. His whole body registers defeat, as though he has already surrendered to the knowledge of our certain treachery, of our world that leaves him out.

When the bell rings, we tumble from the room like a flock of birds just released from its cage. We all walk together down to the Trafalgar bus stop on Broadway, a noisy gaggle of adolescent laughter and brash certainty. An old woman steps down from the bus, and as her feet touch the sidewalk, she grasps my arm to steady herself. I look into her eyes and it is like looking into the portholes of a ship lost at sea. Her eyes a watery grey, her face a map of long-ago journeys. A shipwreck of the past.

And in that moment, for the first and perhaps the only time in my life, I see my place in the Universe. I am a sixteen-year-old girl and the world is mine. I look into the old woman's eyes and I think: *It's my turn now.* And I know in that moment that it's true.

I sit on the bus and rub away the dirt and grime on the window so I can look out and watch my neighbourhood fly by: the red and white sign of the Dairy Queen; our school like a prison, a grey bunker hunched against the green hillside. But all I can see is that sad, tired look on my teacher's face, that giving up and giving in as he returns to his empty classroom, not understanding or remembering the fierce energy of youth. It is a look I have seen in my parents' faces too. That bewildered sense of powerlessness as we stride so carelessly into our bright and limitless futures. And I wonder why they are so burdened with us, with the weight of our untethered dreams.

The next day when we return to class, our teacher says nothing of our disappearance. But that song of freedom still runs through my veins: the glory of that day and the sailor I met and would follow to another port, in the way I would follow many men to many places over the years until I learned to travel my own path. I wish there was something of the magic of that day that I could give the teacher: the gift of remembering the power and the beauty of youth, the gift of vision that could give him clear eyes to see the small nuggets of gold mined from just once flouting the rules, turning our backs on another day of sitting in a stifling classroom that took so much more from us than it gave back.

He would accept such a gift hesitantly, turn it over and over in puzzled uncertainty. And that uncertainty would mar its love- liness, like a stone flung into an untroubled lake, only to disturb its quiet beauty.

I want to tell him all of this, but I know I can't. He is not the one who risked tearing apart the familiar, or the one who unearthed the diamond from the sameness of our days. He is not that brave. He was not made for out-and-out rebellion. So the gifts are not his. They belong to me.

I shove my books into my desk. Feel for the bottles of nail polish pushed into the farthest corner. I pull them out, line them up on my desk. *Be whatever you dream you can be*, says the label on the tiny, pyramid-shaped bottles. Their names—Pink in Paris, Strawberry Kiss, Frosted Ice—conjure images of cotton candy and bubble gum. Hazy thinking: None of these images reflect who I ever want to be. I tuck the bottles back into my desk. Gather my books to my chest. Get up and walk out of the room.

My departure creates not a ripple of interest. The only thing I hear in the moment before I shut the door on this classroom, whose walls I will never see again, is my teacher's voice. A low drone, like a wasp beating its wings against an empty window as it looks for a way in or out; it doesn't matter which. Just another mad fool crashing against an impenetrable wall, an insensate thing that cares nothing for arrivals or departures.

5 — Waiting for Alexandra

THE VIA PASSENGER TRAIN from Vancouver pulled into
the Saskatoon railway station shortly after 9:00 a.m. on May 8,
2012. I had been sitting in the station waiting room with another
twenty-five or so people, all of whom appeared to be waiting
to board the eastbound train heading to Winnipeg and beyond
to Ontario and then on to eastern Canada. I had not been out to
this railway station in the distant southwest part of the city for
at least twenty years. I wasn't even sure people ever boarded or
disembarked the VIA train in Saskatoon anymore, so it was a bit
of a surprise to see so many people sitting in the station, waiting
with the usual impatience of travellers destined for some other
place and anxious to board so they can get on with the actual
train ride that would make their journey a reality. It was an
interesting mix of young people and seniors, with very few in
the large age gap in between. They all appeared to be under
twenty-five or over sixty-five. I wondered whether this reflected
the ridership of Canada's remaining passenger trains.

As I took in my surroundings in the railway station, it struck
me that VIA Rail seemed intent on discouraging train travel,
rather than making any serious attempts to encourage it. There
was one small notice board to inform the public of the two trains

still running through Saskatoon—Train 1 and Train 2. One train ran westbound for Vancouver and the other rolled eastbound for Toronto. They alternated days, so in fact, only one passenger train a day left, crossing the vastness of the Canadian prairies. But while the notice announced the days and directions of the trains, there was no indication of the times of day the trains would arrive. Nor was there any sign of a single VIA staff person anywhere in the building. *Strange*, I thought. As I further scanned the station, I noted a complete absence of a coffee shop or convenience shop or even a food-vending machine. No food, no drinks. Nary a VIA employee to answer questions, inform people of anything, or even provide a guesstimate of the train's arrival time. Or whether there would be a train at all. It was almost an otherworldly place where travellers appeared on the basis of faith alone. The many inconveniences made me all the more impressed to find at least twenty-five people here to catch a train; the romance of train travel appeared to outweigh the determined efforts of VIA to sabotage it.

I was here at the VIA station this May morning to meet a special passenger travelling from Vancouver to Toronto. She had informed me that the train was to arrive in Saskatoon at 8:45 and had a twenty-minute stopover, so would I like to meet her?

I would indeed. I was very eager to meet this woman, whom I had not seen for fifty-three years.

In 1957 I began my teaching career in Yorkton at Simpson School in the elementary public system. For the first three years of my teaching career I taught in that old two-storey brick school that held around five hundred students. I remember those years as being very satisfying and the students as a wonderful and quite diverse group of youngsters. One of the twenty-eight or thirty students in my sixth- and seventh-grade class that year was a twelve-year-old named Alexandra. She was from Ontario, new to the school, living in Yorkton with a foster family while her parents were undergoing marital or other problems that necessitated her having to live with another family a considerable distance from her own.

Alexandra was a voracious reader with a lively imagination, a very bright student in every respect, but there was also an aura of fragility that clung to her, no doubt because she must have felt incredibly lonesome and lost, perhaps even rejected in some ways, separated from the rest of her family as she was. I sensed this, even as a young and inexperienced teacher barely out of my teens, rough around the edges, having grown up in rural Saskatchewan, not so very far from where I was now teaching. Because she wore this vulnerability much of the time, I went out of my way to try to engage her in activities as often as possible. And because she also happened to be a tireless reader with an active imagination and intellect, I would try to challenge her as much as I could without making it painfully evident that I was paying her more attention than some of the others. One of the memories we both retained from that year in Simpson School was of my efforts to make her laugh, or at least break into a smile, on days when she seemed especially melancholy.

In one of the many emails we exchanged across the Atlantic over the ten years or so after Alexandra "discovered" her long-ago teacher on a website, she reminded me that whenever we had our weekly spelling dictation, I would read the words aloud and use each one in a sentence. But to make the drab nature of spelling dictation fun, I would conjure up outrageous sentences, dreadful puns, silly similes, unexpected verbal twists or turns, anything at all designed to evoke laughs, guffaws, or groans. Though I was an inexperienced educator, one of the things I *had* learned by that point was that if a teacher could stir a small measure of frivolity in with the serious matter of learning, the students not only enjoyed the work more but were also more likely to succeed at it. When the matter of trying to master and spell difficult words happened to be interspersed with sheer playfulness and gales of laughter, even the poorest spellers tended to learn faster and learn more, probably because they did not feel under threat in the classroom. Moreover, it was fun— something school generally was not.

On the day we both remembered, Alexandra was looking very grim-faced as we began the spelling dictation, and I sensed she needed a little cheering up. I was determined to make her break down and laugh out loud, so I approached each example sentence with the aim of making it as silly, as verbally playful, as outrageous as I possibly could. But Alexandra remained impassive. As I glanced back and forth between her and my notebook, I sensed that this classroom spelling dictation had now become a battle of wills between Alexandra and me. She was refusing to give in to laughter, and this made me try even harder to be animated and verbally comedic. The rest of the class was in stitches, some laughing so hard they could hardly set pen to paper to write down the words. The rest of the class could sense that this spelling day was different, that something was going on between the teacher and the new girl. The more the wafts of giggles and guffaws swept around the classroom, the more she seemed to set her jaw as if to say, "You will never make me laugh."

In the end, of course, it was inevitable that one of my verbal concoctions would turn the tide; but before she relented and gave in to laughter, I remember her small frame, shaking ever so slightly as mirth broke down even her most determined attempt to resist.

Alexandra returned to Ontario and to her family at the end of the school term, or possibly even before then. I moved on from Simpson School shortly after that to get married, then to attend university and eventually to take a high-school English teaching position in Saskatoon. I suppose that, over time, I might have entirely forgotten the little girl with the melancholy and vulnerable air, the bright young girl who, for a while, had been a genuine concern to me because of her special circumstances and her so-apparent loneliness, the absence of her parents and siblings. Then without warning, over four decades later, Alexandra reappeared in my life; she was a published novelist who had her own website, and she wanted to know whether I was the same Glen Sorestad who had taught school in Yorkton all those years ago. The Internet had reunited the young school girl and her one-time elementary-school teacher, now a writer himself and long removed from the classroom.

Alexandra was living in England when she contacted me. It didn't take me long to discover that the bright little girl who had sat in the front desk near the classroom door, and who had acted as my designated door answerer, had gone on to amply fulfill the promise of her early aptitudes and creativity. She had studied acting and had spent time playing roles on stage and in film before settling in to become a novelist. Over the years she had authored nearly forty romance novels as well as a book on cats. She had also studied at least eight different languages. It turned out that Alexandra was much drawn to the Mediterranean countries and their history, culture, and languages; she now spends part of her time in a home she and her partner have on the island of Crete, in addition to keeping a place in London and spending time in Canada.

When the VIA train pulled into the station platform and shuddered to a stop, I had a few moments of anxiety as I began to wonder whether I would be able to recognize her at all after these many years. And how would she possibly recognize her former teacher in the seventy-five-year-old, grey-haired man I had become? Would we have anything meaningful to say to one another?

I recognized her as soon as she stepped down onto the platform from the coach, and she came into the station and directly towards me without a moment's hesitation. It was like the coming together after a long absence of two family members or very old friends. But of course, that's exactly what we were, though it wasn't until long afterwards that I recognized this. *We were friends and had been for all these years*, though perhaps neither of us knew this, except for somewhere deep inside us. More than twenty years in a host of different classrooms have taught me that teachers can and do form very strong and close relationships with many of their students, relationships that do not fade with time. Often teachers are quite unaware of how profoundly they may have influenced some of their students, and when I sat down with Alexandra in the railway station that summer day to converse with her face to face for the first time in over fifty years, I realized that not only had I had a considerable impact on her but that she had likewise done the very same for me.

Fifteen minutes flew by in the blink of an eye, and before we knew it, the passengers were queuing up to board. We stood, and I embraced Alexandra as if she were my daughter, or my niece, or my best friend. On the drive home, I tried to recall the things we chatted about in our time-pressured reunion, but I only know we shared of ourselves like near and dear friends, and we lived in the moment as fully as we possibly could. I know one of the things I was thinking was how that much younger me in Simpson School all those years ago, that wretchedly inexperienced, young, would-be teacher, may have been intuitively wiser than I have ever given him credit for. Her presence in my classroom taught me that a good teacher was much more than a dispenser or conveyor of knowledge and that caring for each student as a fellow human being came first.

Now, all these years later, I think it is entirely possible Alexandra taught me more than I could ever have taught her.

Scope

6 —— The Art Hospital, ELIZABETH HAYNES
the Floating
Hospital, and
the Burning
House

THE ART HOSPITAL smelled of sandalwood incense. A small
boy in a white knee-length shalwar kameez and a fez patrolled
the common room with a censer. An old bearded man swept
the white floors and lit the tall, silver candles at their corners. At
night, stars shone from the ceiling like the cut-outs in a Turkish
hammam I once visited. I should have liked the art hospital, but
I didn't. It was lonely as hell.

We had to attend daily lectures. Sat captive in a row of plastic
seats, their high sides obscuring us from one another. One day
a young woman who looked like my artist cousin, Charlotte,
told us how painting had healed her. She showed us slides of
her work, but the projected images were small and my glasses
had disappeared. After the lecture, I tried to get out of my
chair, but my belly was too swollen. I couldn't speak, either, so
I rang and rang my call bell. I stared at the artist, hoping she'd
notice I needed help. She didn't. Finally, the small boy came and
tried to lift me. He made a rude comment about me being too

emphysematous. What did that mean? This was supposed to be a rehabilitation hospital. Where were my rehabilitators?

I'd had just about enough of the art hospital. Was going back down to the regular hospital. But the hospital director wanted me to stay. She was tall and willowy, a Balinese dancer in a gold and emerald sarong, her black hair swept into an inverted cone. The dancer danced, extended her Olive Oyl arms, waved her hips back and forth—a shadow puppet at the edge of the room. I kicked and kicked my bed. Let me out of here.

Finally, an orderly appeared. He pressed a button and my bed slid down to the regular hospital. All I had to do was transfer myself to a gurney on the other side. The bed was close, just a few centimetres away, but I couldn't move. There was no one to help me. Exhausted, I gave up. My bed whirred back up to the art hospital.

This time I was in a large cave staffed by Mexican physio-therapists. The walls were decorated with bark paintings of deer and corn dancers. Beaded Huichol gourd bowls sat on the tables. There were roosters, too, but they didn't move, so they must have been sculptures of roosters. The women seemed cheerfully resigned to an overly busy work day, to unpaid overtime, though I heard one talk about filing a grievance with the union.

My physiotherapists manoeuvred my swollen body into various positions, resting me on their strong backs when I was tired. I liked this part of the art hospital better. But damned if I was going to stay here.

⋮ Toxic delirium is a sudden, confused state of mind that comes and goes and affects personality and behaviour. Toxic delirium is a state of acute mental confusion affecting the ability to think, remember, and distinguish fantasy from reality. Toxic delirium can be caused by a number of things. In my case, an emergency operation.

In the ICU, I had a private nurse who had come all the way from Seattle to look after me. This nurse called me "little bear," which was funny because that was what my sister, Leslie, sometimes called me. The nurse kept trying to get me to breathe deeply, which was annoying, because I already knew how to breathe. I thought it strange that the nurse was staying with my friends, Angelika and Garrick. That she came to the hospital in Garrick's borrowed truck, which used to belong to a national park warden, and had a cage in the back for transporting bears. In fact, it was uncanny how much the nurse looked like my sister, Leslie, who was also from Seattle.

One day my favourite nurse, Leanne, told Leslie and me a story. While on vacation in Mexico, she'd seen a fire burning on top of a mountain. A series of burning huts, she was told. A ritual. Before a Huichol woman gave birth, she was put in the last hut. The first hut was set on fire. The woman had to have her baby before the fire reached her hut. Then, newborn strapped to her belly, she cooked a feast for her family.

Seven months later, I can find no reference to this Huichol birth ritual. I learn that indigenous Huichol women usually give birth alone or with a mara'akame—a shaman—present. According to medical anthropologist Dr. Jennie Gamlin, many Huichol people believe that "while western medicine may cure the illness, it will not treat the cause. This will always be supernatural, and any illness treated bio-medically will also require a spiritual cure." One of Gamlin's interviewees, Graciela, explained: "When the baby can't come out because the Nenekate and Kaka+yarixi [gods] won't let it through, this is when the mara'akame opens the doors, by speaking to them."

My parents and I once took a tour to a Huichol community outside Puerto Vallarta. Our guide, Miguel, and a shaman, Santi, took us through Santi's village, where we visited the church with

its altar of deer antlers, bow and arrows, and gourd bowls called
xukuri. Xukuri are symbolic wombs that are filled with blood
offerings to the gods. They are used to contact the spirit world.

The Huichol believe their beings are formed by elements of
the natural world: fire, air, water, earth. Plants, deer, and maize
are ancestor gods who can be accessed by ingesting peyote.
Peyote visions inspire their art: yarn paintings and beaded
xukuris. A shaman artist may sacrifice a deer, and inhale its
last breath, before creating a piece of art.

In Santi's village, my father bought a xukuri. I purchased a
yarn painting: a green shaman with horns holding a medicine
bundle and a torch, a deer below, birds at the four corners. The
painting hangs at the entrance to my living room.

My doctors worry about my cognitive status, my fluctuating
level of mental orientation. I am wheeled down long corridors,
lifted on and off gurneys by singing Mexican porters. My body
is slid into CT and MRI caves. Hot liquid whooshes through my
abdomen. A disembodied voice tells me to hold my breath. How?
I struggle to get enough air. My butterfly lungs are missing their
bottom wings.

In the ICU, nurses ask what I need. I'm getting good at
gestures. Moving my shoulders upward means *reposition me
on the bed*. Pointing to my mouth means *suction*. Pointing
combined with a hands-up shrug means *when will this damned
breathing tube be removed?* "Not yet, not yet," they say. "Your
lungs are full of fluid. You can't breathe by yourself."

Leslie builds me an altar with pictures from my travels:
a Buddha, Indian and Indonesian textiles, a Colima dog. She
writes my history on the whiteboard. She finds me an alphabet
board so I can communicate more than yes and no. When I spell
"sisters" for the nurses, it means *where are they, when are they
coming?* My sisters, Leslie, Jocelyn, and Melissa, are allowed to
arrive early, stay late, because I am less anxious and agitated

when they are with me. When I wake, open frightened eyes, Les sings to me, calling me back from wherever I've been. She drives the bear truck home in the dark, following a string of lights to Garrick and Angelika's.

Doctors come and go, wanting to know where I am. A difficult question. Where I am floats toward then away from me, a piece of driftwood. Sometimes I am in a hospital on the top of a mountain in Colorado. Sometimes I am in Calgary, but at the South Health Campus with the floor-to-ceiling windows that look out onto brown prairie. Sometimes I am where I am, the Peter Lougheed Centre.

The ICU doc weans me off the psychotropic drugs, which he thinks are causing my alterations of consciousness. He brings a machine to suck the fluid out of my lungs, urging me to watch the screen. My lungs are full of green liquid, floating ferns snared on bones. We got twenty litres, Dr. Luc announces proudly. Twenty litres, I think. Enough to drown in.

⋮ I woke up on February 21 feeling exhausted. Thought I'd overdone it with two days of cross-country skiing in Lake Louise the previous weekend. I'd been tired all week. On Friday I overslept, dressed quickly, walked to work. I had just turned on my computer when I felt sharp pains in my lower back. My skin turned clammy. Something in my belly let go, like a stitch unravelling. I called a friend to bring me home.

I lay in my bed thinking that the hard bed in Lake Louise, combined with lack of stretching before and after skiing, had caused the back pain. Then the spasms turned into stabbing knives. I threw up, red-brown liquid. Staggered to the phone and made an appointment with my doctor, called my friend to take me there.

His resident couldn't find my blood pressure. Tried a second machine. A third. The knives were tearing me to pieces now. I remember screaming. An IV. Ambulance. Pain dissolving.

CT scan. A doctor told me I had to have emergency surgery. A woman asked if I wanted a social worker, the chaplain. No chaplain. Yes social worker. I told her to call one of my sisters. They'd call each other and my elderly parents who didn't hear well on the phone.

In a different ambulance. A man asking me my name, where I live, when I was born. Already told you. But he kept asking, flooding my eyes with light, when all I wanted to do was sleep.

This man, I learned later, was the Foothills Medical Centre ER doctor. He had jumped into the ambulance because he wasn't sure I'd survive the ride to the Lougheed where they were prepping for my surgery. Because at ten o'clock that morning, a 9.5-centimetre aneurysm—a ballooning of the aortic artery in my abdomen—burst, flooding my belly with blood. I'd had a triple A: an abdominal aortic aneurysm. Known as the "widow maker," because it usually happens to elderly men, who usually die. Half the blood in my body poured into my peritoneum. The social worker told my family I had a 10 per cent chance of surviving the emergency surgery, where a stent would be inserted through my femoral artery. My chances of surviving after the operation were 4 per cent.

I was given blood, litres and litres of it. Six transfusions in all.

⋮ The snow had started Saturday night and was still falling heavily in Lake Louise by Sunday morning. Pipestone Loop had been track set the day before, but the tracks were obliterated. I clamped my boots into my cross-country skis and followed my friends up the trail, my skis gliding easily on fresh snow. The trees wore crowns of snow, shoes of earth. The four of us moved over frozen ground, through the beautiful silent world.

⋮ The Peter Lougheed Centre could float. Was, in fact, a hospital ship that nightly sailed down the Elbow River. I was inside the boat, though I yearned to be outside on the deck. Wanted to watch our dark passage, hear the lapping of the water, see the stars. But my fellow passengers, nurses all, wouldn't let me get up. Kept telling me to calm down. Sleep, sleep. Go back to sleep.

Leslie told me later that I had been taken from surgery to a windowless ICU room, a little cave. When they moved me to a room with big windows and stars on the ceiling, my orientation improved, and I stopped trying to rip out my tubes.

One night I was drowning in fluid. I rang and rang my call bell, but no one came. I kicked and kicked my bed, and still nobody came. Then finally someone did. She checked my lines, my oxygen levels. I pointed to my mouth, my throat. I can't breathe. Suction me!

Les told me later there had been three code blues in the ICU that night. Three people's hearts stopped. Three people floated out of this world.

Scotty, my favourite respiratory therapist, was on duty the spring day I passed the spontaneous breathing test, the day my breathing tube was finally removed. I coughed ferociously, like a wounded beast, gasping and wheezing between bouts. After the coughing abated, I tried out my voice. It was bearish, a low-pitched whisper-growl.

Scotty's wife and daughter arrived to perform dances of universal peace for patients. They wore long embroidered robes and colourful scarves. While my favourite nurse, Leanne, looked for a place for them to dance, the little girl wordlessly approached me, handed me a red rose.

I fell asleep and when I woke up the dancers were gone. I'd missed them. I asked Leanne when they would return. "Pardon me?" she asked. Apparently, there are no dancers in the regular hospital.

Later that day, I insisted my sister, Melissa, call our parents because my mother was lost. Mel wouldn't do it. A doctor came with a CPAP breathing machine, covered my face with a mask. I kept trying to pull it off. Mel begged me to wear it, said I wasn't getting enough oxygen and if I didn't wear it, they might have to put the breathing tube back in. I stopped fighting and went sailing instead, this time on a sleek sailing ship, tacking into the wind, heading out to sea.

⋮ I was transferred from the ICU to a ward, then discharged. My sister, Jocelyn, installed equipment in my home: bath bars, raised toilet seat, a pole I could use to pull myself up from the couch. She gave me a bell, which I rang ten, twenty times a night. I started coughing again, couldn't stop, couldn't get enough air. Joc called my doctor, who told her to take me to emerg. I had pulmonary emboli, tiny clots starring my lungs.

⋮ Five days later and stabilized on blood thinners, I was home for the final time. My eighty-six-year-old mother came to look after me. She insisted that I do my breathing exercises hourly, made me walk. Supervised, as I slowly inched my walker down the sidewalk, pushing it through thawing earth and tiny shoots of green to get to a bench in my neighbourhood park. My belly was still huge, full of the blood that had flooded it when my aorta ruptured. My surgeon, Dr. Nutley, told me that the blood would eventually reabsorb—that slowly, slowly, my belly would shrink to its normal size.

⋮ In June I told a writer friend about the art hospital. She wondered if I had gone there when I was leaving my body. It had been touch and go for me the first few days in the ICU. Was the night I tried to go back to the regular hospital but couldn't, the night of the three code blues? The night Leslie was tugged awake at three o'clock in the morning, got into the bear truck, and raced along the line of lights to the hospital?

In July I swam in Okanagan Lake. Drove my parents' car down the rutted entrance road to Kalmoir Park, past ponderosa pines and quails. Donned my suit and water shoes, and dove in. My nervous parents paced the shoreline, making sure my head stayed above the surface. I loved being back in water, though the lake was often disturbed, rocked by currents, and stirred by the winds. Ferns brushed against my legs; ducks swam by, dropping feathers.

I returned to the Okanagan in August. Kalmoir Park was closed because of fires. Smith Creek, across the road from my parents' home, was burning. My parents were on evacuation alert, had the car packed with valuables, and were ready to leave at a moment's notice. At night, they set up lawn chairs on the street, watched the flames jump from tree to tree. There was fire all around them, ash dropping onto lawns and swimming pools, but somehow all the houses were spared.

Leslie told me Leanne had been in Mexico but hadn't told us a story about a fire on a mountain. I think she did. I wonder if the woman in the burning hut had her child before her blood womb broke and the fire reached her home? Did a shaman help to let the baby out? Once her water baby was born, did the woman strap the tiny girl to her chest and cook that feast for her relatives as I would, later, for my family and friends who kept vigil, who called and sang me back?

In Huichol mythology, the earth is a pregnant female belly that contains and produces life. Earth was created from the gourd womb of the earth goddess, Tatéi Yuriknake, when Kauyumari, the trickster, entered her womb and enlarged her belly. The ancestral gods and goddesses then created a flood of blood that filled the earth womb and carried them gently back to the surface of the world.

7 — The Past Was a Small Notebook, Much Scribbled-Upon

CORA SIRÉ

ON A WINTER MORNING in June, I open the curtains in my hotel room to the city of Salta sprawling towards the Andes. Gangs of gauchos are converging in a plaza down below. Many are wearing large leather shields—*guardamontes*—to protect their legs against thorns, suggesting they've journeyed from afar. They dismount, lead their horses to the fountain for water, and tether them to *tipa* trees. Wrapped in their ponchos, sharing bottles and stories, the gauchos wait.

From my tenth-floor window, the scene is soundless. Doubt creeps in. Is this real or imagined, and why are the gauchos waiting?

I get out my camera and angle the lens to exclude peripheral signifiers such as the HSBC bank around the corner. This could be the frame of a film's establishing shot: patriots bracing to battle the Spanish in pre-independence Argentina. All presided over by the timeless cordillera jutting into the brilliant, high-altitude sky.

I've arrived in the capital of Salta province to visit my in-laws with my beloved who grew up here. Otokar and I came from Canada as we always do, via Buenos Aires, where we spent some days acclimatizing. Actually, there was an ulterior motive to my idleness in Buenos Aires. I'd been waiting and hoping to meet acclaimed filmmaker Lucrecia Martel. Born in Salta in 1966, Martel has written and directed a trilogy of tightly constructed feature-length films shot in her home province.

I've convinced myself that Martel, who now lives in Buenos Aires, is the only director who could take my book and transform it into a film that would outshine the novel. This is a case of hope bordering on the delusional; *Behold Things Beautiful*, about a Latin American poet returning from exile, has yet to capture the imagination of Spanish-language publishers. My hope degenerates as I pass the days waiting to meet Martel.

On our last afternoon in Buenos Aires, I'm in a bookstore in Palermo, not far from the house where Jorge Luis Borges spent his childhood. I browse the labyrinth of book-stacked tables and shelves until I pick up a novel entitled *Zama* and leaf through the pages. The book opens with an intriguing dedication: *A las víctimas de la espera*.

The phrase is difficult to translate. The verb *esperar* means *to wait*. It also means *to hope*, which is logical, since waiting involves some form of hopefulness. But there's usually also some doubt. Unless, of course, hope is blinded by an irrational faith. Then it becomes delusional.

In a quasi-Borgesian twist, the bookstore employee tells me, when I'm paying, that Lucrecia Martel is about to make a film version of *Zama*.

On the flight from megacity to provincial capital, I crack open *Zama*. Impressively, it's the novel's seventh edition (Buenos Aires: Adriana Hidalgo editora, 2013). I begin with the author bio and learn that Antonio Di Benedetto, a journalist and screenwriter, wrote nine novels including *Zama*, first published in 1956. Twenty years later, Di Benedetto was imprisoned by the military dictatorship, tortured, and subjected to mock executions. The hellish wait for release took eighteen months. Later, I learn that the author, arrested within hours of the 1976 military coup, was never told why he had been jailed. Along with many others who managed to survive the Dirty War, he fled to Spain, returning to Argentina after the fall of the junta in 1984. He died two years later at sixty-three.

The haunting truth is that Di Benedetto's biography corresponds to the fates of many Latin American intellectuals of his time. Persecution by military dictators in Argentina, Chile, Uruguay, and Brazil during the 1970s resulted in the disappearances or incarceration of thousands—a form of calculated erasure.

⋮ The plane trip to Salta takes over two hours. As we fly northwest across the pampas towards the Andean spine, I'm too absorbed by the book to pay much attention to the stunning landscapes down below. Di Benedetto's novel deals with the fraught causality of waiting, a state that resonates after my days in Buenos Aires.

The antihero, one Don Diego de Zama, is a senior official posted to an unnamed outback of the Spanish realm in the 1790s, waiting and hoping to return to his wife and children in pre-independence Argentina. In the nine-year span of the novel's narrative, Zama lurches from scene to scene in a process of moral degeneration and financial ruin. The longer Zama waits, the more delusional his hope and the more perverse his behaviour.

The novel opens with a riverside scene. Zama observes a dead monkey floating in the rippling water, the corpse rising and falling but not going anywhere, and thinks, "There we were: Ready to go and not going." To spend time with this unreliable narrator is to submerge oneself in his downward spiral. Zama's wait goes on so long that hope becomes distant, elusive, and, eventually, absurd.

When we finally get to Salta and check into our hotel, I go online and research the book. *Zama*, it turns out, is considered an overlooked masterpiece. Since the 1950s, the book maintained a cultish following and was translated into German, French, and other languages. (But not English. It was only later that I found out about an English translation in progress that was finally released in 2016.)

I also learn that one of my literary heroes, Roberto Bolaño, paid homage to a fictionalized Di Benedetto in his short story, "Sensini." Alluding to *Zama* as a novel "written with neuro-surgical precision," Bolaño writes that while critics (mostly Spaniards) dismissed the novel as "Kafka in the colonies," *Zama* endured, recruiting "a small group of devoted readers." Bolaño describes the protagonists of Di Benedetto's fiction as fabled gauchos, "brave and aimless characters adrift in landscapes that seemed to be gradually drawing away from the reader (and sometimes taking the reader with them)."

"The wait went on. I did not know what for."
A few days before witnessing the gauchos in the plaza, Otokar and I find a driver to take us south from the provincial capital to Cafayate, a smaller town in fertile wine country. The two-hour journey snakes through mountain passes and crosses largely uninhabited plains where red-hued rock formations stand as immense sculptures, as if waiting to be discovered.

The landscape hasn't changed much in hundreds of years. Except that this winter, the scrubby vegetation and wide riverbed are parched. A trickle of water is all that's visible of Río Calchaquí, the once-tumultuous river celebrated in Salta's music and folklore.

Our driver entertains us with stories as if to distract from the drought devastating his province. Jauntily dressed in a blue cashmere sweater under a leather jacket, Francisco knows the road very well, anticipating sudden turns and narrow river crossings. Like most Salteños, he's an affable raconteur. He tells of his past, how he grew up poor in Salta province, joined the army at a young age and made a career for himself.

The dusty mountain landscapes stream past my backseat window to the soundtrack of Francisco's narrative. It turns out Francisco served in the honour guard of the presidential palace in Buenos Aires at the time when Isabelita (Perón's third wife) took over as president in 1974. Her reign, which lasted until the 1976 military coup, is generally considered disastrous, paving the way for the atrocities committed by the junta. When I ask about his role during the dictatorship, Francisco changes the subject to the newly named pope.

"He picked an excellent name for himself," Francisco says, turning to look at me in the backseat. Otokar laughs and after a few seconds, I get it. The Spanish version of the pope's name is Francisco.

In Cafayate, Otokar stops for a music lesson with his *quena* teacher and I continue with Francisco to the centre of town. He parks by the plaza and tells me to meet him here in an hour. I'm glad to walk and relieved he doesn't want to join me. His chatting's become a monologue in urgent need of an intermission.

I circle the plaza, passing benches with backpackers resting their feet and school kids huddling over solar-powered tablets. After visiting a church, I enter an alley that turns out to be an artisanal market. Women sit behind the stands knitting and chatting. It's off season. They're not expecting any business; they're not even hoping or waiting.

I stroll through the alley then loop back and return to the street. Turning the corner, I catch a blur of Francisco's tan leather jacket before he ducks into a shadowy colonial archway. To shake off my paranoia, I pivot into a side street and enter the first shop. After the brilliant sunshine, it takes some seconds to discern the man with the ponytail and tie-dyed shirt dusting knick-knacks on a counter. There's a basket of *quenas* on the floor. I stoop to check them out. The shopkeeper comes over, picks one of the flutes and plays a quick tune, his fingers dancing over the holes of the hollow cane, an instrument dating back to the time of the Incas. The Andean melody pierces like a gust of wind over a white-watered river. A tan swath crosses the entrance. Francisco looks inside.

Later we meet up at the car and Francisco drives to the *quena* teacher's house. Through the open windows, a nimble rhythm wafts from the house, carried by the wind, through the vehicle and up the mountainside, gliding like a condor—all nobility and purposefulness. Francisco is silent, almost brooding. Perhaps he's unhappy I noticed he was tailing me in the town, motivated, I conclude, by some lingering sense of duty from his days as a presidential bodyguard.

On the drive back, we overtake groups of gauchos on horse-back at various intervals. "Where are they going?" I ask Francisco.

Just as the car swerves into a harrowing hairpin curve, he turns to the backseat and looks at me. "To the city of Salta, of course."

⋮ I've spent years trying to discern Salta's complexities. At first, this process was entwined with trying to figure out my husband. Otokar grew up in Salta and left Argentina in 1976. Every few years, we travel back to visit his family and each time, arriving in Salta, I'm besieged by a conflicting mix of inertia and antsiness.

Part of it is geographic, the recovery from twenty-four hours spent in planes in between long sojourns of waiting in airports and adjustment to the city's altitude. Sudden exertions leave me breathless and my heartbeat keeps me awake at night. Another part is cultural as I adapt my thinking to Spanish and to Salta's enigmas, such as the distorted notion of time and the casual regard for weapons.

Even though Salta's a city of about one million, everyone seems to know everyone else, or *of* them, which gives the place a self-contained feel. Salteños generally have three or more children and they have them young, so extended families are large and multigenerational. Not many who are born here ever leave, and if they do study or work elsewhere, they often return. Buenos Aires, almost 1500 kilometres away, feels as detached as a glittering, distant planet.

In Salta the days exist as long bouts of nothingness between sporadic flurries of activity, an existence held together by the unique texture of an Andean culture with deep indigenous roots. I learned to speak Spanish here, which, early on, established a point of view that feels childlike, that of a naive observer who doesn't totally understand what's going on or get the jokes. No matter how hard I try to adapt, I will always be an outsider, never entirely sure of what's expected of me.

During one long afternoon *asado*, or barbecue of pampa beef, I'm advised by an earnest Salteño that if I ever discover an intruder in my room, I should "shoot the thief immediately, then shoot at the ceiling so you can tell the police you fired a warning shot." He looks at me, expecting thanks for his advice.

In the past, when Salta's quirks, dangers, and weird temporal rhythms perplexed me, I assumed I was just maladjusted and/or overly *gringa*. But in 2002, I saw a film that deepened my understanding of the place.

"The past was a small notebook, much scribbled-upon, that I had somehow mislaid."

In a cinema in Montréal, I watched *La Ciénaga* (*The Swamp*) and saw my various disjointed reflections on Salta explained to me through the lens of an insider's camera. Written and directed by Lucrecia Martel, the film depicts the dramas and inertias lived by two related families. The film's early scene shows the parents stumbling by a pool outside a summer residence near Salta. Kids lie around in a state of heat exhaustion or boredom. Nearby a band of boys, some armed, track through a leafy forest with a pack of dogs. Thrums of thunder intensify the sense of foreboding.

With close camera shots, Martel captures the family discon-
nect, neglect and danger. We're minutes into the film and the
mother, weaving poolside with her wine glass, trips and drops
her glass. It shatters on the tiles and she falls onto the shards.
She's bleeding, and since the adults are drunk, her daughter,
sixteen or so, puts on a shirt over her bathing suit and drives the
mother to a clinic. This inversion, where adults depend on their
children and children take care of them, is a recurrent phenomenon, as is the bleeding woman. Most of the adults and children,
and some of the animals in the story, are wounded, sometimes
fatally. The angles of Martel's shooting style and off-camera
dialogue evoke my sensations of being a naive observer of Salta,
like a kid trying to make sense of an unfathomable adult world.

The kid's perspective matures into adolescence in Martel's
second Salta film. *La Niña Santa* (*The Holy Girl*) also features a
swimming pool, this time indoors, at a decrepit hotel where a
medical conference is taking place. Two young women, about
seventeen, observe the interactions of the mostly male doctors,
some of them blatant sexual predators. Martel plays up the
women's hyperawareness and their adolescent fervour, both
sexual and religious. The film competed in Cannes in 2004, and
when I watched it in Montréal, I looked for and found the signifiers of Salta: Catholicism, incestuousness, and the decaying
bourgeoisie.

In the final installment in Martel's Salta trilogy, *La Mujer Sin
Cabeza* (*The Headless Woman*), the point of view ages further,
and we see through the eyes of a middle-aged woman. Early
in the film, driving alone on a highway, she appears to have
struck a dog or a boy. Her head slams the windshield after she
hits the brakes. Tightly constructed scenes show the woman,
confused and wounded, trying to make sense of her condition
but never owning up to the accident. When she learns of the
death of a boy on the highway, she admits to her husband that

she killed someone. The husband reacts with silence. Her lover, a cousin, handles the cover-up and repeatedly tells her, "Nothing happened." To emphasize her willed blindness, after confessing she puts on her sunglasses and, choosing not to see, waits out the fallout from the accident.

The 2008 film deals with the morality of indifference and silence. Given Argentina's recent history, it is political with a powerful subtlety. The first time I travelled to Argentina, in 1984, the country had just held its first democratic elections since the dictatorship. Yet when I asked about the disappeared, the 30,000 Argentines who had been abducted and executed during the preceding seven years, the answer, more often than not, was silence. *De eso no se habla.* Of this, one does not speak.

Martel's trilogy conveys an awareness of Salta that is recognizable and deeply perceptive. But more than a mirror to Salta's middle class, the films' stories are universally relevant in revealing the degradation of relationships, family life, and society.

In a 2009 interview published in *Bomb Magazine* after a retrospective of Martel's films at Harvard University, the director says, "In Salta, repeating the lives of others is a goal...In this city, traditions—not in the good sense that traditions can have—are a connection with the past, an affect...You conserve something that is not alive, something that no longer functions, that is rotten."

History—including the epic battles for independence from Spain—looms large in Salta. But the same pride and spirit that overcame colonial oppression can, over centuries, become degraded and frayed when people cling to traditions that no longer have meaning; they can constrict new generations with untenable expectations. This is what Martel conveys in her films. She introduces elements of the fantastical to raise doubts about reality, giving her films the feel of real experience. The scenes in her movies feel as vivid to me as my interactions with Francisco on the trip to Cafayate.

Martel's next film, *Zama*, which she has written and directed, was released in 2017. It is her first feature film set outside of Salta. Although Di Benedetto never specifically names his setting, various geographic markers point to Paraguay, especially the river that has special meaning in Zama's state of waiting. Boats arrive with or without his pay, with or without news from his wife, and leave with his messages, his lover and colleagues, but never with Zama himself.

In an interview in Argentina, Martel recounts how she first read *Zama* during a boat trip on the Paraná River from Buenos Aires to Asunción in Paraguay. When she finished reading the novel, she found herself in a strange euphoric state that triggered the idea of writing and directing a feature-film version. Since then, she'd been submerged in the world of *Zama*, comparing the adaptation process to being possessed by a kind of viral infection.

Reading *Zama*, I'm struck by the enormity of Martel's endeavour to transform the book into film. Narrated in first person, the novel is largely internal thought as Zama's situation degrades from that of a high-ranking official drawn into various intrigues with women and his colleagues to that of a participant in, and then prisoner of, a small cavalry bushwhacking into the interior of Paraguay. Zama's shenanigans and convoluted self-analyses are, at times, laugh-out-loud ludicrous.

The story is compressed into three parts according to year, 1790, 1794, and 1799, and it's the final part that evokes cinematic scenes of encampments and the Spaniards' confrontations with indigenous tribes who tend to show more compassion to their conquerors than is bestowed on them.

In the summer of 2016, the first English translation of *Zama* was published by New York Review Books. Translator Esther Allen spent several years in the anguished world of the novel. She has said that recreating Di Benedetto's *sui generis* style in English was one of the greatest challenges she faced. When I open the English version of *Zama*, the first thing I do is read the epigraph, curious to see how Allen translated the duality of waiting/hoping in the dedication. It reads, "To the victims of expectation," brilliantly capturing the essence of Zama's condition.

"The sun was a dog with a hot, dry tongue that licked and licked me until it woke me up."
After photographing the gauchos from my hotel room, I descend into the plaza to capture them untying their horses from the *tipa* trees. They pay no attention to me or my camera. The waiting's almost over. Something is about to happen.

The first flank of gauchos rides down the avenue on paso finos, horses known for their smooth lateral gaits. Otokar explains that every year, hundreds of gauchos converge from all over Salta province to file past the monument of their fallen hero, General Martín Miguel de Güemes.

The gauchos in the plaza mount their steeds to join the current of horses on the pavement. It's a visceral sound, the four-beat rhythms of hoofs: we remember, we remember, we remember.

In the fight for independence, Güemes led his cavalry of gauchos against the Spanish royalists in ebbs and flows of victory and defeat. Until, in 1821, under cover of darkness on a cloudy winter night, Spain's army fired a barrage of bullets. Wounded and clinging to his horse, Güemes rode to a nearby ravine and delegated command to his colonel: "Swear by your sword you'll fight for independence until Salta's lands are secured and free." Ten days later, on June 17, the general died.

After the parade of gauchos, I enter Salta's fine arts museum, housed in an elegant, early twentieth-century villa. I am alone, except for a security guard who follows me from gallery to gallery. On the second floor, I encounter a portrait of General Güemes. With his fearless, brown-eyed gaze and dark, curly hair, the gaucho-commander exudes dashing arrogance and high-octane machismo.

So the rumours whispered by his rivals might be true. His death, they insinuated, was really caused by a bullet fired from a jealous husband's weapon. Güemes might have died for a woman rather than his loyal gaucho cavalry, another hero corroded by the ambiguity of history.

Not unlike Don Diego de Zama.

At the end of his long wait for deliverance from the hinterlands of the Spanish empire, Zama is arrested and obliged to ride on as a captive of what's left of the ragtag cavalry. The Spaniards are greedy to discover precious gems, called *cocos* by the indigenous peoples, and deliver them to their imperial patrons. Zama decides to tell his captors the truth:

The *cocos* were an illusion, I said.
They did not contradict me with incredulity or mistrust.
I had said yes to my executioners, I knew.
But I had done for them what no one had ever tried to do for me. To say, to their hopes: No.

8 —— Beyond the Horizon

JULIE SEDIVY

OCCASIONALLY, we hear of the woman who died waiting for the man she loved, laying down a supper plate for him every evening for thirty years in case today was the day he walked in the front door, looking a little sheepish, a little breathless with anticipation, but mostly relieved of the great burden of being elsewhere, relieved to be home at last. Or we hear of the man who, after bullying, belittling, and bellowing at his children all their lives, alternately demanding everything of them and turning his back on them, is finally sucker-punched by the disassembling of his sturdy body and unyielding mind. He sends messages through those who will still talk to him, pleading for his children to come and grant him absolution. But no one comes, and he dissolves in the acid of his regrets, each day becoming more and more entangled in his bedding and his longing, until he is gone. And we think: That is the saddest thing. How sad to die in such a state of unmet yearning, how sad to die robbed of the resolution that should accompany death like the smoothing of sheets.

For decades, my father waited for the Iron Curtain to part. He'd fled Czechoslovakia in 1969 with his wife and three small children—a fourth on the way—crossing the Austrian border and then launching us across the Atlantic Ocean to Montreal.

His mother and brothers had said their goodbyes, knowing they might never see him again.

And yet, my father spoke often about the day the regime would fall. He talked about how I would play with the cousins I'd never met—or certainly didn't remember. His eyes became moist when he described the plum dumplings our mother would make from the fruit that grew so abundantly on his family's land in Moravia, the southern part of the country. Even as he built a new life in Canada—and build it he did, constructing the very house we lived in—his spirit seemed to be always oriented toward the east, as if he could hear strains of his country's folk music, or the whispered promise that soon, soon, soon, things would change and his homeland would open its borders like loving arms to welcome him home.

To my young self, who'd been born into the repressive regime, and who had yet to realize that history is perfectly capable of stopping in its tracks, wheeling about, and striding off in an entirely new direction, my father's state of anticipation seemed akin to waiting for anti-gravity cars, or gleaming cities on Mars, or a medical cure for death. It was an abstract future, nice to contemplate. But pinning any actual hopes on it was bound to lead to hot disappointment. It seemed yet another one of my father's sad little fantasies that was sure to slam up against the brick wall of reality. Like his dreams of prosperity and success in a new land running up against the reality that he—lacking an education and being master of neither English nor French, and not having absorbed those subtly oppressive Canadian norms of politeness, distance, and dominance—could do no more than inch his way up a rung or two on the socioeconomic ladder. Or his expectation that we would retain our Czech language and all the traditional customs of our home country. Or his deluded hope that I might find, fall in love with, and marry a young Czech, of whom there were precious few in Montreal.

What was strange about my father's choice to live in this suspended state was that I'd never thought of him as a patient man, as someone who could tolerate the stillness of waiting. He was inevitably the one we were waiting for, as he scrambled to find his jacket or his tie or his comb as we were heading out the door to church. If he happened to be ready before one of us, he would stand by the door twitching and calling out for the laggard among us to hurry up. He caused each of us many moments of anxiety about whether we'd make it on time for our school plays or music recitals—I remember rushing onto the stage, psychically dishevelled after having sat in a traffic snarl on the Metropolitan highway, growling at my father who merely shrugged and said, "If we'd left any earlier, I'd just be sitting in a chair waiting for things to start." He had an especially hard time waiting for us to grow up. "How is it that you don't know this already!" he would exclaim, eyes pointed at the sky and arms dropping to his sides.

But now, through the revised sight of an orphaned daughter, other things come into focus. I remember him spending countless hours in his garden, or, before spring unfurled, in the greenhouse he'd built on the second floor of our house. He pressed seeds into soft potting mix, waiting for them to germinate, then waiting for the spindly seedlings to become strong enough to set outdoors. Though his relationship with time was often fraught, he seemed to accept the totalitarian rhythms of nature with something exactly like serenity. Every year, he brought the amaryllis bulb up from the cellar and waited twelve weeks for it to bloom on my mother's birthday. On my wedding day, he presented me with a tiny cactus plant that had thrown a single white blossom, a flounce like a miniature taffeta skirt. This cactus bloomed for only a few days each year, he told me. It took me years to realize that its flowering that day was no coincidence and that he had acquired and nurtured the plant in anticipation of my wedding.

Maybe his waiting for the political situation to change in Czechoslovakia was a bit like this, more to do with the affairs of nature than with the hearts and habits of humans, who so often proved themselves to be flagrantly unpredictable and would disappoint you for all your waiting. Maybe he felt certain that there was an order to the universe that, on a schedule still unknown to him, would inevitably draw back the tide of oppressive occupation that had submerged his homeland.

Or maybe his decades-long wait had nothing to do with certainty, or belief, or expectation, or even anything to do with reality at all. Maybe his waiting was exactly like hope—not the kind of hope that sets store in any version of the future, but hope as described by my father's countryman, Václav Havel. While Havel waited in prison for an indeterminate time, sitting out his punishment for failing to absorb and reflect the lies of his government, years before the tide turned and he left his jail cell to become Czechoslovakia's first post-Communist president, this is what he wrote:

> Hope is a state of mind, not of the world. Either we have hope or we don't; it is a dimension of the soul, and it's not essentially dependent on some particular observation of the world or estimate of the situation. Hope is not prognostication. It is an orientation of the spirit, and orientation of the heart; it transcends the world that is immediately experienced, and is anchored somewhere beyond its horizons... Hope is definitely not the same thing as optimism. It is not the conviction that something will turn out well, but the certainty that something makes sense, regardless of how it turns out.

My older self is better able to make sense of waiting for something that you may never live to see. There is yearning, yes, of the kind that cultivates the pain of disappointment. But there is also openness, the welcoming of a certain possibility, remote as it may be. There is a readiness of the heart should that possibility come to pass, a certainty in how we would respond to it if it did.

Whatever the nature of my father's long wait, he was ready when the fraying Iron Curtain was torn to the ground in the waning days of 1989. By 1991 he had moved back home, reunited with his mother and brothers. In the generous soil and mild climate of his native Moravian countryside, he planted fruits he never could have in Montreal: apricots, plums, grapes. He sank deeply into the warm folds of his mother tongue, which he could now use to freely express his views, even with strangers and without closing the door or shuttering the windows.

But new yearnings soon replaced the old. He had failed to persuade his wife or any of his children, who had not lived in the same state of waiting, to move back with him. He and my mother remained married, visiting each other in their respective countries, and my siblings and I saw him on his annual visits to Canada. His campaign began: he wanted us to visit him there, to become reacquainted with our roots.

I don't know why I didn't go. I suppose I felt at the time that there were things in my life that couldn't wait—graduate school, children, an absorbing career, putting out the fires in a marriage that was increasingly on the verge of full conflagration. A visit to the fatherland, I thought, *could* wait.

One day, I was wriggling out of yet another request to come for a visit. And the next, my mother called, waking me from my sleep to tell me that my father had died in his.

He'd been unable to wait for a more opportune moment; he died just a few days before the beginning of my divorce trial, the kind that sends your kids into a tailspin and locks you legally and emotionally into place. I wasn't even able to attend the funeral in the town where he'd been living. I heard that it overflowed with mourners who greeted the Canadian relatives and spoke with feeling of my father's great influence on their lives.

It was a number of years before my life settled down enough for me to make an extended visit to the land that had birthed me and taken my father back into its body. Then, for two months, I lived in a corner of the sprawling family compound where he'd spent his childhood, sleeping on the very same bed on which he and his brothers had been born. Every morning, I woke to the peal of church bells next door and walked through the village, watching the early sun anoint the fields and vineyards that stretched far behind the houses, hearing the soft calls of mourning doves. I ate most of my meals with my cousins or uncle, sipping the wine they had made from the grapes they had grown. It was on this land, which my family had occupied for nearly four hundred years, that I began to understand how it had made sense for my father to wait all those years to go home.

In Canada he had always seemed cramped and uncomfortable, as if wearing an ill-fitting suit. The poor fit was apparent, and embarrassing—to me, when he failed to behave like the other parents I knew, and to him, in the way people spoke louder upon hearing his accent or were offended or wounded by the blunt instrument that was his humour. His discomfort was clear in the way he held his opulent Slavic sentimentality in check with those he didn't know well, acting like a slouching man embarrassed by his unusual height.

It was only by visiting his country after his death that I came to know who my father had been, how, once restored to his native soil, his full self stretched out to grow into the eloquent, courageous, humane leader that his Czech compatriots knew him to be—the sort of man who knew how to support an alcoholic trying to stay dry in this wine-soaked region, and the sort of man whose version of religious piety would not stand for the shunning of a young unwed couple living "in sin." How often,

I wondered, do we know others only as they are in a poor soil, in a corner of the world to which they are not suited—refugees violently transplanted, Indigenous peoples severed from their lands, women barred from the public or professional life for which they were designed, transgender people sorted into bins in which they will never belong.

Before I returned to Canada, I visited my father's grave. Beneath the flowers that I left on the polished stone bearing his name was a letter I'd written him. I told him about the places I had been to in his homeland, the people I had met, what I had seen and learned. I wondered—and wonder still—whether at the moment of his death, he was still waiting for me to come visit him.

I hope he was. I hope to God he was.

9 ___ Two Women Waiting

REBECCA DANOS

WAITING. The impressionist artist Degas created a painting entitled *Waiting*, featuring two women side by side, doubled over on a bench. One is dressed in drab black street clothes, and she holds an umbrella. The other wears a white tulle tutu with a blue silk ribbon around her waist. You can lose yourself, as a voyeur, observing these women in the painting. I know I have. What are they waiting for? Is the ballerina a woman with a romantic career, waiting for her turn in the ballet? Is she catching her breath before she radiantly returns to the spotlight? Or is she waiting for the ballet to finish, so she might take refuge in a bath? As for the other woman, is she living a pedestrian existence, trying to escape a cold, wet day in Paris by taking refuge in the theatre before she must again face a dreary life? We can imagine endless scenarios as we ponder why these two women wait. And if we imagine ourselves on that bench, we can ask ourselves: are we spending our own lives waiting, waiting for our lives to change, or maybe even for our lives to begin?

Isn't the experience of waiting for news or an event to transpire universal? Our minds clench. Hands chill. Alternative scenarios play out in our minds. We try to read others' thoughts as we wonder what delays them in responding to our emails or phone calls. Our human minds, generators of pessimistic outcomes, concoct tragedies and rejections. Our pulses race. Muscles contract. Obsessive worrying bombards our consciousness.

Life is a string of such empty moments, fraught with anticipation for the surcease of the mundane and the incipience of the dream. We await cessation of the pain of the human condition. Isn't this what we all are really waiting for, anyway, and not just for that elusive promotion or aspiration? To be human is to suffer, Buddhists might tell us. We engage in distractions and dreams, fantasies and escapes, to evade our suffering for a little while, to lose ourselves in someone else's story, a mathematical calculation, a painting, a performance, a novel idea, or an imagined future.

The pain of waiting is a tautology. Throughout my life I have waited for the suffering to end with an expectation that it would once I attained my goal. However, this anticipation only precipitates more anxiety and pain. Am I only augmenting my suffering by spending my time waiting for it to cease? How can I leave the bench?

The two women on the bench embody much of how I have experienced the great majority of my life. As a child, my inner life was dominated by my fantasies of escape from the misery in which I was imprisoned. Like the pedestrian woman in black, I felt trapped by the monotony and cruelty that defined my life: ceaseless subjection to berating and bullying and the performance anxiety and perfectionism that claimed my mind when it came to exams and everyday activities. At an early age I envisioned that I would one day dance into the spotlight by becoming a professor of theoretical cosmology. My life would have been as dark as the ordinary woman's clothes, were it not for the redemptive anticipation of college, graduate school, and my version of the storybook ending in which I became, not a ballerina, but a faculty member. Life as a professor would include probing the secrets of the universe, engaging in

intellectual discourse, and tackling the great unsolved cosmo-
logical mysteries such as the nature of the universe in its earliest
moments. Plodding through all the childhood years and those
that followed, populated by bullies and emotional, academic,
and physical hardships, I never questioned that one day I would
trade my black garb for a gorgeous white ballet dress and evade
toxicity by dancing in a harmonious academic waltz.

But the ballerina must also spend her days waiting as she
prepares for roles in ballets or to be promoted from an apprentice to the corps or from the corps to a soloist. She must also wait
to hear if she is awarded a part in the ballet. And so I waited as
well. I waited for high-school graduation and news of college,
graduate school, and postdoctoral acceptances. I waited for the
bestowal of the degrees. I waited to check off each goal on the
ladder leading to the promise of fulfillment as a theoretical
physics professor.

Through each stage of this waiting, I engaged in a flirtation
with the glamour of physics and a life in physics. There was
the captivating beauty, not just of my undergraduate campus,
Wellesley College, but inherent in the mathematics, physics, and
astrophysics I studied there. Linear algebra inspired me with
a romanticism that would rival *Giselle*, laying the framework
for quantum mechanics. Then in quantum mechanics, I saw
how two possibilities can coexist, like Odette and Odile in *Swan
Lake*—or as the two women on the bench. In college I glimpsed
the glamour of physics scintillating not only through the intellectual spectacles of my studies but also through travels to
Harvard's Mount Hopkins telescope in Arizona and internships
at MIT and Harvard, universities where research shimmers like
the ballet dancer's pointe shoes. I had fallen in love with the
story of the universe, with its cosmic dances, and felt ready to
sacrifice life's pleasures for my ambition, forgoing sleep and
participation in the many Wellesley traditions and activities.
This was just the beginning, I rationalized; I was a member of

the corps, on a path to being promoted to a prima ballerina, and I would wait patiently for the realization of the dream, a faculty position where investigating theoretical physics questions would occupy my waking moments.

The paths we envision for our lives are often more circuitous than we hope. My path to completing a master's in Physics from UCLA, a PHD from McGill University, and my postdoctoral fellowship was punctuated by difficulties from every direction, and I came to realize that while the dancer might wear a ballerina's costume, she nonetheless suffers unforeseen injuries threatening her auditions and performances. Or perhaps she sits on the bench, cast away by an irate artistic director. Maybe her understudy outshone her, and she has been demoted. As a graduate student and postdoctoral fellow, I grew to realize we embody elements of both women in all the possibilities each could experience, a superposition of states as in quantum mechanics. I danced on the stage when I gave talks at such exotic locations as Paris and when I enjoyed the glitter of cutting-edge seminars and discussions with my McGill group. I also sought shelter from the rain when I encountered difficulties with collaborations or research problems. I began to realize that these two women and their lives are complex and entangled, not as black and white as the clothes they wear. But I never ceased to wait to become a professor when I could spend most of my hours pondering profound research questions.

Do we wait for a change of circumstances so that we might unfold ourselves and exit, erectly, the waiting room where we reside most of our day-to-day lives as we strive for our goals? The woman in black street clothes might await a fantasy that is, indeed, just an illusion. Was I deluded that meeting a professional goal would transform my life from one steeped in darkness to one haloed in light?

Now after tasting life as a university instructor of math and physics courses and observing my husband, a professor of theoretical physics, I question the fantasy. Is it really so romantic to balance teaching, administrative, service, and research duties that devour all one's waking moments? Is this really my dream? I sit, as the woman in black, still not a professor but with a glimpse of the profession, studying the ballerina's bloodied toes and strained tendons. Have I waited my entire life for a goal I might never reach? And, as in the painting, I realize that even the woman whose life might be a patent success must endure periods of inactivity, when she might need to nurse sore toes or tolerate aching muscles. Or sit on a bench. Waiting.

As I look at the painting and ponder the human condition, I wonder, would I rather be the woman in black, wishing to be the ballerina? Or be the dancer, exhausted from a performance, who fantasizes about a life more ordinary and structured, surrendering late nights of exertion for an evening resting in a bath? Which fate do we really desire? The answer is that both women's lives represent all of us; we truly are a superposition of both. Both are also subject to the interminable in-between moments that suffuse most of the hours of our lives. We all live dual identities, the dreamer who conceives of glamour and the one who desires just to be a member of the audience. Sometimes we land the role and have the opportunity to dance our lives on the stage. At other times, we struggle just to stay dry.

I don't know what lies in my future. My dream is no longer the singular one of becoming a professor, as I realize research is just a small part of a faculty position, and I have other passions to explore. I desire, instead of holding steadfast to a specific dream, to be open to a range of possibilities that might unfold. I don't regret my preparation for one profession, even if another might replace it. Life holds many question marks regarding the directions we might follow. However, I have discovered, the act of working towards our ambitions becomes the substance of our lives, regardless of its destination, not a passive waiting for our lives to begin. A cessation of suffering occurs when we realize that each moment, even the captured image of two women on a bench, possesses meaning as a scene from life. Maybe we can recast our time spent on the bench into poetry or art. We need to make peace with who we are, as embodied by both women. We need to accept that we cannot, to avoid life's hurts, move freely through time, speed it up, or slow it down, as Einstein revealed to us in his theory of relativity. We need, instead, to embrace our trajectory through time, whatever it is, and endow it with meaning and purpose. We might never reach our planned happy ending. The ballerina might never become a principal dancer or secure the role of Giselle. Or if she does, she might find fulfilling the responsibilities daunting or the emotional demands of dancing the mad scene to be too overwhelming. She, too, might realize that life is an ongoing timeline of waiting punctuated by interruptions by events, rather than its converse. We can choose to wait. We can choose to find solace, without suffering, in our variegated fates and roles, even in our distress. Because even in pain lie the nuanced colours of the human condition from which we can learn, grow, create art, and develop deeper human connections. And should we find ourselves waiting on a bench with someone, perhaps we can enjoy her company.

10 ── Esperando

MY FIRST SPANISH WORD: perro. I smear white paste on the back of the small square of photocopied paper and squish it into a lined notebook. A simple drawing of a dog. Thick black letters form the word. Perro. In my head, I can hear the rolling middle, the rounded ending. But my Grade Four teacher corrects me, again and again. Perro. Perro. A squat Peruvian with over-sized glasses, Señor teaches us "La Cucaracha" and flips through a slideshow of his trip to Machu Picchu. It's not part of the curriculum; we're learning his first language. This should be the moment that Spanish takes hold. The moment I can later point to as fortuitous, since the language has seeped into my every day. But I am still waiting.

Spanish resurfaces, this time as an optional course, when I am in Grade Nine. After years of compulsory struggles with French, I hope Spanish will be easier. The pages of my textbook smell faintly of vinegar. The teenagers inside wear platform shoes and bellbottoms. They frequent the discotheque. I suspect places like Mexico, being poor and far away, can't escape the 1970s. My teacher wears flowing, earthy dresses and piles her fine dark hair into a bun. Señora encourages banal conversations en español. We are acquiring vocabulary. I peel una naranja inside the cubby of my desk, digging into the thick rind with my fingernails. The lunch bell will ring soon. "Who is eating an orange? Who?" Señora marches down the aisles. "We are not leaving until someone admits to eating an orange." Esperamos. We wait. We wait until long after the bell rings, and Señora gives up.

Spanish isn't offered in high school. For many years, I don't think about the verbs, the nouns, the odd way adjectives are arranged. Wanderlust takes me through a dozen countries, places where students sweat over English grammar. I memorize a few polite greetings in the local languages. On a bus leaving Cape Town, I meet a South American backpacker. Before we part, he writes a message in my travel journal. I can't decipher the Spanish. I don't want to show anyone. I don't want to look it up. This message is ours. The following year we are engaged and living in Canada. I find an office job to pay off credit card bills from a year of travels. On Tuesday nights, we drive through the rain to take non-credit classes at the college. He studies astronomy. I study Spanish. This time, it's the easygoing Spanish of travellers. The students exchange greetings, order huevos revueltos, chat about the weather. My fiancé also writes out lyrics by Colombian pop star Shakira for me. This technique helped him learn English as a teenager. I can pick out words, but even pop music is incomprehensible. Before my last Spanish class, I chop fruit for sangria. His class plans to meet at Tim Hortons for star gazing, so he asks me if I know where Tim Horton lives.

I return to university that fall, swimming in disconnected palabras. I pick Spanish for Beginners as an elective, hopeful that I can finally succeed at a language, until I see my Grade Nine Spanish teacher at the front of the class. Not the ghost of my Grade Nine Spanish teacher—my actual Grade Nine Spanish teacher. She returns my first quiz scarred with red pen marks: half points for missed accents, zeros for misspelled words. Spanish wraps its hands around my leg, pulls me down into the depths of its dark water. I panic, imagining my grade point average falling, along with future scholarships and grad school. I won't improve. I can't improve. Before dropping the class, I visit Señora in her claustrophobic office and I ask if she remembers la naranja. She looks surprised, maybe embarrassed, and says she doesn't like the smell of oranges. At home, my fiancé is understanding. He's also learning a new language. He needs a thick dictionary. Avionics monitor, approach speed, auxiliary rotor. Those are just a few in the As.

A few years later, my husband is flying a Twin Otter in the Arctic and I'm between jobs, living with his parents in Montevideo, Uruguay. I'm determined to finally learn Spanish. Angular apartment buildings line the cracked, patchwork sidewalks. Drivers honk, buses spew diesel fumes, and garbage pickers load acquisitions from trash cans into donkey-pulled carts. Summer approaches, warming the city. The air is thick with the promise of barbecues and trips to the beach. My in-laws speak English, but outside the apartment, I'm isolated by language. Each morning I catch a bus, packed with dark-haired men in suits and flawless women in pencil skirts paired with heels. My tutor lives in an old, but elegant, white house. I'm her only student in a windowless room with a few desks. She is unmemorable, except for her patience and outdated slide projector. We move quickly through the pleasantries of Spanish. Soon I'm conjugating verbs. I learn that the verb to wait in Spanish—esperar—also means to hope. At lunchtime, I buy a baguette sandwich, en español, at a crowded deli. The nearby park has cool grass under the shade of arching ceibo trees. I watch people nap or sip mate through silver straws from dried gourds. Spanish is washing over me. I'm starting to understand. I no longer stand by the door, my bag packed for the beach, when everyone else is discussing the dark clouds and planning a trip to the mall. But the words still feel like marbles in my mouth. I make mistakes. I feel embarrassed. A friend laughs, says my lessons remind her of little kids in a jardín de infancia. I speak a little less. Once I've flown home, I speak some Spanish with my husband, but we soon drift back into English. Over the years, I take more night courses but don't really improve. Frustrated, I tell my father that people like us can't learn a new language. He takes Spanish lessons anyway. He's hopeful, even at seventy.

A baby's brain is like a vast dark room, capable of any language. Light switches flip on for every sound. At least, I read something like this in a book. I cling to it, hope it's true. I tell my husband he must speak in Spanish to our baby girl, and I will speak in English. She'll speak both languages without effort. Her first words are a mixture: mama, papa, cat, bath, agua. But as those words congeal into sentences, it's mostly English. And my husband starts to respond in English, unable to resist sharing a language, sharing a connection, with our toddler. The Spanish words start to disappear as she eases into English, her brain sopping up streams of sentences and encouragement. I realize I can't hear my husband's accent anymore. I double check with other people. They laugh. Yes, he still has an accent.

When our daughter is five, she starts to study Spanish in school. She sings in Spanish, counts in Spanish, learns the words for desk, pencil, chair. I volunteer in the classroom, calculating simple sums and playing games en español. As she gets older I try to help her study for dictado, but she says I'm mispronouncing her spelling words. We wait, we hope. For years she won't speak more than a few Spanish words to her abuelos and primos during visits to Montevideo. Then, one day, she finds me struggling to speak to a grocery store clerk, fighting to string together the words, to spit out the marbles. So my daughter corrects me, laughs, and takes over. Maybe she makes mistakes, but she keeps going. The clerk, delighted, calls her niñita, asks her how she learned Spanish.

At home, lying on the bed with my daughter, her head on my arm, I ask her what she did at school today. Her hair smells like watermelon shampoo. She can't stop wiggling her toes. "I'll tell you in Spanish, okay?" she says. She begins to speak quickly, and I can pick out phrases and many words. But I don't understand everything. So I stop listening. Instead I feel the words reverberating through my body, through my bones. I thought I could conquer this language in a classroom or during a month-long trip. But Spanish might take me a lifetime. I can wait. I'm still hopeful.

11 — Currents

ALICE MAJOR

FOR THREE YEARS NOW, we've been waiting to see what we'll think of it, this massive development on the old railway yards just north of downtown. The tower cranes—their strutted jibs, slewing units, cables, and counterweights—have sketched preliminary engineering diagrams against the sky, but it's still difficult to imagine what this new arena and these towers, meant to house hotels and civic offices, will actually feel like at ground level.

I'm not at all sure I will like it. A giant limb reaches out from the arena to cross the avenue and plant a massive paw on the far side. During construction, we have driven below this arch as though our cars were plunging into the maw of a dark cave. It is architecture that doesn't seem to have anything to do with our story. This isn't cave country—it's a landscape of slough and poplar, of wide river valleys open to the sky. It's not a landscape of heights either. I feel despondently that the new skyscrapers seem interchangeable with towers anywhere on the planet— buildings not much more distinctive than the tower cranes that are erecting them, designed as much for Minneapolis or Mississauga as for Edmonton, Alberta.

The arena's design does make some gesture towards this particular area's economic heritage. Seen from above, it is supposed to be shaped like a drop of oil—and oil has been shaping us for about half our official existence as a city.

I arrived here in Edmonton, Alberta, thirty-five years ago, at the tail end of the boom that had surged through the 1960s and 70s, after the Leduc No. 1 well blew in southwest of the city in 1947. When I got here, the downtown skyline was still hiked up with construction cranes; their long booms hovered over new buildings rising from the drawing boards of prosperity: the pink glass curtain wall of the Government of Canada's tiered structure, the grey-blue edifice of Commerce Place.

But by 1981, a worldwide recession was finally catching up with Alberta's heated economy. The price of oil sank to $10 a barrel. Politicians were looking desperately for some mega-project to keep the province's growth going—a magnesium processing plant in the south, a huge hydro dam in the far north. But nothing much materialized. Our skyline settled into a decade and a half of construction lull.

I didn't really notice the hiss of escaping energy as I settled myself into this new place. Even if I had been conscious of the economic slump, I wouldn't have minded. I was coming to like this city very much, its openness to the sky, its modest downtown. There was a lot of energy at ground level. We were starting arts festivals and arts councils, writers' guilds and poetry groups. I remember an electricity in those days, a sudden feeling that I had been plugged into a socket, really could become a writer.

⋮ I came here because of electricity—quite literally. I had a new job working for an electric utility company, another bright-eyed young woman in the public relations department. Along with articles for the staff magazine about the Vegreville office or the new generating station at Sheerness, I began to write a lot about the planning of an electric system.

I liked the engineers whose ideas I was helping to communicate—thoughtful men (yes, pretty well all of them were men) who were able to see different sides of a question, were idealistic about serving customers well. Still, there were assumptions they (and I) took for granted and didn't question. For instance, it made sense to have an electric system with big central plants (where you could more easily and tidily control emissions) and long transmission lines that pushed across the province into smaller and smaller tributaries, like river systems in reverse. It made sense to burn the abundant subbituminous coal to generate power and save our more valuable oil and gas to sell elsewhere.

I scribbled notes as the engineers told me how you need to carefully plan a mix of generation sources: big "base load" units that go on pumping out power round the clock, plus "peaking" units that you can switch on and off quickly to meet the daily rise and fall of electrical demand. That's because electricity is a funny thing, a careful balancing act between what's going into the system and what's being drawn out. If you don't get the two matched within a hair's breadth at every moment, the whole system will flail around and fail.

Nor can you just stick extra juice in a bucket and freeze it until needed. Battery storage is pretty useless at the scale of an electric utility—you'd need batteries the size of hills. No, the best thing is just not to make any more than you need at any given moment. Just make sure you have options like hydro units that can be turned on and off like a tap to meet the electricity rush hours.

This system didn't leave a lot of room for things like wind or solar power. (You can't turn the wind on with a switch, the engineers pointed out. And what does a solar farm do for you at midnight?) But on the whole, the system worked pretty well for the 1970s and 80s. The big utility companies in the province sat down together around a table, figured out how the load was growing, and came to a gentlemanly kind of agreement about which company's unit would get built next. It was best for consumers if you made such additions in a planned way, with an orderly flow of new generating plants and transmission lines.

⋮ During those years, I took part in corporate scenario-planning sessions with the engineers to try to prepare for different futures that might be coming at us. Those exercises were a lot of fun. But the thing is, you don't actually see change coming. You *think* you're planning for it, but it comes through a side door or announces itself in a newspaper story on page three that you missed.

I wasn't all that anxious for change anyway. I knew my city. I had an idea of its shape. I liked it. I laughed at the bumper stickers reading, "Please, God, send us another oil boom. We promise we won't piss this one away," knowing that I didn't need or even want an oil boom.

Then one day my husband came home and mentioned how he'd been at a meeting where companies expressed concern about not having enough skilled labour in the province. "It's happening again," he said. We were ramping up into another feverish, fifteen-year cycle of rocketing house prices. Suburbs began stamping their cookie-cutter feet farther out over the farmland around the city and, once again, the construction cranes were rearing their angular heads downtown. Condo towers were making 104 Street trendy. Finally, a developer closed a deal with the city to build this dizzying new arena district on the weedy, puddled railway land that has been waiting so long to be used again.

And then, again, the air blew out of the tires. It wasn't a slow leak this time. I couldn't help but notice the headlines, the tumbling price of oil, and I could recognize the pattern. We'd had the oil boom and pretty well pissed it away.

Oh, well, you might think. *It will come back. We could use the breathing space.*

⋮ My city is only a little more than a century old, though Indigenous peoples have camped here beside the river's rolling current for eight thousand years. The petroleum industry has been a factor here for only a single human lifetime; I was born just a year or so after Leduc No. 1 started to flow.

You can see the industry's stamp in how the city has been built—the vast, flat-roofed warehouses of equipment manufacturers in the south, the fractionating towers, flare stacks, and squat round storage tanks of Refinery Row at the eastern edge. We were a service town, not a head-office one, so the city centre had relatively few of the tall buildings that erupted in Calgary.

Changing technology has altered the shape of most cities, even ancient ones. I was born an ocean away from here, near Glasgow, which has had city status for nearly a thousand years. I used to be taken into the heart of Glasgow by train, to the massive railway terminus of Central Station. Below the overhead rail platforms runs a dark tunnel-stretch of Argyle Street, lined with small shops. My mother and I would come down from the smoky train platforms to an urban landscape built of dense stone blackened by soot from burning coal.

The whole edifice of Central Station was built over the top of a small port village known as Grahamston. The railway terminus represented an enormous redevelopment, a nineteenth-century planning mess driven by competition between railway companies and built in spite of objections from the village's residents. Six hundred homes and businesses were pulled down and thousands of people displaced to bring the railways into the city.

It seems mildly ironic that I have ended up in a place where it's the railways that are being buried under redevelopment. The railyards here were enormous: twenty tracks wide, with boxcars packed as close as cattle jostling in a pen. A stately column-fronted station welcomed thousands of immigrant settlers from countries like Ukraine and soldiers returning from the battle-fields of France—surging currents of people who move around the world, as people do.

Sometimes I think wistfully of medieval Italian towns—Padua, for example, whose core has been magically preserved for five hundred years. Footsteps echo at night over its cobblestones, shut off from the current of traffic. No construction crane will raise a head over the Piazza delle Erbe or the Prato della Valle. You can still walk into the classroom where Galileo taught or find a table in the Caffè Pedrocchi where Stendhal praised the coffee. The town planners have held up their hands and said, "No more. It stays as it is."

Of course, I'm being romantic. Padua isn't a medieval town in any sense. Its economy has changed profoundly since Giotto's day. For fifteen centuries, from the time the town went by its Roman name of Patavia, agriculture had been at its heart; the poet Martial praised Patavia's fine wool and the warm tunics woven from it. But today, the stores and restaurants lining its quiet streets and the goods sold in the market square bear little or no relation to what people of the fourteenth century consumed. The seven-hundred-year-old Scrovegni Chapel is now an air-locked space where tourists shuffle in for a fifteen-minute scrap of time with the famous Giotto frescoes. Outside the historic centre, Padua is ringed by motorways and the giant struts of high-voltage power lines; it is home to one of the biggest industrial zones in Europe. You would wait a long time to smell horse dung or to buy cloth in the market stalls that isn't imported from somewhere else.

Of course, we don't, can't, wait for the past—even though sometimes we would like to preserve it in amber. The past always looks easier, as though people back then *must* have known how it would all turn out, how the story would end.

⋮ The word "electricity" comes from the Greek word for amber. The phenomenon that inspired its name is the paradoxically named "static electricity"—the prickly, hair-raising sensation that the ancients noticed when a piece of amber was rubbed against cloth, ripping apart negatively charged electrons and positively charged nuclei.

We don't think of electricity as *static*, standing still. We usually think of it as *current*, as something that moves purposefully in a definite direction, through the metal wires that run down our back lanes and inside our walls. However, those moving circuits represent only a subset of the much larger phenomenon of *charge*, a force that creates the familiar structure of our world, holding atoms together. Charge doesn't like imbalance; if electrons and nuclei get sheared apart, it wants to herd them back together.

Our world is like a huge vat of electrolytic fluid, positive and negative charges all swirling around together until a switch gets closed. Then current has to start moving through the completed loop. But "current" isn't necessarily the flow of negatively charged electrons that runs through the artificial situation of solid metal wires in our planned circuits. In other states of matter (in fluids, like batteries and living cells, or in gases like fluorescent tubes and the ionosphere) positive and negative currents move simultaneously in opposite directions.

Even in solid wires, electric current is not the massive, organized, onrushing flow of electrons we might imagine. Within a circuit, individual electrons drift back and forth, up and down, colliding with each other and making surprisingly little headway—a metre or so in an hour. It's still something of a mystery what actually moves through a circuit, but its force has to do with potential, the difference between the two ends.

It's a little like the river that moves though my city. The river itself is a single big thing, a flow pulled by gravity from the Rockies to Hudson Bay, three thousand miles away. But it's also a collection of very tiny things. Every water molecule feels its own specific combination of forces, up, down, sideways, sometimes moving, sometimes stuck. The river isn't one big determined, and determinative, flow. It's also backwash and sidestep, loop and eddy.

So, change, any change, often means just sitting in a state of potential, in which it is hard to see what the gravity of the future is pulling us towards.

⋮ Up until about 200,000 years ago—the tiniest sliver of time in the planet's history—there were no modern humans around. Then we arrived, with whatever combination of genetic tweaks that made us different from our ancestors, and it was as though a switch had been closed. A current began flowing. From our source in Africa, we pushed ourselves out all over the globe. The impact has been, from a planet's point of view, almost instantaneous and our great worry now is that the current is negative, that the ecosystem that supports us is starting to flail around and fail. We're here like small animals sniffing the air, trying to figure out what's coming for us, for the future. Where is this narrative heading?

There's a sense of real change abroad, a sense of potential. It's not just because of the negative sense that we *shouldn't* contribute to destabilizing the planet's climate, but the positive sense that we *could* do things differently. There are all sorts of small signals: The train ride I took through Germany a year or two ago, when I was startled to realize that all the rooftops on the quaint farmhouses were shining because of solar panels. The article I read last week about a new technology—solar cells so gossamer-light they could sit on a soap bubble. The net-zero laneway house that a neighbour down my street has built at the back of her lot.

That picture of the electric grid I learned when I came here is becoming out of date, a planner's picture from a century already passed. It could be replaced with small, distributed sources of power—solar panels on rooftops, a wind farm here, a biomass plant there—that move energy in small, back-and-forth pulses. If you have enough small, varied sources like this, you don't need as much backup storage. (Your windmill is generating tonight, but my solar panel will pick up the slack when the wind dies down.) Nor does it take as much energy to move power down the street as it does when you're pushing it for hundreds of kilometres. The electric system could become less a centralized grid and more like an underground root system, extracting what it needs from nearby.

We can't entirely abandon planning and forethought, of course. Humans need to undertake shared initiatives if we're not going to electrocute each other. Electricity is still a subtle, back-and-forth force that needs to be kept in balance. We'll still need the engineers.

But much that seemed pie in the sky during those scenario-planning sessions is now becoming practical. The world may not need drops of oil forever—or at least not the growing flood we've been pumping out of the ground around here.

⋮ So, I sense the oil boom may well *not* come back. What will become of my city, then? Will we become like one of the rust-belt cities of America, bulldozing abandoned suburbs and trying desperately to reinvent our economies?

What will our oil-drop arena become in fifty years? In a hundred? In fifteen centuries? A roofless, abandoned ruin reclaimed by aspen trees? (They have already reclaimed the abandoned coal-mine shafts that were burrowed into the river valley's walls more than a century ago.) Or could it become like the ancient, still-standing Roman wall that surrounds the Scrovegni Chapel? A structure whose original purpose is no longer relevant but that still offers its familiar curve for people to stroll beside.

Our arena's design gestures to a very narrow layer of time, a transient bubble in the flow of our narrative. However, even when newly built things don't seem to belong at first, they can eventually pull stories around themselves, the way that rubbed amber attracts nearby fibres.

That tunnel under Glasgow's Central Station became known as the Hielanman's Umbrella. Highlanders from the north, dispossessed by the Clearances and desperate for work, arrived in their thousands by rail. They used the archway as a spot to meet their Gaelic friends, sheltering from the weather under the cast-iron-and-glass Victorian pile overhead. They'd gather there after church on Sunday or on Saturday nights to exchange gossip and news from their homes, or to walk out with sweethearts.

As construction proceeds on the giant paw of our new arena, its tall windows and silver cladding are starting to remind me a little of the glass arch of the Hielanman's Umbrella. Inlaid in its floor, there will be more glass—a giant mural designed by Aboriginal artist Alex Janvier. It's circular swirl of colours represent the flow of paths in this region, circuits that have been broken and rejoined.

Perhaps this building will, like the Highlanders' meeting place, become a stone in time's current where stories eddy and gather. Such stories may well have nothing to do with that viscous fluid, oil, but they will shift and change; they will be positive and negative at the same time.

Meanwhile, I am left waiting. My own story here is not a dramatic one; I'm simply one of the many molecules in the movement of time past this place, one of the hundreds of thousands who have flowed here from around the world, as people do.

But I am curious about the future of here. I've often said I don't particularly want to be immortal. Still, I *would* like to be able to drop in every fifty years or so. Just to find out how the current, the energy, has gone on.

Moment

12 — Letter of Intent Rona Altrows

WHY AM I HERE? It's the question I asked at age four when my beloved uncle Al died, have asked repeatedly since then, and find myself, at twenty-six, asking again. Twice in my late teens, steeped in deep depression and unable to find a logical answer, I tried to end my life. What helped me most then was what often comes to my rescue in despair—a book. In that case, it was *The Confessions of St. Augustine*. Not the religious content of that book. Just the fact that the guy had so many questions. I once decided to count them. Twenty-five in the first three paragraphs alone. What a comfort.

But today I'm nowhere close to despondency. I just want to know why I am *here*, in the hall outside Room 32, Chancellor Day Hall, McGill University, seated in a straight-backed wooden chair. There's only one way to keep nerves in check: write in my notebook. Write anything. Take control of time. Don't just let it pass. Make it pass. Is it fair some people are born all nerves and questions?

Law-school classes are held in the ugly concrete tower immediately west of here, but the building I wait in, a grand limestone mansion built in château style, is the home of the law professors' offices. At some point I will be called in to Room 32 to talk to two of those professors. Three quarters of an hour ago, I knocked tentatively on the heavy wooden door of the office. A man in his forties emerged, perspiration beaded on his forehead. He left the door ajar, stepped out into the hall, and told me that he and his colleague would need a few more minutes to prepare. Mind you, I arrived fifteen minutes early. Still. What on earth can they be talking about? Is my application that intriguing? That problematic? I know what they're doing. They're scrutinizing my letter of intent for the fifth time, dreaming up trick questions. They're going to try to trip me up—that's their strategy. Oh, why did I write what I wrote? Why didn't I compose something more clever or scholarly or legal-sounding? They'll ask how a degree in English Drama can be expected to lead to a career in the real world, for example, in law. How a person with a permanent, well-paying job as a high-school teacher decides to leave that stability behind and invest in a rigorous, multi-year program of studies in a totally different field. How my fixation on a British prime minister, Benjamin Disraeli, has any connection with my application. Well, I'll tell them, Disraeli took the first steps toward a law career. Yes, one of my interviewers will point out— the one who studied in England—yes, but did Disraeli stick with the law? He did not. Why do I regard him as a role model? Then I will pull out my trump card: Disraeli wrote novels! Numerous novels. Long novels...

Mind you, I may have something going for me here. In Grade Five, my classmate Gail and I made a pact that each would nominate the other for Red Cross rep. I followed through but, to my horror, she reneged. For me, that experience crystallized a preoccupation with fairness. It's why I initiated a petition to the National Assembly last year, requesting a two-word addition to our Civil Code that would allow tenants to get in front of the courts quickly if they needed to, so they would not have to go through a long, expensive legal rigmarole to force their landlords to do essential property repairs. I collected many signatures, and I got my way—those two important words did get added to the Civil Code. Because, eventually, the legislators came to see the situation the way I did: the old way had not been fair to tenants.

But is that what the practice of law is about? How badly do I need to find out?

Maybe my two interviewers will wonder whether I have shown up just to make a personal point. After all, when I received the secretary's call the day after my mother's funeral, I declined the interview. I explained that my mother had died of accident injuries earlier this month, and my father, who had not been in the accident, was critically ill. The secretary had a warm voice, so I let myself talk a bit, at least enough to say that it was all too much, and I should probably return to teaching in the fall, forget my law-school dream. Well, it's up to you—you can withdraw your application, the secretary said. I told her I'd let her know within a week. But once I got off the phone something that I had not counted on presented itself. A voice. I barely had time to put down the receiver when I heard it. *Roncha, what are you doing? You want this. Call back and go see those professors. They'll enjoy talking to you. Call back right away.* Well. What do you do when your mother has been dead for only a few days and her disembodied voice is telling you what to do? The situation is unfair. It does not allow for options. So, I did call back and said I'd attend the interview after all. I asked who would be talking to me. I recognized the names of both men.

I'm uneasy sitting here. It's not that comfortable sitting anywhere when you are seven months pregnant. And will my interviewers notice? That's the main thing. I mean, maybe they are not as observant of such things as women are. And I do have the evidence hidden under a long, fringed, royal-blue cape that comes down almost to my knees. Under that I wear black dress pants. Surely a black garment creates a slimmer look, even if it features a wide, elasticized panel at the waist? After all, my interviewers will not ask me to lift my cape. That would be rude. They may think I am mentally unstable though, for wearing a heavy woollen garment in this weather. It is only late May, but Montreal is in the midst of one of the blistering heat waves it is famous for, most common in July and August but not unheard of earlier in the year. There is no air conditioning here. To make matters worse, I'm reacting to the musty smell of the old building with a hint of the nausea that laid me low in my first trimester.

How to find relief from the heat? I've got a white cotton blouse on but dare not reveal it, as one of those professors may open the door at any moment. If he sees me capeless, he'll be able to tell right away that I'm pregnant. I mean, I am not carrying big, but the bulge is not exactly invisible. I set down my ballpoint pen and notebook, grab three fringes of the cape, braid the fringes together. Repeat with another three. Repeat, repeat. I can't help it. Can't simply write. Must do something else with my hands too. Otherwise I will scratch my arm, head, ankle. Scratch to the point of drawing blood. Since childhood—since earliest memory, really—I have done this compulsive scratching at times of stress, unable to stop once I start to scratch, especially when I am also hot. Better to put those fingers to work on the fringes.

My father thinks the law-school plan is a mistake. "The legal profession is not what you think, Roncha." He has said it many times—most recently, yesterday, at the hospital. "Law is not all about making things right for people. Law is business," he said. "You like politics, not business. Teach now and run for Parliament in a few years. People are sick of lawyer-politicians. A teacher who goes into politics, that's a politician people can get behind."

But when one parent is still alive, however tenuously, and the other is freshly dead, the words of the dead one carry greater weight. Unfair but true.

My high-school friend Pat graduated from McGill Law School three years ago. That's how I recognized my interviewers' names and knew something of their backgrounds—both had taught her. When I applied she gave me a warning: they don't like to admit students with part-time jobs. They believe you can't meet the demands of the program if you are also working at something else. Maybe the interviewers will quiz me on whether I intend to take on some part-time teaching. I can truthfully tell them no.

Of course, it's not as if I won't have any distraction if I get in. This baby is due at the end of July and I've heard that care of a newborn takes up time. How much, I have no idea. I've never had a baby before. I've applied for a space in the university daycare centre for September, but they won't reserve it because I haven't been accepted into law school yet. I'm single so it'll just be me looking after the baby—me and daycare if I can get the baby in. Kind of scary but I can do it. I'm healthy and I have tons of energy and I can get by on five hours of sleep a night if I have to. I can make it all work. I think.

Twelve more minutes gone. What are they up to now? Maybe they're figuring out how they will carry out the interview. Maybe they'll take on roles and they are rehearsing. Who'll play the good cop, who'll play the bad cop. Or maybe they have already decided my transcript and letter of intent and references are all golden, and there's nothing to worry about, and they're 99 per cent sure they will take me, but they just want to look me over and talk to me for a couple of minutes to make sure I am not off my rocker or inarticulate or a Martian. That may well be what we're headed for. A quickie corroborating interview. Pro forma, like Perry Mason says.

If I could just get some water. Why am I here? Something beyond the obvious has brought me to this place, I'm sure of it. Something to do with—what? Justice? Honour? Fairness? I'm a spaghetti-western hero, crawling through the Nevada desert as the sun beats down on her head. Struggles to eke a final drop out of her tin canteen. Empty, damn it! She throws the canteen onto the barren ground. It clatters, jangling her raw nerves.

Should I knock on the door and ask for a small glass of water? Or would that seem too demanding? I gather up three more fringes of the cape, braid, repeat.

There don't seem to be any people wandering around. Sure, it's between academic terms and maybe some professors are away, but still. All of them? They're all away, except for the two in Room 32? Or are they actually here, noses buried in heavy legal tomes? Do law professors lock themselves in their offices all day every day during the intersession?

Of course, there are advantages to not having access to water. I don't have to pee. And that's a good thing, because what if I'm not here when they finally open that door? Will they assume I am gone, and scratch my name off the list of applicants? So unfair. No. I will not let that happen. Even if they would be inclined to conduct themselves in such a lax and cowardly manner, I will not give them the opportunity. I will not drink, therefore will not pee, therefore will not leave this chair until they call me in. Bastards.

It's going to be crazy if I make it. I won't be able to tell my mother I got into law school. How is that fair?

The baby doesn't like it when I get wound up. The baby delivers protest kicks. What if I get into the room and the professors start asking tough questions and I get all nervous and the baby kicks hard, and the interviewers see movement under my cape? Never mind. I'll tell them I have indigestion.

I should have brought a book. Something deep, about law and ethics or law and society or, best of all, law and property. Then if I happened to forget the book, they'd be impressed with what I'd been reading, and the absent-mindedness that has always plagued me would actually help my case. But I didn't bring a book and if I forget my notebook, what they will see is what I am writing right now. They'll know they shouldn't read my notebook; they're not stupid, they realize it's personal and not for their eyes. But read it they will, human nature being what it is. And without saying so, they will deny my application on the basis of what I have written here. My whole academic and professional future depends on my not forgetting this notebook in Room 32. Unfair.

I can hear the doorknob being turned. In a second, I'll be in there, with the two of them. No time to unbraid the fringes. And out of nowhere, I need to pee.

13 —— The Next Minute

THE SCENE is a doctor's waiting room. I fidget, watch the clock, absently flip through dated magazines, and begin to resent the doctor who is keeping me waiting. Waiting brings out the worst in me.

Thirty minutes into this cycle, I see a patient leave one of the rooms and walk back to the waiting room, a doctor by her side.

Everyone looks up. No one else is called. As person after person returns to their old magazine with varying measures of disappointment and frustration, I guess that this is my doctor, one of six names on the door. I watch for clues to see what he is like. Will he listen kindly or be dismissive?

The patient is unsteady. The doctor's hand is at her elbow as he ushers her to the raised reception counter and guides her to the opening in the glass. He dictates rapid instructions to the nurse. I overhear snippets. An urgent MRI.

I realize what I am watching and feel sick. I have the terrible sense of being at an accident scene, transfixed by the horror, staring. I am back in time, in my twenties, with paramedics pulling me out of a car wreck and passers-by staring at me. Unable to speak, I try to send the bystanders urgent telepathic messages to look away. I don't know if I am clothed, if I am gruesome. I don't want to be a spectacle lying in shattered glass. I don't want to be seen like this.

And today, here is this woman, exposed to me in a way she could never have imagined. She has cancer. I don't know another thing about her, but I know this intimate, crushing fact. I know it only minutes after she does, and well before she knows what to do with it. The least I can do is spare her the indignity of my staring. I look away and pretend to read, suddenly grateful for the old magazines.

No one else seems aware of the drama happening a few feet away. I look at her again with my peripheral vision. I can't help it. I am in awe. How she can stand there and fill out forms without her legs buckling, without crying, without screaming? How is this possible? What was she thinking when she came here? Before she saw the doctor, had she assumed, like me, that she had some weird virus? Had she been worrying about her in-basket at work? Mentally cataloguing her freezer to find tonight's dinner ingredients? I think about how plans are utterly meaningless.

I realize the self-absorption of my own petty impatience just a few minutes before and am truly penitent. I direct positive thoughts towards her in something akin to prayer.

And then she is gone, and I am called. I decide to like this doctor. With a new willingness to wait, I wish he could take a break before he sees me. His day has been difficult. He has been the bearer of bad news. I promise myself I will try to make this visit easy for him, get a prescription and go.

He sits down, heavily. He has reviewed my ultrasound. He looks me in the eye. He looks in my throat. He feels my neck. He says something. I cannot comprehend it. You think I have what? Say it again. Please say it again. I can't hear you. I'm sorry, please say it again.

I don't know how much time passes before I am at the counter with the doctor at my elbow requesting another urgent

MRI and handing me forms. I don't know who is impatiently waiting to see him, watching me fill out the forms. I don't know if they understand what they are witnessing. Pen in hand, I do what the woman before me did. I understand now how she did it without her legs buckling, without crying, without screaming. I am grateful for the way the form anchors me to the present and creates a way to get to the next minute, and the next one and the one after that. I write my name.

14 —— Frozen

LORRI NEILSEN GLENN

WHEN THE DOG AND I WALK along the shore this morning, the water is hammered metal and the wind stiff. The seaweed thrown up on the path frustrates the dog's paws; no clamshell treasures today. I find myself wondering what ice does to scent. When I peek out from under my jacket hood, drawstrings tight as I can make them, I can glimpse the bay. No boats in sight; yet I know someone is out there fishing, possibly for tuna. What is visible: the cliffs beyond, white with bird shit, and blocks of ice heaved along the shore like chunks of a collapsed igloo.

I watch my feet as they navigate ice-glazed rocks; step and tap and turn. These mid-winter days, everything seems tottery, uncertain. This morning, after I finished reading a satisfying novel, I felt bereft. Then, poring over family history, I found only more mysteries: a rogue with a seven-shooter and a bag of cash who left his wife with twelve children, a CPR engineer whose train crashed into a landslide, a Cree ancestor elusive as a deer at dusk. I had started my day before sunrise, taking deep breaths, awed by the Big Dipper splayed across the sky, both my hands cradling a warm cup. Still, dark; pure calm before the clatter of breakfast and trash pickup and local trucks roaring off to work. Where are the poems? They aren't thawing in my hands, and they aren't riding the constellations. Where am I these uncertain days?

⋮ Waiting time. It's eight weeks before spring. The dog and I pick our way back to the house, turning our chins down against the gale. On the beach, greys and reds layered in the mounds of frosted shale; when I look up, the bitter skeleton of the larch against the blue milk sky. New deer tracks circle the barn. At the porch, the chickadees are break-your-heart frantic from the feeder to the bushes. Eight weeks. Cold holds its promise close to the chest these days, hiding what glints, what stirs in the veins of the earth.

15 ___ Harder, But Still Not Painful

ROBIN VAN ECK

NINE MONTHS. Unless you're an elephant, that's how long it takes to grow a baby. An eager sperm head butts a shy egg. They unite. A reaction begins. And then the wait.

I always wondered how my mom felt when she found out she was pregnant the first time. For some reason never asked. Did she experience the *squee* of excitement felt by many women? Or did she have the nauseated feeling that her life was over and wonder what the hell had she gotten herself into?

I never imagined a life with children. Arie and I married in September of 2007. He, an immigrant from the Netherlands, had had enough of the flat green, the constant rain, the tulips and windmills and wooden shoes. We had the talk. Kids? No kids? Both of us were okay either way. If it happened great. If not, life would go on.

Four months later I stand in the bathroom leaning against the counter, clutching the stick in my hand. Two pink lines.

I stumble from the bathroom—light-headed, drunk, motion sick—my focus intent on the brown carpet, every stain, every worn thread, all the gunk I can't see, buried layers deep. *We need to steam clean the carpets. What's down there? Leftovers from previous tenants, my own crumbs, tangled in the knotted threads.*

As I enter the living room, Arie launches off the couch, panic stretching across his face. I sink into his arms, feel the throb of his chest against my ear, and begin to breathe.

What's wrong, he asks?

I show him the stick still clutched in my hand. His face slackens then explodes into a smile. He holds me tight and says, we can do it.

Barely out of her teens, the mother cradles her baby girl, newborn slime smeared through the dark brown hair, but it doesn't matter. In that moment, nothing else matters. The baby suckles, an intense connection between mother and daughter forms.

The baby girl doesn't know what came before, nor what is happening in this moment. All she knows is the blanket wrapped around her, the mother's breath on her skin.

The father lingers in the corner of the room, a shadow, hackles raised, skin bristling. He smells of cheap beer and cigarettes, sawdust and grease. The woman lying in the bed he doesn't know how to love, the baby, another mouth to feed.

We don't get a say in who our parents are.

I was born in May, the year Dave Barrett called a snap election and the BC NDP lost to Bill Bennett and the SoCreds, the year *The Rocky Horror Picture Show* debuted on Broadway and Bill Gates formed Microsoft.

My mother and father lived in a little house at the ass end of someone else's property, near the confluence of the Fraser and Nechako Rivers, where each year the rivers flowed so slowly they froze and melted, froze and melted, leaving areas around the city of Prince George gasping under layers of water. My mother, an immigrant from the United States, sought adventure across the border. My father followed the music, guitar strapped to shoulder, going wherever he could find work. Hippies high on life and copious amounts of hash, living in a tiny pocket of the second-largest country in the world. My birth, a mere blip.

But I am nearly thirty-three years old with my first child on the way. We live in an apartment. Happily married.

The little girl is seven years old. She walks to school. Across the train tracks, through the sawmill. She waves at her grandpa standing outside the mechanic's shop, cigarette dangling from his lips, smoke curling around her head in a halo. He waves back.

She is away from the house, from the windows rattling from their skin each time the train thunders its annoying hello, from the old boards grinding and twisting with the vibrations, barely holding the tiny three-room home together. Away from the beat-up carpets bleeding beer and sour whiskey, purple cherry wine stains ground deeper. Away from the air ripe with diesel fumes and powdered bleach. The floors scarred from childish tantrums, angry words, broken plates, and bleeding lips. Despite the wood stove cranking out heat, the rooms are always cold.

The girl gazes into the sun-soaked air, feels its heat wrap around her. Gravel slips under her feet, crackles and skips along the ground, as she begins the hike up the hill. Even with the logging trucks, dump trucks, and tractors grumbling past, she loses herself in her imagination.

She reaches the top and sees something in the middle of the road. A black-and-white cat, barely recognizable, congealed to the road, brain and eyeballs spreading in a snowflake pattern. She knows this cat. It belongs to her friend on the other side of the trees, in the big brown house. She can't see the house, but she knows it's there.

Parents are supposed to be excited about grandchildren. I've seen it on TV. The kids make the announcement, the parents almost faint, and then they start making plans, buying obnoxious gifts that a new baby wouldn't need.

A couple of months in, I make the phone call.

I'm pregnant, I tell my mom.

Silence.

You still there?

Yeah, I'm here.

I could practically hear her chewing on her words.

Are you sure that's wise?

Of course. Why wouldn't it be?

It costs money to raise a child. Arie isn't even working yet.

We've informed Immigration Canada.

But what if he's not working by the time it's born?

We'll figure it out.

He doesn't even have a driver's license.

More silence. Then, finally, How far along are you?

Just a couple of months.

Have you considered an abortion?

I fight back tears and swallow my burning anger.

That is not an option, I finally say, and hang up on her.

Arie sits at the other end of the couch rubbing my leg.

The phone rings.

Do you want me to talk to her? he asks.

I shake my head and let the phone keep ringing.

A few weeks later my father comes for a short visit.

Sit down, I say. We have something to tell you.

You're pregnant, he says. You got a beer kicking around here?

Just before the little girl turns eight, she gets a brother. At first it seems like it will be fun to have someone else to play with, but he's just a baby. He plays by himself, he screams, he stinks. All the time. The little girl tries to feed him dirt. The mother doesn't like this either. She yells at the little girl, sends her crying to her room and then cuddles the baby. The little girl ignores the mother and runs

*outside, curls into her red wagon, refuses to go back in the house.
The father comes out and kneels beside the little girl.*

Hey, Robinowitz Munchkin Worm. Why don't you come inside?

*The little girl likes it when the father calls her silly names. She
smiles through her dried-on tears but shakes her head. I don't like
her. She always yells at me.*

She's tired.

*She's not fun. The little girl folds her arms around her and
sticks out the pouty lip.*

Tell you what. You dry that face and we'll go fishing, okay?

The little girl's eyes light up. Just you and me?

Just you and me.

How much shit can one baby possibly need?

Sure, 1975 was much different than 2008. I slept in a drawer
because my parents couldn't afford a crib. Seat belts weren't
mandatory, so why would you need an infant's car seat? Cloth
diapers versus disposable.

I make lists. Scrawls of everything we may need: diapers,
bottles, formula, breast pump, blankets, crib, playpen, soothers,
diaper pail, bottle sanitizer, bibs, high chair, toys, car seat, mobile,
Jolly Jumper, books, cute outfits, socks, booties, hats, sweaters.

As months click by, items get checked off the list—some
generously donated by friends and family, more purchased by us.

What am I forgetting?

*The father rushes into the house, sawdust clinging to his pants,
to his hair.*

Where's your mother and brother?

The little girl shrugs.

Get your shoes on. We're going for a drive.

Where?

Never mind that. Just hurry.

The little girl climbs into the truck. Dust and gravel kick up behind them. Soon she can't see the little house.

The father parks in front of the old hotel and runs inside. The little girl close behind him. The father darts past the Greyhound Bus sign.

The mother is seated in a chair holding the baby brother. Her face tightens, and she looks away when the father and daughter appear.

You're not going anywhere with my son.

The father tries to take the brother. The mother holds on tight. They struggle. They fight. People are watching, stepping closer. The father softens and sits beside the mother. They speak quietly while other passengers watch. The little girl stands against the wall. Where is the mother going? On a vacation without her? Not fair.

Finally, the mother stands, shoulders slumped, and follows the father out of the bus station.

No vacation today.

I stand in the middle of the Walmart clothes department, a kaleidoscope of pinks, purples, reds swirling around me. Fleece sleepers with princesses. Plush stuffies: puppies, kittens, seals, koalas, frogs, baby ducks. What good does any of that do in the first year when all a baby does is sleep, poop, drool, and eat? I still want to buy up everything, but without definitively knowing the sex of the baby, I can't.

I fill the basket with green and yellow onesies and blankets and grab a stuffed puppy.

The girl hides in the corner of the front stoop. The dog lunges around the corner. The girl is fast, but the dog is faster and will always find her. The dog presses its nose into her neck. She laughs and leaps over the porch railing, to the ground. She runs. The dog chases. Around and around the house. She hurtles herself onto the wooden garbage bin before the dog reaches her. Then down and

around the back of the house into the back of the father's truck.
She falls to the floor of the box, laughing. The dog stands on its
hind legs, sniffing the air, a smile on its lips.

    The girl smells smoke. She sits up and searches the sky. Black
clouds curl upwards. She runs inside the house. The mother stands
over the sink, scrubbing, always scrubbing. The father perches on
the couch, his legs stretched onto the coffee table, a beer in one
hand, the TV louder than necessary. The brother stands in his
playpen.

    Fire. The girl straddles the gap between her parents.

    Where? The father sits up.

    On the hill. Come look. The girl grabs the father's hand and
leads him outside. The mother grabs the brother and follows close
behind. They stand and watch until the father ushers them into
the truck and they bounce along the pitted road to town.

    Hundreds of cars have pulled over to the side of the highway,
gawkers snapping photos, gasping as the hotel burns to the ground.
The girl has her camera too. Snap. Wind. Snap. Wind. The air burns
her nose, the heat reaches across the street. Firefighters move in
slow motion trying to corral the blaze but it's too late. Even the girl
knows this. The fire is strong, gulping down the rooms, the restau-
rant. The Greyhound station.

⋮ Subtle flutters of movement, a foot pressed against the inside
of my stomach, skin stretched and released. I need to pee. A lot.
These little moments, and my ever-expanding abdomen, the only
reminders that another life is growing inside me, depending on
me for survival.

    I lie on the table in the doctor's office. Needles. I've been stuck
so many times I've lost count. And there may well be more to
come. But this time, we will hear the baby.

    How are you feeling? the doctor asks.

    Good.

    No morning sickness?

Nope, nothing.

The doctor squirts warm gel over my stomach. She moves the probe over my belly, searching. I hold my breath. What if she can't find it? Then, before I can worry myself to nausea, there it is. A beat, and another and another. I exhale.

Have you found out the sex of the baby yet?

Not unless I believe all the old wives tales I've read up on. Carry high it's a girl; carry low it's a boy. Faster heart rate it's a girl; slower heart rate it's a boy. At the last ultrasound they'd said 60 per cent chance of a girl. It sounds to me like 60 per cent chance of rain, which in my world means nothing.

The doctor listens. She times the beats. Today it's a girl, she says with a chuckle.

I smile. Does she really believe that hocus pocus?

The little girl is almost nine years old. She huddles under the blanket, presses her tiny hands to her ears, hugs her stuffed bear, tries to block the shrieks and cries slamming through the thin walls. Shadows creep around the small room looking for a place to get warm and settle, but there isn't one. The brother sleeps in his crib beside her.

The father thunders, the mother snaps.

Slut.

Bastard.

I'll kill you.

Broken glass.

The girl wants the noise to stop.

She slips from the bed, feet plodding along the cold floor. She feels her way in the dark, leery of the monsters under her bed, terrified of the monsters outside her room. She opens the door, hugs the frame, tears drying on her cheeks.

A plate flies across the room, shatters against the wall. Spaghetti noodles left over from the dinner the father has refused to eat slither to the floor. The mother clutches a frying pan in her hand. *The big heavy kind. She raises it to shoulder level. The father doesn't see.*

The girl cries out, Daddy.

Both pairs of eyes turn to the little girl.

The pan clomps to the floor.

The noise stops. A drowning silence.

The wall, stained orange.

In the middle of the night, the mother wakes the little girl. The girl wipes away the sleep and yawns. We have to go, the mother says. Eyes wide, puffy from crying. The mother's lip is split, blood stuck to the corner of her mouth.

The words are confusing. The girl dangles her legs over the edge of the bed, lets her mother dress her. The mother hurls clothes, toothbrush, not-too-minty toothpaste, into a small bag, then pulls the girl to her feet.

My bear, the girl whispers.

No time. Be quiet. Don't wake your father.

The girl lets the mother lead her from the room, silently waving goodbye to the little bear, watching its peeled nose and button eyes peer out from under the blanket. The brother is still sleeping.

The father snores on the pull-out couch as they tiptoe to the door.

The floor creaks. The mother stiffens, then curls her hand around the little girl's, and together they slip into the night.

The night is not scary in this small town. Street lights spray the road orange and yellow.

Where are we going? the little girl asks.

It's going to be an adventure, the mother replies.

They hurry to the highway. The mother holds out her thumb. The little girl does the same. A car pulls over. A woman rolls down the window.

Where you headed?

Castlegar, if you can get us there. The mother squeezes the little girl's hand.

You're in luck. We're going to Christina Lake.

The girl falls asleep in the back of the car, her head resting on the mother's lap.

I lie awake nights. Questions, buzzing, stinging. What if we can't do this? Will I disappoint my child? Mental illness? Shit. I'll have to tell the doctors about my maternal history. I'm not worried about myself, but what about the baby? I'm sure I've heard somewhere mental problems can skip a generation— but what if it hasn't skipped me at all and is lying dormant? Postpartum? Will it come in the form of some psychotic break after the delivery? Will I hurt my baby? Will I know in time to do something about it?

What if Arie and I started to hate each other?

What if my mom was right and this is all a big mistake?

The father finds the mother and the little girl a few days later in Castlegar and brings them home with promises to do better. The mother becomes quiet. Sad. Doesn't seem to care what the little girl does.

The little girl begins to take on the role of mommy. Feeding the little brother, changing his diaper without stabbing him or herself with the diaper pin. She's good at this job and the mother doesn't yell at her anymore.

The mother is sick.

She goes to the hospital.

The little girl doesn't like the way hospitals smell and the old people always look at her funny, but she visits anyway and she hears the grownups use words like psych ward and nervous break-down and depressed.

Heartburn. Acid reflux. I've heard people talk about it but never really understood what it was until now, several months into the pregnancy. Stomach acid traipsing up my throat, settling into that little hole in the back of my mouth that no amount of swallowing or guzzling of water or milk will dissolve. Tums have become my friend. A fruity candy treat. When I complain, Arie doesn't get it. He tries but unless you're living it, you don't really get it. No matter what I eat, the stomach acid fights back.

Heart. Burn. An indescribable fire growing inside. I run my hand over my belly, imagine cradling the new baby. All the things we will do together. I glance over at Arie as he sleeps, peaceful and unaware. Is it the same for a father? Will that bond form instantly? I'm the one doing all the work. What if the baby loves Daddy more?

Summer crawls closer. My feet begin to swell.

⋮ *At school the girl lies face down on the centre post of the merry-go-round. Her hands grip the bars in front of her, her feet tucked securely under the bars behind her.*

Go, she says to the girl and two boys. Her friends.

The three grip a bar and begin to run. Faster. Faster. Feet digging into the dirt. The merry-go-round spins. She hears other screaming kids, laughing, rolling over one another, all wanting to be the next king of the castle.

Her world blurs.

Faster, she cries out. The force tugs at her. She holds on tighter. Her long brown curls whipping out. She closes her eyes.

She is flying.

⋮ Five days overdue. The tightening starts in my abdomen, significant but not painful. Contractions? Not contractions? I haven't slept well in months. Gestational insomnia. Is that even a thing?

More tightening. I check the clock—almost two in the morning—and time the intervals. They are close. Too close. But no pain. There should be pain.

I dump my purse out onto the couch, searching for the number for the Alberta Health Services after-hours hotline. Year-old squished tampons, wallet, wads of old receipts, tissues, lip balm in multiple flavours, body spray, elastics, paper clips, pens, notebook, mints. Screwdriver—where did that come from? So much paper but no phone number.

I pull up Google on my phone and find the number, jot it down, and question the phone. Should I call? I'm overreacting. Braxton Hicks. It's not time yet.

No response from the so-called smartphone.

The baby is ready.

The phone flops to the couch and I sink into the brown leather alongside it.

I am not.

⋮ *When the girl is ten, the father loses his job and in a desperate attempt to keep money coming in, he takes off to Toronto. Says he'll send for them when he settles.*

A year later, the mother and the girl and the brother still live alone. The father has sent no money, but telephone calls promise it's coming. The mother is sad. The girl is hopeful.

She spends her days solving mysteries with Nancy Drew, writing stories and plays, performing with her dolls.

One day a bearded man comes to visit. A friend her mother met when she first crossed the border so many years ago. The girl lies in the middle of the living-room floor eating her popcorn, watching Fraggle Rock, *while the mother and the bearded man laugh and talk. The girl has forgotten what the mother's laughter sounds like and she is happy.*

The girl doesn't cry the day the mother leaves. She sits on the edge of the bed watching the mother pack items into a suitcase.

Why can't I go with you? the girl asks.

It's only for a few days. You and your brother will stay with Grandma and Grandpa until I find a place for us and then I'll come get you.

The lure of adventure excites the girl. A new house. A new room. A new school. What will the other kids be like? Will she make new friends?

The girl doesn't cry the day the mother leaves. Because she doesn't know the mother isn't coming back.

I can't decide if I should wake Arie or call the hotline. I pace. I sit. I lie down, counting the seconds between each totally not-painful contraction. They are different from the Braxton Hicks. Tighter. Harder. But still not painful.

I place the call.

I think I'm having contractions, I tell the nurse on the other end of the line, but they don't hurt. Aren't they supposed to hurt?

How far apart?

All over the place.

When are you due?

Five days ago.

You should go in.

I don't like the idea of traipsing into Emergency, being a nuisance, and being sent home to wait it out. But since the nurse said I should, I guess I should.

I wake up Arie with a poke and a nudge. He lurches out of bed, panic rinsing away the sleep.

Relax. Make coffee. I'll call Shelly.

Shelly, my best friend and ride because Arie still doesn't have a driver's license and apparently it's inappropriate for a woman in labour to drive herself to the hospital.

On my way, she says.

Don't rush, I tell her. I can wait.

16 —— Alterations WENDY MCGRATH

ON THE LEFT SIDE of the business card is a replica of the Eiffel Tower. Paris Tailors is on the street level of a downtown Edmonton high-rise. The air moves so hard and fast against this building sometimes—opening the door is like trying to move a piano.

I have alterations to pick up and I wait in the front room of the shop along with bolts of fabric, which are suits and shirts still unimagined and waiting to be made. I see the potential. "Every man should have a shirt made for him once in his life," the tailor said to me once. I had been trying to decide on a birthday present for my husband; weighing the sentimentality in the weft and weave of fabric, thread, stitches, and seams. There is deeper meaning in Oxford cloth the colour of sky and clouds, in smooth shirting, or in a suit of fine gabardine.

On this particular Saturday, also in the front room of Paris Tailors, are beautifully carved instruments. There is a red drum. The drum curves, slopes, and narrows, and on its skin rest boxes of silver straight pins. The instrument waits to be played and I stare at its potential. I imagine the movement of bodies around the sound of this drum—the language of rhythm, the feel of silk, the taste of gold on my tongue. Another instrument at the front of the shop looks like a harpsichord stripped bare, carved brown wood with the strings exposed—a piano without the casing.

The tailor plays two instruments for me. First, he opens a case and lifts a long cylinder of dark bamboo from its place inside the box. He plays. The music is low and moody and mournful on this soft grey Saturday morning. A single sharp threads its way through the weft and warp of sound, fabric, and music. The tailor then chooses a smaller flute to play for me. "This one is for happy songs, like at weddings." He plays—high notes that travel back a hundred years to touch a thimble that pushes a needle through time and sound, a needle that may sew the dress for a bride who waits for her wedding day.

The tailor plays a third instrument for me—the *erwu*— a violin with only two strings. It has the head of a dragon and a base that looks like a black mallet. Where are the reference points? How can he find the notes? There are no frets, nothing to go by, but I've heard him play this instrument before, in the back of the tailor shop by the sewing machines, by the fabric waiting to be made into something, trousers waiting for repair, dresses and skirts waiting to be hemmed. The time before, I just listened and waited. I could see his reflection in the three-way mirror as I waited. Now, the bow's weft and weave makes a sad sound of longing, the music in my dreams I forget the second I wake.

Today I have come to pick up two pieces. In one motion the tailor lifts a long camel-coloured coat and a vintage-looking purple jacket and when he hangs them on a cascading metal rod I hear a soft sound like a long, icy glide on skates. "Is that you?" I ask him. I look up to the speakers above the change rooms—but the resonating sound is closer to me, a soft brush against metal. "Yes," as he motions to the hammered gold circle suspended and hidden at the far end of the front counter—the gong that makes the sound when waiting clothes disturb its rest. The counter is smooth, white, and strewn with names on slips of paper, silver straight pins, tailor's chalk, measuring tape that snakes like a dragon.

·I motion to the gong. "What is that called?" I ask him. *Fung Loh*. He writes it in blue ink for me on the back of a small square receipt. The character is beautiful. He breaks the word into pieces for me. "Fung Loh," he says as he writes. "This contains the sound." He continues to write, and I wait as he breaks the sound down into other pieces: gold, four, silk, good.

We struggle to find the word for *Loh* in English. He rips the edges off each side of a sheet of printer paper—now narrow strips with regular punched holes—and then he takes a pen from the counter. "You know when you take something and go in and out, over and under..." he says as he places one strip over and one strip under the pen. "Weaving?" I say. "From dead trees over and under," and he bends from the waist, holds imaginary handles, picks something up and waits for me to connect the charade to the word. "Basket?" I say. "Yes, basket. This holds the sound."

The tailor knows the length of my arm, the slope of my shoulder, and the circumference of my waist. He understands how alterations must make clothes move as part of the body, how fabric can be translated into line and rhythm. But, I think, he also understands how music makes alterations inside us, how it waits to be imagined and made beneath articulated surfaces and beyond time.

Soul

17 — Who Will Find Me

THE NEW MOTHER was kind at first, she swept me up in her arms and tucked me into her lap as I ate red candies from her hand. She came into my life when I was five and a half, when my father remarried after my mother's death from breast cancer two years earlier.

Childhood is a dark ledge I've always shied away from. Others see it as a window through nostalgia at what might've been. For me, all sensibilities are dark, leading out to an expanse that risks misunderstanding: that sense of falling. So, if I could stay here alone, away from those colours and galaxies, locked against hurt and regret, I would somehow remain myself.

But the ledge is always there. My eyes see the child I was, who tolerated pain through erasure—I was too young, anyhow, to measure myself against others. That would come later, with the recovery that comes from being taken away in small increments, not unlike a child who grows up and notices, one by one, the scattered toys in the toy box slowly disappearing.

This house is safe. It has nothing to do with me because the space around me has been muffled by a week's worth of yesterday's fabrics. Socks, underwear, forgotten Kleenex in pockets, leaf dust in pant cuffs, dirt, punishments, disappointments. All

in a dismissive heap, as I lie myself down now on the bathtub.
Step-mum piles the dirty laundry on top of me—a surprising
contradiction as I think of it now—dressed in my pony rider
pyjamas, freshly bathed, smelling of Ivory behind the ears. Why
would Step-mum, fearful of germs and all that was unruly and
unsightly, let me be buried in such filth?

It is Sunday evening. My sister is watching the Julie Andrews
show on TV in the other room, and as much as I want to be
beside her, it is nearing 9 p.m. The cuckoo clock will chime soon,
and Dad will be home early.

⋮ To be an outer layer worn and discarded with the succeeding
days: the repair-cost of being human. Same for the echo of voices
separating from the fleshy throats that made them.

I was a child casting thoughts out from their blood flow
around spine and brain. Each day severing me from the event of
my birth.

I'm thrown into a room full of screaming kids. I'm age three.
Side by side in separate cribs, my sister and I wait in the children's
shelter (orphanage was a word that wasn't officially used for it,
even in 1968). Someone faceless provides a dark blue toy piano.
Was it dropped into one of our cribs? All I remember upon waking
up is that my sister presses out notes on its tiny, perfect keyboard.
Right away she invites me to put my hands on it and create those
tinny, sharp, precise, beautiful notes. But I'm also scared of touching
the piano, so I sit in my little cage, looking through the bars at her,
unsafe and separated by these bars. Why can't we sit together?

I grip the crib bars, noting their solid regularity. If I were a
little older I would know the importance of counting them.

I'm afraid of the quiet darkness of this giant gymnasium or
hall, with its tall high windows shuttered with heavy curtains,
the air stirred and slowed by far-off cries and shuffles of other
children in the many cribs I see in the bare distance. But the one
presence I understand is my sister Sook Mei. She does not cry.

124

Two years older than me, her small mouth and short-cropped hair framing those large laughing eyes. How calm she seems, bouncing on the balls of her feet as she stands and passes the toy blue piano over the crib bars to me just before I start to cry.

Dry heaves, followed by waves of uncontrollable tears.

Press them. There. See?

This is the voice in my head I might've manufactured ever since I was a young child. I need to hear something, play a mother's words over and over to calm that rising tempest tearing at the thing it hasn't yet learned to reconfigure. This voice could have as easily been my sister's, instructional and wise, telling me to never let the piano—and by extension herself—out of my sight.

It works—sharp-edged notes shoot out from pressed fingers on plastic. Soon, and for the moment at least, the music I make is all encompassing. I look into my sister's face with a slow delight that lifts away tears born of questions that I don't yet know how to formulate.

Other evenings, this piano would be our sedative. Right away, as soon as the crib and the piano presented itself to us, we would lose the use of our legs. We'd plop down into our respective cribs as if crippled. What we wanted was to lie next to each other, soothing ourselves with a few notes on that piano in the dark; the cribs that stretched as far as the eye could see in that darkened gymnasium demanded that we lie down as one animal and be in one cage.

We as a group had each other only in the sense that we knew we were being cared for by a means that had no precedent. Was Sook Mei too young to recall what that other means was? Certainly, I do not recall ever calling out for a mother or father as such, nor even conjuring a mental picture of them during this time at the children's shelter. It was as if memory had reset itself, its former parental nurturing wiped clean. Perhaps as a survival instinct, I could now move forward not expecting anything.

Only after my father remarried did life seem to gradually stir itself from the yawning grey of the gymnasium, tensely hushed, and from the two years in a foster home that followed, years in which I seldom talked, and not simply because of the foreignness of English.

The usual sleep and waking routines with a new stepmother in the house, balancing morning dish-clatter with skillet and stove banging, welcomed me after those two years at the foster home.

It was only at age six that I began to recall images of a mother's face.

And only after seeing some small black-and-white photos of that first mother's face, did I recall anything of her at all—a hand on my back, balancing me on her hip. Fleeting snatches of her anguished and sickly moans.

These moans I would never recall audibly, but my body would continue to reverberate with what I saw, through the eyes of a two-year-old, etched on her face. Waves of panic have submerged me, building a wall of grief, those few times when some failure in my life took on the guise of her suffering eyes and open mouth. It was enough to pound me down under.

Years later, when I'm driving my father home from hospital, he'll tell me how I dragged a toy behind me and then ran to touch this shadow-mother's hand. This mother who I only have five memories of. I talked to her in my baby-voiced Chinese—*Look! See how my toy duck shimmies side to side as I drag it behind me!* I wanted her to take the duck on a leash and make it waddle too. I wanted her to stand up, but she was too weak to get up and follow me.

Truth was, I'd already learned to substitute all that she was to me and all that I was to her, for a heavily starched anonymous voice with giant hands putting me to bed and shutting the lights in an endless hall where all you could hear for the next hour before sleep were the baby cries of strangers.

No wonder then. My two recurring nightmares, during the first month of my new life with Dad and Step-mum, were the giant flying squirrels and the sentinel of the cuckoo clock. At night when my sister and I were in our cots in the tiny living room, lying in that deafening pitch darkness punctuated with headlights that pivoted across the living-room ceiling, I would fall into those recurring dreams:

The sky would be menacing as I looked upwards. Then I'd be running for it when the giant squirrel sped down from the sky, its giant teeth bearing down on me.

The other dream was worse. It seemed to grow from inside me, panic enlarging it until it constricted my heart. All the while, the mind's eye would zoom in slowly upon a mechanical cog. It wheeled and clicked, catching on a tooth. Then a darkly crouched figure would rise, holding a sharp weapon. His arm would begin arcing down in a deadly stroke, as my heart tried to beat its way out of my chest. Then I would waken.

Our stay at the orphanage could not have lasted more than three weeks. I was too young to know for sure, but the brief flashes of memory—of being in a lineup of freshly washed toddlers in robes, each in turn lifted up to a chair and struck in the knee with a silver hammer, the doctor's whites and the white walls smelling of phenol—don't seem to span much time.

But it was long enough. One day I decided to stop talking. I screamed instead. The orphanage had a central room. A chaos arena full of toddlers. And me, uncontrollable, screaming at the top of my lungs and punching and kicking at anyone who approached. I can only guess that I was missing something that I couldn't name, though I must have called out the names of my mother and father. But by then they were abstracted beyond concept—certainly beyond the sterile confines of this hellhole. And it has taken me a lifetime of revisiting my past to conclude that those strands of identity in my three-year-old mind had already compartmentalized that previous life in a Chinese family, to this present horror of noisy, strange, screaming children run amok. I do recall falling to my knees in front of a half door that the other children closed in front of me, their eyes all googly and uncomprehending due to my crazed outburst. Finally, I was picked up by an adult and taken to a quiet room where I could be alone with a carpeted floor full of toys, and someone new to watch over me.

I calmed down, exhausted, and fell asleep.

After that, I remember always being with my sister. They allowed us that, although we were two years apart, and the institutionalized system seemed to prefer segregation by age.

I was nearly five by the time Dad had saved enough money to arrange for an overseas bride—a widow, a "broken shoe"—to be sent to Calgary from a sister village in rural Kwangtung province. It was understood that only a widow would be desperate and chastened enough to marry an overseas Chinese suitor— and one already saddled with young children.

Only now, my stepmother must have thought to herself, as she got off the plane that took her from Hong Kong to Calgary. *Only now my new life begins.*

⋮ Maybe the comfort of waking in my own bed, with my sister in the other cot in the living room, with Dad and Step-mum asleep in the room just beyond the kitchen, is the permanent and stable home life that has eluded my sister and me until now.

In this perfect house, my cot in the living room will turn into a narrow sitting sofa by morning. Even as a child I sleep less than eight hours. I wake early, my hands brush the leafy textured wallpaper already twice painted over, first with off-white, now with the palest blue (my favourite). My sister and I, having been reintegrated with Dad into this new family, take turns rolling out of our cots and tumbling awake on the hardwood floor of the living room. No wonder: we're comfortable and secure again. Sleeps are deep, dreams ever vivid, in spite of the infernal cuckoo clock that still gives me the occasional shuddering nightmare, where the crouched executioner pivots on the balls of his feet at the chimed hour's conclusion; or another anxiety-dream involving the clock's two cone-weights, whose chains let go so that the cones crash through the floor, opening a sinkhole that collapses the walls of our home.

I wake up to wind gusts rustling the ash trees. The front storm door is open, and only the screen door is locked. It's summer, and I tiptoe out of bed, seeing Sook Mei still burrowed under her covers, one ear peeking out. I sit on the doormat with my nose pressed to the screen mesh, amazed at the warm wind and its welcome, the thrusting undersides of leaves tethered to entire branches that hint at a hidden presence, of sap beneath the skin of trees, of birds and bird nests buffeting somewhere in the foliage. It's late May, eight in the morning, and already the neighbouring girls are playing hopscotch on the sidewalk, Connie's dark hair bouncing up and down in spite of her seriousness. Red-haired Angela is more carefree, her pageboy hair framing happy eyes.

An hour later, Step-mum gets the coffee going, then peanut-butter-and-jam toast and milk. It's Saturday, and Dad sleeps in from a late Friday night at Lantern Chop Suey. Sook Mei downs her milk and we go outside to bat the badminton birdie back and forth. My breath still smells of peanut butter, the default means of keeping an empty stomach happy. I feel the neutral buoyancy of not talking to Connie and Angela, who often want nothing to do with us. Last year their mom caught us calling Connie "wop," as if returning the favour for Dad overhearing Angela call me "chink." Those are the terms of dread-turned-consolation for having a foreign home life in need of defending, when it is clear that envy or apology are going nowhere. We all feel the need to adapt to this misplacement, justifying our appearance by mocking the other. And if you are on the receiving end, invisibility is key.

Before long, Step-mum appears from the side door and plops down a full basket of wet laundry. Sook Mei throws down her badminton racquet and runs to the back porch, placing a stool in front of the pulley line. Her mouth holds two clothespins at a time. Deftly, she starts feeding the pulley line after each shirt or towel is shaken and pinned. I'm tired of badminton, so I sit pulling grass from the lawn, and before I know what I'm doing, I'm running around and making roaring noises at Angela, just to make her big green eyes go buggy, make her shriek. Connie stands her ground, pushes me away, but I laugh. I throw a small blue ball at Angela and say, "Let's play pig-in-the-middle. I'll be the pig."

This unexpected concession draws Connie's suspicion. Angela, though, is game. But being less coordinated than her younger sister, Connie tries to extricate Angela from our game of catch by bringing out her set of six Barbie dolls. I don't think anyone else on our block owns six Barbie dolls. I am enthralled with their outfits and the plastic house with its small compartments and painted interiors and moveable chairs. There are beds and a fridge. A plastic dog perpetually frozen in a sitting position.

"Play more badminton?" Sook Mei pokes me in the side, totally uninterested in the doll house.

"No. Look, let her jump from the roof. Like this." I take Connie's Barbie and send her flying.

"Don't! You're wrecking it!"

In an instant, Connie packs up our entire world of make-believe and the sidewalk is deserted.

By lunchtime, the sun is shining down, Sook Mei and I are tired of each other, we're hungry for lunch, but there's nothing to be done about it until we're called in.

Then I see Angela traipsing back and forth across the front porch of her house, humming and singing to herself. She is holding a bowl of French fries, her lips slurred like a clown's— and seeing her stuffing French fries into her mouth, lost in her own eating and singing leisure, freed from the kitchen table, I'm more than jealous. I want to erase her using the very space that permits her to walk free.

I amble down the sidewalk until I'm across from her front porch.

"Angela? Where are you? I hear you but I can't see you—"

She's confused. "Well I'm here, I'm right here," she says over and over again. My eyes dart everywhere as I approach her porch, avoiding her direct gaze.

"I smell something. What are you eating, Angela?"

Giggles. Guffaws.

"Hey, but what—what if—maybe what you're eating makes you invisible!"

Such an easy trick.

Leave it to Sook Mei to break the spell when she comes to get me for lunch:

"Hey, ketchup-face, hey Angela, you look like a pig!"

My own mouth smeared with ketchup.

Which tips off Angela that I had been lying to her. That I could see her plain as day all along.

⋮ Now I'm under the pile of laundry dumped in the bathtub. Playing invisible is an art. It feels like hell only because the favourite game will always come to an end.

Last Sunday evening, I hid inside the Hoover vacuum box. It took Dad forever to find me. I could hear Sook Mei giggling and then shrieking uncontrollably every time Dad exclaimed in that loud, friendly booming voice of his, "What? Not here?" My in-out of breath, first soft, then seized as he approaches: you throw another invisibility cloak around yourself to confound the searcher.

Dad is at his best when in search of me. Sook Mei hears it in the jibing singsong of his voice, the gesture of a hug afterwards.

Tonight, he'll pick me out of the heap of laundry, maybe swing me onto his shoulders. Sook Mei isn't too old to have this happen to her: yet it never will, and I'll have replaced her as the child who inherits everything; so much can be read into a grand, sweeping, innocent (for the house is a breathing lung for that kind and all-encompassing) gesture.

I remember raking leaves with Sook Mei, jumping in them. Burning ants with a magnifying glass during the annual ant wars, which would see migrating streams of ant invaders crawling up the side of the house from subterranean cracks in the cement. We were keen to kill the winged ones, which were the mating queens and kings.

I realize now that behind all that unsupervised play was a shadow economy.

Where was Dad? I recall how he would hide in the garage he built, chain smoking, lifting out the engine of his Plymouth Fury II. Fine mechanical details lifted him away from everyone else. At times I would enter his world, curious as to what it involved.

"A-Meen, ga-loo-thlu-pai." Get the screwdriver, he'd tell me, the air smelly with car oil and his no-nonsense purpose. He was never more himself than when confronted by a large project he could oversee—running his own restaurant and keeping the bills paid so completely occupied him that any small concerns from our day-to-day children's games had to be kept to a minimum. We were distractions he had to get away from, to focus his energies on working and making money. The drive for survival clung to him like an odour.

Sometimes his face would darken suddenly. Sook Mei knew what that was about. One night, after he'd slapped her around for coming home hours late, he came to the living room and hovered over her cot. He placed his hand on her head. Sook Mei flinched away and said something amazing: *No more hitting.*

I fell asleep while they talked. In the morning Sook Mei told me the story of how, during the war, Dad had had to sell his younger brother. Everyone was starving; Dad's father had already died. Later, in 1962, Dad's mom took her first and only trip out of that village in Hoi Seng, to America. She followed many leads over several months but couldn't find the son she had given away.

And then there was a time when Dad was out of a job. He didn't get along with the boss at Lantern Chop Suey, so he quit, and he and Step-mum could be heard at night tensely whispering, their bedroom door shut. Next day, the badminton net appeared outside. He taught Sook Mei how to bat the birdie around, while I tried and failed to hit the damned thing, Dad laughing, Step-mum silent and brooding.

My pyjama-flannel belly warming the metal enamel tub, I'm excited for Dad's arrival. An old argument between Sook Mei and Step-mum, from maybe about a year ago, runs through my head. She's asking Step-mum if both of us can hide downstairs, in the basement—"So many places down there! He'll never find us!"—but Step-mum, busy with the dishes, only grunts, "*Lut-tut ek-dai! Nee mao loon-ne gow-ne-yeh, mu-thlum, mu-thlee*"—meaning, don't disturb the junk down there. We knew what Step-mum meant when she mentioned the *mu-thlum, mu-thlee*. It was the bric-a-brac of pictures of our first mother, now a spirit who could come back and haunt her through those photographs. It was important to her success as the next wife that the power of the first wife be broken. All traces of her had to disappear, including the fur coat, which was put out with the trash within the first week of Step-mum's arrival. The wedding photographs, along with any recorded history of her with this family, were necessarily removed so that her presence in this household would never again see the light of day. Luckily, Sook Mei on one of her snooping expeditions found them.

Sook Mei is more than a head taller than me. Though she knows that it isn't simply because of her height that no efforts are made to include her in my parents' hiding game, she accepts this. After all, Dad is visibly tired after a full day plating food from a blazing wok. His forehead perpetually tanned, his red face glazed like crisped duck skin. As he hunts for me, his jovial out-loud muttering announces where he is going next. Wedged beneath the low chesterfield, or folded behind the plastic base-ball bat of the broom closet, when Dad ventures nearer and nearer, I make a point of being excited for both myself and Sook Mei; it will be over soon; Dad will yell *Ha-ha!* yank me out of the hiding spot and I will smell his neck, the restaurant grease; his grimacing day-shouts have now ended, and he is relieved to be safely home, participating in a mock hunt. In search of a son he never lost.

He'd been broken for a while, after losing our first mom. He'd stopped working in order to pay for her cancer drugs, which in the end made no difference. He lost her, and then he lost Sook Mei and me for two years at the foster home. I found out many years later that he hadn't trusted that Anglican family in Airdrie to raise us. Their dairy farm was beautiful, and he got along well with Auntie Nancy and Uncle Fred and their three children, but only to the extent that whenever he'd visit in a smart grey suit, and have us sit on his lap, there would be an underlying strict-ness. Giving us Chinese candies like Haw Flakes and coconut toffees, he'd prompt us to say please and thank you. I recall in those years still understanding the words he spoke to us in Chinese, though by then I was surrounded by English.

All of us hear it now. A banging on the front door. Violent pounding. At this point I'm looking through Sook Mei's eyes. She and Step-mum are both in the living room while some guest on the Julie Andrews show is singing. Is it Robert Goulet? Sook Mei will eagerly hum along whenever Julie sings.

Where I am, under the pile of dirty laundry, is so comfortable. I'm suddenly scared for everyone, but I don't move out from the safety of my hiding place. How lucky I am to be out of sight with intruders at the door!

We both look at Step-mum. She's always warning us to lock both front doors as soon as we get home after school. She unlocks the doors precisely five minutes before our scheduled arrival, and so the demand to be punctual is unwavering.

Out the windows at night you can't see much. Step-mum has been sewing a crotch tear in Sook Mei's pants, and is frozen in place, clutching her rosewood ruler.

Earlier that day:

"Angela! I can hear you but I can't see you. Can you see me?"

"Ha, I'm right in front of you. Why can't you see me?"

"I know! You're eating something magical, maybe your mom knows magic that makes you invisible. Moms can do that, you know. Maybe I can vanish if you let me try some!"

Angela teases me with a French fry at first, holding it in front of me while I aim my face in its vicinity. I let the ketchup get on my forehead, my ear, my neck. Each attempt to ferret out the "invisible" French fry is followed by Angela's billowing laugh. Each one worth the delicious effort.

Angela continues feeding me, with the continued hope of making me disappear, when Sook Mei arrives and bursts the illusion.

Burrowed under the laundry, I'm too scared to move. Sook Mei is the bravest, inching her way to the front door, followed by Step-mum wielding large fabric scissors. Incessant banging. There he is, crouched on the top cement stair outside, unable to walk. The low slant of his fedora hat, coupled with the evening dark, hides Dad's eyes. Sook Mei wants to see into his eyes but can't, she can't tell whether she's supposed to sit down beside him and join in, or whether this is different—dramatic, urgent. That she's supposed to somehow rescue him. He appears fragile, lost, yet so very smartly dressed for a Sunday evening working in the steam-billowing kitchen of a restaurant.

They get under his arms so Dad can get his legs working. They can smell the alcohol. I hear his booming voice as they get him inside. That other voice he uses, the one that accompanies the plastic blue bat when it is patiently taken out of its closet and used for anything but baseball.

So why do I keep waiting in the bathtub, cozied under the stack of fragrant, protective laundry, cloaks of ordinary, uncontested, play-the-role-you-wear laundry that smells of all our easeful days that first year of being back together again as a family?

Looking through Dad's eyes, it's easy to figure out what he was looking for: the invisible one, the one in the fur coat, whose otherwise obvious traces have been extinguished.

Maybe she would have preferred it this way.

18 — in the event of STUART IAN MCKAY

I KEEP COMING BACK to lilies. Out the window of my studio, I imagine there are thousands of them clustered in the ravine. Soon, after years of waiting, I will be free as they are. Soon, in the sanctuary of my studio, in the deep sanctuary of the words that have led me here—up the mountain, down the path, through the door, to my desk—I will share in the sanctuary of their opulent waiting.

The call from home came a few minutes ago, my mother with life-changing news. Every hope I have ever held onto is justified, every vision a great deal clearer. I sit at my desk, my books, the pages of my nearly completed third book of poetry spread all around me. I take in this moment, the one that marks the departure from an old life to a new life. "You got it," my mother says. "Got what?" "AISH." I'm an artist with a permanent disability. For the first time in my life, through the Alberta government's Assured Income for the Severely Handicapped program, I have a source of income. For me, AISH will be like an extended artist's grant: I will receive a certain amount of income every month to cover my needs. The amount is not extravagant, but, to me, it is a blessed miracle.

I write this good news from the Evamy Studio in the Leighton Artists' Colony at Banff Centre, where for decades, artists from all over the world have sought solitude, community, and their own creative high. Finally, I am here, and I can celebrate so many things. My getting AISH follows other good news. I have been awarded a grant for this residency. The launch of my second book of poetry, *a cognate of prayer*, was only a few months ago. Just as my book was about to go to press last year, I had my first comprehensive, and personally liberating, assessment of my disability—essential knowledge for myself and for those who decided my case. This could not be any more poetic. I think of thomas, the central character in the second of four long poems in my book. He stands in the doorway of an abandoned building downtown, overwhelmed by his circumstances, but passionate in his understanding that his life is more than what it appears. He reaches out, beyond his disability, as I have done, into the unknown, and asks why he must wait.

To me, thomas is no stranger; I have been him many times, in many phases of my life. Like him, I have had to confront the bare fact of my disability, then wonder if hope does eventually win against despair.

In the classroom, in the few times when I have had a job, in those encounters with friends who simply could not understand why I am the way I am: can I find a place where my disability is not an end, but a beginning?

Writing this question feels like an invocation. This long slow chant started when I was a child. Words brought clarity, order, and comfort to my confusion. I knew I could survive and even thrive despite my learning and visual disability because of the words I gave to my experience. Language was a companion in whom I took refuge. The tortuous bafflement of a math class or the too fast, too much action for my eyes of a gym class might haunt me for a few hours, but I possessed the freeing ecstasy of language that nothing could violate. Words and I slowed down together. We made a life of our own, as if we had been waiting for the other to arrive.

The more I come to love language, the more I come to embrace, even love, my disability. The two intertwine, I have discovered. An outstanding feature of my learning disability is how it affects the speed with which I process information. My thoughts, my words are always slow to coalesce, as if each is in some dark corner of a cluttered museum or library, and I must seek out, with great labour, all things I need to express. This approach has an in-built advantage. Instead of racing through my work—"Look at this poem! I wrote it in ten minutes!"— I live with impressions, thoughts, patterns of language for a substantial period. I take even longer to write my poems. I edit each word, line, and poem over and over again until I know I have what is meant to be on the page. Perhaps it is an echo of the essential conceit of *a cognate of prayer* that it took a writer with a disability five years to write an account of what it is to be disabled.

What slows me down further, and, curiously what turns the act of writing into a ritual, is the fact that I write longhand. My visual disability—low vision in my left eye, good vision in my right—means that I have poor depth perception and difficulty with peripheral vision. A keyboard and a computer screen tend to accentuate the eyestrain I suffer from most of the time. It is as if I am back in gym class, a visual cacophony at odds with a single letter, a single word drawn out by faith onto the world of paper.

But what a holy, passionate love affair it is to create! What an event it is to dwell within this creation! Now I can release the pain of my past. Now I can reconcile with adversity and know how it has focused the creation I treasure. The friend who thought me lazy and unmotivated, who pushed me away, is only someone who does not understand what I understand. The eight hours I once worked in a café before being fired are nothing compared to my real work and its riches. The twenty-five years I lived well below the poverty line prepared me to appreciate the pleasures of life, while knowing their ephemerality and the joy of a simple choice.

I waited. I never gave up waiting. My imagined world was, is, a real thing. I insisted I would reach it someday.

I did.

Today in the welcome solitude of my studio and the quieting beauty of the trees and mountains that frame it, I better understand the last words in "thomas." He says, "all my life I've gone down hills." I like to think that he says these words to someone, that he walks toward something. I want to tell him, to tell the part of me he comes from, that his waiting has not been meaningless. There is a lesson in any kind of waiting, because it motivates joy and passion and deepens their importance. I'll put it this way: Breathe in this mountain air with me, then imagine not waiting. See where that leads.

19 —— Whisper Talk ANNE SORBIE

HAVE YOU EVER spent the night waiting for sleep? That purveyor of the dream world. That other who lets you visit your own other. Yes, that's right. That vehicle of dream. That filibuster of fulfillment. That suspender of body and soul. That ever-elusive harbinger of escape. Not me! Take last night, for example.

At 2:34 a.m. I dreamed about dreaming. I walked to the window, watched and worried. About the fog. My husband slept on, oblivious to my whiteout anxiety, which is much like the feeling I have when I think about a blank page. My father used to tell me, during similar childhood episodes, that my "heed wis full o' wee sweeties." But. *I'm* looking out into the white night. *I'm* obsessing about the groundless effect of the mist around my aerie.

And suddenly I realize it's as if there's someone else to which certain things happen. That Anne person. And I'm sometimes sure I have no clue who she really is. Could it be as Borges once said? That I'm living just so that Anne can live.

She spent her first thirteen summers in Scotland. I lived in Glasgow, then Cumbernauld. A new town when my parents moved there with my brother and me, to Stonylee Road. To a house with its own garage. The last time Anne googled the name, the town was described in *The Scotsman* as the ugliest in the country. I remember it as a fleet of concrete battleships. And the largest one, the Town Centre, the 1955 utopian engineering brainchild of architect Geoffrey Copcutts, still makes me lick my lips. Why? It housed shops and a hotel. But best of all. At its brig. A library. A scintillating storehouse of stories. The first story Anne ever wrote was a parable. For Sister Margaret. *My* English teacher. Do you see what I mean? Anne's first story began like this: *One day a man called Jesus came to the Town Centre.* I remember where it ended too: on a walkway outside the bakery. A scuffle had broken out in the midst of the disbelieving crowd that collected around the man. *The crowd was like an octopus*, Anne wrote. *It had more than two sets of eyes and four sets of arms.* And the arms sent the man over the railings. At first the crowd didn't realize what had happened. Then. When they peered down from the walkway, which was really an early form of a Plus 15. The man was gone. The character Anne had dared to call Jesus *fell* to the parking lot below. Anne was pretty sure she'd done exactly what Sister Margaret had asked her to do. Yes indeed. Anne was convinced she'd written a parable. For my part, I knew there'd be a lesson in it somewhere. Especially when Sister Margaret opened the door to my French class and asked my teacher to send me out in the hall. Because she wanted to speak to me. The class full of girls held its collective breath. I was terrified of Sister Margaret. Everyone was afraid of her: the bat cape gown she wore and the strap she always carried. It had three tongues. She had used it on the entire class of forty-two girls the week before. That was Anne's fault as well. She was the one who got everybody singing while the substitute teacher was out of the room. In principle, it may not have been the singing that caused the problem. Instead, I'm sure it was the fact that the song wasn't a hymn. The song was "School's Out," by Alice Cooper. But back to Anne's parable. I was sure I was going to faint. Then I couldn't believe my ears when Sister Margaret praised Anne's story. Until then, I thought Anne just suffered from too much imagination. She used it whenever she felt restless and that usually got me into some kind of trouble. Like the time Anne passed out pretending to be Wonder Woman while wearing a sheet for a cape. It got tangled in the back wheel of my bike instead of fluttering behind her at shoulder height. Although, when I think about these things now as the city lights continue to wink at me, I thank the Gods for that Anne person. I mean, she could've been Isadora Duncan. If that were the case I wouldn't still be at the window dreaming about dreams.

It's 3:26. I'm going downstairs to the living-room couch. I think my nervous system has been, and always is, affected by that Anne. Otherwise why would my imagination still be running amok? Although. Anne once wrote: *imagination is the vehicle of dream.* I love this couch. And my mum, who is dead and gone now, loved it too. She took the odd nap on it. So maybe it'll work for me too. My mother was a lot like that Anne: she also had an imagination. She envisioned beginning her married life in New Zealand. But her dream of another place didn't come to be until I had three siblings and my granny, whom my father refused to leave in Scotland, alone, died in 1973, in August, right about the time school went in. By Guy Fawkes Day of that same year, a plane landed me and Anne and my family in Canada. Six thousand miles from the site of the gunpowder plot, in snow-covered Calgary. Winter put a damper on Anne's image of the Wild West. Her mind had been full of the cowboys painted there by BBC coverage of the bucking broncos in the Stampede. Likely what dulled her enthusiasm a tad was what I got for my first Christmas in Canada. Anne insisted that I ask for pointy-toed boots. What I got instead was a pair of second-hand ice-skates that were three sizes too big, so that I had room to grow into them; a wooden pencil case with a sliding lid; and a journal. Anne took over the journal immediately, began a story with another absurd sentence. One that went like this: *Once upon a time, a wee girl left her house and went on a journey to look for home.* I have no idea what she meant by that. Because I was always out of the house. School. Friends. Fumbling my way through half a year of Grade Nine, while Anne tried her best to sound more like my new friends every day. By the time I started high school less than a year later, Anne had convinced me that she sounded just like any other Calgary girl—and I think she was right except when I heard her say words like *book* or *boots*. Anne drove my mother mad with pleas for halter tops and money to go to movies. She carried on phone conversations. In Scotland my family couldn't afford such luxuries. By the time I finished Grade Twelve at the tender age of sixteen, Anne had been a cheerleader, played field hockey in the celebratory local 1976 Junior Olympics, and fascinated yet another Catholic teacher, a priest this time, when she asked for permission to write my Religion 30 project on Zen Buddhism. She had certain ideas about higher education. And. For sure those came to be because *I* wasn't the kind of person who spent very long lazing on the living-room couch.

4:14 a.m.: Did you go to college or university right out of high school? I didn't. I did what my parents had done just before the age of seventeen: I went to work. But that Anne. She went camping, dancing, partying. She discovered skiing and drove me to the mountains every chance she got until at nineteen, I imagined myself into a marriage to a gentle man with piercing eyes. The truth is, I almost left him at the altar, because Anne, who was fascinated with the TV show *Rhoda*, envisioned me running along Seventeenth Avenue, Bay-bought dress and veil flapping in the September wind. Just before we divorced, shortly after I turned twenty-one, Anne wrote a poem about that man. It began like this: *His eyes are boyish and blue but clever.* The division between him and me was absolute. I knew nothing about him until he stood behind me in a queue at the post office twenty years later. That's when I found out that his then-wife was a nurse who occasionally worked on the same hospital unit as my sister. It was 1997 and I still hadn't finished college or university.

⋮ 5:01 a.m.: A few years following that, I fell deeply in love and married again. I gave birth to two children and began a post-secondary journey. I became a Canadian citizen and got a passport. Anne wrote in travel journals. I visited Scotland, Greece, and Nepal, trekked the Everest route with my brown-eyed partner. We used umbrellas in defense of the deluge of rain at the start of the trip. Were glad for the shade they provided at elevation later on. The top of the world was a fantastic place: exciting, beautiful, moving, and dangerous. Anne travelled in our group of seven, recorded every breathtaking moment. But strangely, never had I felt so intensely alone. Something was missing. Anne did her best to describe the atmosphere, which like the Himalayas, had as many ups as downs. Her journal entries seem prosaic when I look at them now. Their Moleskine covers seducing her years before she understood why. Her first Nepalese entry begins like this: *Kathmandu. The noises grow. The city awakes. Voices rise. Prayer wheels turn.* I continued to spin. Out of love again.

⋮ 6:25 a.m.: At Anne's urging I took another path. With my two daughters. I worked while Anne studied. I tried to ignore the stories that began in her head and rarely made it onto the page. Then, I fell in love again. So tenderly. With a gentle soul and his three sons. I worked less. Anne studied even more. Claimed a corner of our house in which to scribble things down. Later, she took over a vacated bedroom. Made it her own. She convocated while I freelanced from a home overrun with five teenagers. I drowned in the kind of melodramas my mother had suffered from me. Anne continued writing for herself. I wrote for other people; they paid very well. I was hooked. I encouraged my young adults to work hard too. I cried buckets when one of my stepsons handed me his high-school diploma as he came off the stage at graduation. Anne marked the occasion in a new Moleskine. Still later, when there were no teenagers left, Anne

convocated again; now she is a master of her own art. I walk yet
another path.

⋮ 6:59 a.m.: I teach in a college while whispering that I am really
a writer. Anne pens a single postcard story during the course
of my three-hundred-and-eight-day term position. She submits
it to a magazine along with a stunning photograph of a bride's
feet. The editors publish the piece. It begins like this: *All your
life you fantasize.* After a few years I come home to roost. I give
up commuting to another city to teach. Spend time alone in an
empty house with Anne's journals and story ideas. She goes
to workshops and I read read read until my eyes bleed. I speak
these words: *I* am really a writer.

⋮ 7:30 a.m.: It's then that things begin to go out of focus. The
five burgeoning adults have careers or post-secondary journeys
of their own. Anne continues to write. Fiction. I accept another
corporate job. It promises gobs of Calgary money so my grown
children can continue to have, have, have. Anne watches me.
She is unfazed. Then it happens: I lose my balance; suddenly,
my giddy-up life comes to a grinding halt. I have an accident at
a lakeside dock. Fall between it and our boat. The only reason
I am not crushed is the quick reaction of another stepson. As
I hang from fingertips clutching at wood and fibreglass, he
scoops me up like one of the babies he is yet to have. Sets me on
sun-drenched grey planks where I writhe in pain. I avulsed the
common tendon that attaches three of the longest muscles in
my body to my sit-bone. I am hamstrung. Literally and figura-
tively. Anne marks the moment in a new Moleskine. Strangely,
soon after that, things come back into focus.

⋮ 8:10 a.m.: Anne thinks and meditates. I am unable to read. I am
supine, eyes weeping salt on my tongue. I am nursed by my
husband, my daughters, gentle friends, and people I don't know.

I convalesce from a major surgery that repairs my leg. I do physio-therapy, massage therapy, rehabilitation exercises, workouts with a personal trainer, healing touch. I do whatever I can to recover. I want to write but I don't. Instead I do everything required for the eighteen months it takes to heal the fifteen-centimetre incision, the scar tissue in the epidermal layers on the back of my thigh, the soft tissue damage, the deep muscle trauma, and the tendon newly attached to my sit-bone. Anne writes poetry. My response is pure. I pick up a pen. Touch it to paper. Words spill. They fill pages. The scrawl sometimes illegible. Then I write this sentence: *I am a lake.* I think and I meditate.

8:24 a.m.: I miss the important things: my children's company, curling against my husband's back, my favourite sexual posi-tions. Summer ends. Fall comes and goes. Christmas is a blur. A new year begins. I keep track of it all. I am healing. And like Anne, I'm not writing for anyone but myself. I begin to under-stand: writing is an important thing.

8:27 a.m.: The fog recedes. It moves away from my aerie and down the valley until it's like a wisp of cotton wool suspended over the Bow River. I see the province's easternmost stand of Douglas fir, the remaining artificial snow below the Olympic ski jumps, the tips of the mountains jutting up behind them. My husband sleeps late. I leave the sofa, climb the stairs and lie near him, enjoying the first rays of sun. They climb through the windows and heat up our bedroom. Next to the nearest pane of glass, resting on the stucco outside, is the blue-black length of a giant dragonfly, wings fanned. I think of an idea for a story. I smile. Anne smiles. I understand now. That purveyor of the dream world. That other who lets you visit your own other. That vehicle of dream. My husband stretches. I turn, move into the sunlight, hold my hand, palm down, fingers spread tenderly against his chest. My story is here. And here is home. I sleep.

20 ___ Waiting for the Impossible   ARITHA VAN HERK

W H Y are these square blockades, these rooms where chairs back against the walls as if in surrender or trepidation, called waiting rooms? Professional planners call this a part of "visit workflow," the space between arrival and "service." As if humans were automobiles, or packages, objects on a production line. But instead of providing a relaxing moment that enables people to recalibrate, take a breath, the waiting room is a containment space, a version of jail and impatience and frustration.

I have begun to tabulate the time each of my health care providers makes me wait, in the process ranking their professional courtesy. My doctor is a prompt and respectful woman, and I seldom wait more than five minutes. She has an effective system, caring and present. My optometrist, another woman, is equally prompt, and seldom keeps me waiting for more than seven minutes; she will come to her office early in order to fit me in with an emergency. My family dentist, a woman too, is reliable and I seldom wait more than ten minutes. But then there is the "other" dentist, the specialist, a man. I've waited up to an hour and a half, without a receptionist or a nurse giving me any indication of why, and no apology, no recognition that my time might be valuable, or that I might have another appointment that will need to be postponed or dealt with. When I inquire, the inevitable question is "oh, are you worried about parking?" No, damn it, I am worried about my life flashing in front of my eyes while I occupy a space that is about as aesthetic as a fishbowl from the inside, the décor a plastic/glass/dead carpet space that pretends to have been designed for comfort (there must be an incredible business in designing waiting rooms—perhaps I should change my profession) but is usually so anodyne that one would be inclined to take indelible marker to graffiti the plastic on the functional chairs and a blade to the inevitable reproductions of mountain scenery or treed meadows and tired Group of Seven landscapes. I've never seen a picture of a grain elevator in a waiting room. I've never seen a Chris Cran painting in a waiting room. I've never seen a photograph of a kick-boxer in a waiting room. I've never seen a waiting room with a shelf of contemporary Canadian literature.

Truth is, I always carry a book, and I read, but while reading occupies me, it does not assuage my contempt. I measure the inches of my breath, I note the surroundings and mock the questionable taste of the dentist, the lowbrow magazines, the truly ghastly art reproductions, the coffee-table books of doubtful provenance. Some years ago, I encountered a medical waiting room with a bank of computers, meant for patients to play games on or to catch up on email, both fun and practical. But that arrangement, I would wager, has long since been discontinued.

It's common knowledge that waiting rooms are cells of incipient discontent. Innumerable studies have suggested that the way to make the wait in waiting rooms less testy is to fill the time with validated questionnaires, prompt question sheets, or "education material," like a film about breast examination, a condescending pedagogical approach to habit. There is a movement toward waiting-room managers, but people are expensive, and can make the wrong impression. A bubbly but ungrammatical assistant who sets out to screen, monitor, and educate me simply arouses more of my contempt.

And so, I track the number of times that my dentist keeps me waiting and plot my revenge. I resist the urge to vandalize the waiting room, and instead plan retribution. Probably in words, probably a story in which an irritated patient tries to tax her dentist for the time she has lost. She endeavours to fine him for the hours he has wasted, sues him for callous disregard of her waning moments, to no avail.

Such repetitions of time lapsed and lost exert their immediate vexations, and then dwindle. Once we no longer plumb that limbo, eager to unstick from the plastic upholstery, we forget the miniature torture of our detention, and hurry onwards in life's accelerated pulse. Such disremembered waiting fades to inconvenience; the nuisance of disruption becomes acquiescence, a shrug, and manageable.

But some waiting performs a ceaseless threnody. That hardened expectancy refuses respite, refuses intermission. Its delay incites a throbbing misery, persistent and inconsolable, for it is a waiting that will not allow waiting to come to a close. It hovers behind the curtains of life in flux, the constant push and pull of emotion and loyalty that are in league with waiting. Why do we love those we love? Why do we forgive some more readily than others? Why do we wait happily for friends and lovers? Why do we bear a grudge, carry old aggrievements like knapsacks? And when do we let go?

I have begun to recognize, now that I've waited for more than a decade, that I will never receive a certain apology I am due. The original insult (vicious and verbal) has been exacerbated by the wait, by my paused expectation that the offender will come to her senses and extend me the courtesy of an expression of regret. But having waited so long, I am brought to the understanding that this suspension was a slice of foolishness on my part, a strange certainty that I lived with, craving reconciliation.

I let a callous cruelty take up space on a shelf in my tender pantry. I waited for that cruelty to dawn on the perpetrator as a regrettable act. I waited for the perpetrator to come to terms, to become human, to understand the pain she had inflicted, to recalibrate, and to express some regret. Instead, I have received nothing, no explanation or "I'm sorry," no acknowledgement of harm done. Nothing, as absent as waiting for the blurred moment when the bikes crossing the finish line at the Tour de France blur past.

This peripheral expectation is a cruel form of argument, a burn that does not cool, the irritant of a hangnail that will not heal. It gnaws. And the waiting for apology becomes itself painfully calumnious, the hurt migrating from insult to the long long stretch of waiting for resolution. Until, in one of those insights that ambush the soul on crisp fall mornings, I realize that this waiting can go on forever. There will be no apology. I've waited for nothing, my expectation a form of self-punishment that serves a chronic affliction.

And so, I've stopped waiting. Such liberation, to refuse to wait. When we wait we do not see the sands of time. We forget that miracles do not happen. We remain in thrall to our offenders. When the waiting is over, we can begin to console ourselves, assuage the ache of time's forfeiture. Sail onwards, no longer disappointed, and drudge to no affront.

21 —— On the Pleasure RICHARD HARRISON of Waiting

I KNEW that waiting would be a complex topic when I began, and that in looking for words for that complexity, I'd feel contradictory feelings. I was surprised, though, at this line that kept coming back to me while I was writing: Perhaps other than death, waiting is the most mortal of experiences. And that has changed how I've thought about it ever since.

Now every opportunity to wait (and *there's* a phrase I didn't think I'd ever use) is a chance to consider mortality, my mortality, and the gift of mortal life, which is an understanding of just how precious time is. Most of my experience has been spent translating the preciousness of time into the value of work. Time may or may not be money, but it is a coin of the realm. Time is wasted if nothing is produced. Time is an obstacle between the intention and the goal.

I was reminded of that the other day when my wife Lisa and I went out for breakfast. There on the table, right beside the menu, was an ad for an app that would let you sign up for the first available table at the participating restaurant of your choice. Instead of standing around with your fellow future-diners, you logged on, and were notified when you should leave your home to get to your table without a second to spare. That's a good use of your time, the ad promises. The app's perfect name for proof: *Nowait*.

We are aiming for it: a waitless society. That made me consider something I hadn't thought about for decades. My undergraduate years were spent at Trent University, in Peterborough, Ontario. Trent was built on the two sides of the Otonabee River. The original university buildings constructed along its banks retain the rough first-pour look of limestone—a sign of a time when things were built towards their natural setting rather than away from it. The river is the heart of a large watershed, so many rivers flow into it from the glacier-sculpted landscape.

Trent faculty and students have both an academic and a personal affection for their rivers. And a friend of mine figured out something about waiting and silence that could only be found there: she realized that the only time that people who knew you and saw you alone and quiet and didn't come over to start the noise of conversation was when you were fishing. So even though she was a vegetarian, she bought a rod and a reel and tossed a line into the water while she read her book or thought her thoughts under a tree. At the weighted end of the thread, usually tempting and deadly to fish, she tied a note, "Get Your Own Food."

And she waited as long as she wanted.

Fishing may be the only activity that treats waiting like a sport. It's the only sport where people's shared love is expressed not just in silence but by it, not in the activity of moving the body just so, but in doing nothing but waiting together. I am writing this a week after the death of Muhammad Ali—a death that has made people around the world consider his mortality and their own. In an interview I just saw online, George Foreman, the man whose life was turned around and ultimately set towards happiness by Ali, and who loved him for it, found a moment of mortality in the otherwise godly champion, and he expressed it this way: "You'd never take him fishing, he loved to talk too much." That sentence makes both men even more human to me.

So that's what I'm thinking about now. Waiting is the chance to consider life while it has slowed, or stopped, around you. It's a chance to think the way the dead think, without the power to reach into events and change them. It makes sense that waiting is a frightening thing, but it is also freeing. Camus pointed out that Sisyphus, condemned to roll his stone up a hillside only to have it always roll back down before he reached the top, is considered one of the most imprisoned figures in mythology. But in fact, at least half the time, he is the most free: as he walks back down the hill to his rock, no one can ask any more of him, he has as much time as he wants—the gods gave him an eternal mortal life. Likewise, we have a glimpse of Sisyphus's freedom when there is nothing we can do but wait. And think. And answer to no one. And experience time, with a little unseen note hung in front of us for the hungry world to read, and reading it, leave us be.

22 ___ Storage

SHARON BUTALA

ON OCTOBER 31, 2013, six years after my rancher husband's death and five after my move to Calgary, I finally emptied my five-by-fifteen-foot storage locker in Swift Current. The locker held mostly books, boxes and boxes of them, along with a few containers of household items that ranked at the top of the "no use" list: tablecloths and matching napkins and odd items such as the nineteenth-century perfume bottle that had belonged to my Scottish grandmother and that before that had come from a relative of her stepmother who had once been a "companion" to great ladies, or at least, to wealthy women. And there were more boxes containing records that the tax department required I keep and lug around for more years. Plus pictures—some framed paintings, some framed photographs—that I didn't really want anymore, but couldn't throw away and also couldn't find room to hang in my new big-city condo.

I had been emptying the locker for the five years I'd lived in Calgary. I was by this time driving a new small car with a tiny trunk, but I couldn't simply hire a truck and move everything at once because in Calgary I had no place to put any of it (except perhaps the pink and gold perfume bottle), and I was prevented from moving it to a closer storage locker in Calgary because here lockers cost about five times per month what they cost in Swift Current. I suppose, if everything in the locker went up in flames

I wouldn't miss any of it, unless of course, Revenue Canada started demanding documents that had turned to ashes. So year after year, odd trip after odd trip, I carted three or five boxes back to my condo, emptied them bit by bit, giving away some things, integrating others into my new life, and throwing away—with tremendous difficulty—a part of each load. Finally, after about four years, I was down to nothing but books. After one trip I managed to find, by sheer luck, two book sales at the same time and got rid of six boxes that way.

Understand, I never wanted to lose a single book from the three thousand or so I had owned, but I had come to face that some were precious to me and some, out of a mixture of vanity and curiosity, I merely liked owning. They were the ones that had to go. I was even reduced, near the end, to throwing away paperback novels. They weren't in perfect condition, nor new novels by a long shot, and most of them could be had anywhere; there was nothing precious about them. I got rid of them when nobody was looking, feeling like a philistine, or like the beleaguered librarians trying to make room in the library in the digital age and nobody—but nobody—understanding how they could throw out thousands of books *just because in fifty years nobody had checked them out.* What had that to do with anything? The destruction of the Library of Alexandria came to mind, all that ancient knowledge lost forever, and the digital age, those fragile pieces of celluloid and then of apparently nothing at all: gigabytes of nothingness. Preservable through the ages? I doubted it.

But this dispersal was the dying of a dream of myself as an intellectual. This is what the books had represented to me, and I always knew they had—my pride in them was based on that. I cherished the books because their ragged and usually dusty rows in a room full of bookshelves said to me and to others what I didn't dare to say out loud: I am not just another ignor-ant country woman with a mind dulled by too many children, too many years driving the baler or the combine, chasing cows on horseback or with a truck, making too many pickles and Hallowe'en costumes, watching too many peewee hockey games, running too many bake sales or cooking too many fowl supper turkeys. I am a mind.

I *had* to be brave; I had no alternative that made any sense to me. I discovered, as I took the last five boxes of books to the regional library, and stored yet another box of papers in my car to take back to Calgary where I would have no idea what to do with it, as I drove across town to the owners of the storage units to return the key and get back my deposit, I found that instead of the elation I'd been expecting, that weight-off-the-shoulders feeling, relief simply did not come. I felt instead a mixture of small pleasure that I would not have to make such a trip again, that I had tied up one of the last of the ends severed by Peter's death, and uneasy melancholy because, aside from the regular trips to my husband's grave, I'd seen the last of the countryside where I'd lived for so long and now seemed to want nothing as much as to escape forever. But for all the years I'd wanted—with something close to desperation—to be rid of that storage locker, to see its contents evaporated, to have the burden it represented put down, it was a wonder that I was not elated, and because I had expected to be, had planned to be, the fact that I could not muster one shout of joy worried and puzzled me. Even stranger was the feeling that I could not believe it was empty and I couldn't figure out why, in the place in my mind, or heart, or soul where I stored tasks, duty, responsibility, encumbrances, it was still there, filled to overflowing, impossibly burdensome still.

It was my past I couldn't dismiss, although I urgently wanted to. On the highway heading back to Calgary I thought of how I had come to terms with the loss of my childhood as everyone does eventually. Mine was certainly interesting, but on the whole, not really that great to live in; I could view it as I might view a movie in wonderful colour—rich greens, crimson-tinted shadows, and unexplained movement, lots of passion, sorrow and shame, but still in some way very real, though I viewed it with a distant warmth and sometimes an equally distant pity; that was now disconnected from the grown-up me. That was just fine with me. Nobody lives that pioneer life anymore or that small-town life of rafting on sloughs on the edge of town, of racing through poplar forests, stick in hand, screaming for no particular reason, skating wherever there was a patch of ice until your feet were so cold you could hardly get your skates off to walk home. No, my childhood was a visceral dream that I could visit if I wanted to, but mostly, I didn't want to.

I had put my adolescence and teenagehood behind me too, partly because I had written it out, mostly in my book *The Girl in Saskatoon*. With both parents dead, and the people I knew from those days for the most part gone to wherever they had gone, living lives unknown to me, I felt I had absorbed that person into my larger self, not without sadness, not without shame, and sometimes with a kind of woebegone pride; that *was* me; no need to revisit it. I had come to the resolution that I would never rid myself of my long first marriage, which had produced my only child, my beloved son, now a man of fifty years, but I tried never to think about it; my second marriage, more than double the length of the first, and with its terrible ending, I was just beginning to emerge from. The storage locker held my past, it represented what I had lost; finally shedding it should have meant I was finished with that past, it should have at last freed me for my future. Yet my joy, which I was making an effort to sink into as I raced down the highway, was bemused and incomplete, laced with an emotion at which I didn't dare look too closely.

Days later I continued to feel as though I still carried the burden of that storage locker and its contents on my shoulders. I have had through my adult life (or so I've always believed) a capacity to put things behind me when I am done with them, to wash my hands of them, to walk away as if they had never happened or been. This ability or desire was part of what kept propelling me forward in life, and although I wasn't exactly proud of being able to do it, I refused to examine it; I had a mental picture of myself striding away, back straight, chin up, into the future. But the storage locker I continued to drag behind me, just as the penitent played by Jeremy Irons in *The Mission* drags up and down mountains his load of iron vessels and objects connected to the Church. In the film, someone eventually takes pity on him, walks over and with his knife cuts the rope that attaches the load, freeing him. But nobody would free me from the storage locker. I would have to do it myself, and *how* I would do this became a subject that I continued to mull over, day after day.

I was learning that no matter how I finessed all my memories, they would come back to strike me in the middle of the night when they would wake me and then I wouldn't sleep again no matter how hard I tried to shove them back below consciousness. Or they would strike me as I crossed a room, and I would slow my pace and tears might suddenly form in my eyes so that I had to wipe them even as I called myself a fool and expelled air through my nose in exasperation at myself. My past on the ranch and the hay farm, the smell of cut hay, or sage in the spring, the semi-annual heart-stirring passage of the great birds, the way my husband had sometimes smiled at me, but also, I might suddenly find myself submerged in whole, long-forgotten scenes. This, however, was not omnipresent, was not a daily or nightly occurrence; those dream-memories had mostly faded, but it was true, I was coming to know and slowly to accept, that this storage locker would, in my lifetime, never be emptied.

The other matter preying on my mind was the fact that though at one time in my life I had often (by rising very early) made the five-hour trip to Saskatoon from the hay farm in southwestern Saskatchewan and back again in time to cook a late dinner and didn't find ten hours of driving too daunting, I now was being worn out by a mere six-hour drive in excellent weather and on perfect roads from Calgary to Swift Current. Not just worn out, but left with thighs that ached as though I'd run a marathon, my always fragile left shoulder—a childhood injury compounded by an adult one—too painful to move, and my wrist and forearm aching steadily from what I suppose must be another arthritic intrusion, and I knew I had made my last six-hour drive in one day—barring, of course, racing ahead of a flood, typhoon, or invading army.

I had begun to feel old. I'd already been old, depending on how one chooses to count, and I'm going to start at sixty, for thirteen years. However, I had never before felt old; that was the difference. Every senior citizen can name the year when he or she actually began to feel old, sometimes can even name the moment when the truth struck home at last: in the middle of a golf game, after a surgery, or an illness or a fall, or unexpected heartbreak—death, departure, retirement. Or even just walking down a street and without actually noticing, avoiding the effort it takes to step up onto the curb and suddenly realizing you've been avoiding stepping onto curbs for some time. When I got out of the car after my drive from Swift Current to Calgary, it took me a minute to creak upright.

A few days later, still recovering from the twelve-hour trip made over two days, as I lay on the sofa reading, something went funny in my head. I thought that maybe I was having a stroke: I blinked, I looked around, I counted to twenty mentally to make sure I still could, I sat up, puzzled, and everything was exactly as it had been before that moment, both inside and outside. Not a stroke then. It had been on the left side, deep inside, impossible to describe; my mind's eye had seen dark red shading to the blackness of the body's interior, but nothing was moving, no blood was flowing; there had been a sort of sudden, muted buzzing, a break in the middle of this, whatever it was, a milder repeat, and everything went back to normal.

I am still puzzling over it, but it was within a few hours, reading something else, although I've forgotten what exactly— somebody's discussion of aging—that I suddenly realized that I had fourteen years left of life at the very least, barring the usual catastrophes, but one doesn't plan for catastrophes, one plans for normal life. Therefore, I would live at least another fourteen years. I would then be only eighty-seven, the normal life expectancy for a North American female who has already reached my current age. I had made just such a calculation after Peter's death when I told myself I had twenty years left, and each year since I had knocked off one until I was now at fourteen. And yet, despite thinking this in a perfectly rational way, even saying to friends, "Fourteen years is lots of time in which to do things," and smiling smugly, I had not really understood a word I was saying. That afternoon, lying on the sofa, my brain did a major shift of understanding and for the first time, the truth I had been mouthing became real. Everything around me shifted, grew clearer, brighter, developed the sharp edges and outlines of real, solid life. I saw how I had begun to drift, begun to give up things (even while telling aged friends that old age was not about giving up but about gaining—sententious fool that I was). I threw off the afghan, swung around, put my feet on the floor, looked around, considered what this shift meant.

In high school I'd had a plan for my life: I would go to university, I would get at least one degree if not more, I would then go on to a profession and I would join the middle class. It wasn't much, but it was a plan. I would marry, apparently I would have children, I would rise in my profession, I would buy a house and a car, and so on. Now, finally, I had come to the inevitable realization, which was that I needed a plan for my fourteen remaining years. I would doubtless become ashamed of myself if I began to behave as if I were living in a dream that would soon end, so that I didn't have to keep on with my studies, or work hard at my writing, or my reading, or travel if it felt like too much effort (and it certainly did), or put myself out in any way if I didn't feel like it; but it was just that in the face of my approaching end it had all seemed futile. This was not despair; it was not depression; I was having a good, interesting life, even if it was not a goal-oriented life. Besides, I told myself, hadn't I been an extremely hardworking woman all my life? Wasn't it time I got a rest, time I just floated around and did what I felt like doing without having to look after anybody else, or meet even my own expectations for myself? Even the closing of the storage locker, constantly nagging at me, was only partially buried, and I still had to keep reminding myself that it was emptied.

I lived now in Calgary; I was perched there. Of all the ways in which I could not conceive of a meaningful future as I had had a meaningful past, I focused, of course, on myself as an artist, a writer. If I had another self I did not know what it was; I didn't think I had another self; I didn't want another self. And so I tried to go back to my writing life—I had never stopped writing—but my writing life refused to return, by which I mean the hours of absolute concentration on whatever work I was doing, the afternoon hours I devoted to serious reading, the way I woke early in the morning and went straight to my desk.

Finally, a couple of years into my Calgary sojourn, for so I still thought of it, not as *my life*, but some sort of an interlude before—what? I did not know what; I didn't examine it—I signed a contract to write a new book. This was, I thought, exactly what I needed to turn me back into a real writer, instead of a mere scribbler playing at writing, imitating the real writer I had been before my husband's death and all that so relentlessly and implacably followed it. I would be single-minded again; I would be obsessed; now my life would once again smooth itself out to be like a river, its steady flow undisturbed by any but the most catastrophic events. Or so I thought.

Instead, I struggled for a week, or two weeks, perhaps even longer, to mentally (or was it spiritually?) *conceive* this book. I had written a proposal for it, of course, plus a fairly detailed outline, and the next step, that first page or first paragraph or even first sentence should have been easy. But I couldn't seem to get started. I backed off and sharpened metaphoric pencils, washed the kitchen floor instead, went out for a walk while the temperature was just right, then came back to stare at my computer, then to turn on the television. Finally, I knew I had to stop all this avoidance, I had a contract after all, I had to write, and to do that I had to figure out what was stopping me. I remembered how I had solved writing problems in my old life in the country before my husband's death wrecked me as surely as an earthquake takes down a building and turns it into a crumpled heap: in those days, I would choose a time when there would be nobody around and when I had no pressing tasks to do in the house, and I would spend some moments in quiet contemplation in order to find focus before putting on my jacket and, with no object in mind other than to solve my problem, going out to walk the fields.

I emulated myself now, and did all these things, setting out for the nearest wild park at a time when there would be few people around. As I walked by myself, I concentrated and began a lawyerly cross-examination: I knew what the book was to be about and how to write it, so that wasn't the problem. The problem was, I concluded to myself, that I could not find that writerly place inside myself, that steady inner state out of which the actual words and sentences begin to flow. I knew from past experience that I needed only to put my finger on exactly what it was that was unsettling my long-honed ability to find that place, and so, as I moved down the tree-lined, asphalt path by the city reservoir I began mentally enumerating all the things that could be blocking me, some large, some trivial—including one I wasn't aware of at the time but later recognized as my own fear of failure. I was jittery, my mind skipping from one thought to another without resolving any one of them, so that in sheer exasperation with myself I stopped walking, looked up to the high tops of the trees that lined the trail on each side and imagined myself throwing a stone at them as hard as I could, angrily, in sheer frustration.

The most obvious of the things keeping me from being a writer again was what was on the morning's news: the Russians had just annexed Crimea and everybody was worried about what they might try next; a Boeing 777 with more than two hundred people on board had just disappeared in mid-flight causing an endless round of helpless, baffled questioning and searching; a helicopter had crashed in downtown Seattle, killing the two people on board; and the day before Los Angeles had a significant earthquake plus aftershocks making West Coasters worry that it might be the prelude to the final Big One. All true, all horrifying, but unless you are personally, directly involved, it isn't hard, when you are about to begin a new book, to push that sort of thing out of your head.

I went on to my immediate family. True, there was serious illness there now that we were getting old but, defining "illness" in the broadest way, there has been serious illness in my family since I was seven and the 1947 polio epidemic in Saskatchewan hit four of us children, nearly killing one and leaving her disabled for the rest of her too-short life. Worry about my sisters' ill health wasn't what was keeping me from writing. True, I had two days previously buried a forty-two-year-old niece whose life had since puberty been the cause of constant foreboding among all the family members, but now she was gone, safely underground now, prayers said, tears wiped, her tragic life ended, or as close as it can be for the living who loved her. Not that then.

Casting about for any other reason for my agitation, I thought of my own health. Thinking something *had* to be wrong (I'm old am I not?), I had a checkup only a couple of weeks ago and the doctor was amazed by my continuing good health. At seventy-three years there seems to be, annoyingly, nothing wrong with me that is worth mentioning. So what on earth was driving me crazy like this? Why was I so anxious and frightened? And why, no matter how carefully I dissected my thoughts and feelings did the source of my anxiety refuse to reveal itself so that I could vaporize it with logic, or at least push it well enough away for a few hours each day so I could sink into my already-precious new book?

I exhaled loudly, gazing around at the black-mottled cotton-wood trunks shining white, or a muted, hopeful green in the early spring sunshine, and higher up to the sky blazing through the fretwork of leafless, finger-size tree branches, then down to the melting snow at their bases. It was not all these *issues*. All those things were there bothering me, but never before had any of them stopped me from writing; even 9/11 stopped me cold for only a few days. I was managing to shove my various worries and concerns far enough back that I could see in the distance the mental peace I was struggling for, but that peace still would not come. There had to be something else, and the longer I walked, pondering as I went, the more I began to understand that there was, accompanying me, distantly, threateningly, a silent, anonymous, dark mass. More relaxed now than when I had begun walking, it crept nearer, and suddenly, I *knew* what it was.

It is true that as with many—if not most—old people, like those West Coasters trying not to think about the one big earthquake threatening them, I had begun waiting for the Big One too: the cancer diagnosis, the stroke, the heart attack, the diagnosis of MS or Parkinson's or dementia or ALS. Every breath I took was at some level being examined by my subconscious to make sure it wasn't going to be my last, or the first of the disease that would, probably sooner rather than later, finish me off. But even this fear I already knew about and had firmly—well, sort of firmly, especially after my checkup where I was informed that my body was in near-perfect working order—dismissed as pointless, neurotic worrying. I no longer allowed myself such disquieting thoughts.

My book, the purpose of my stroll, vanished from my head as the realization hit me: the dark cloud blotting my personal horizon was Mr. Death himself, hanging around, waiting for me to give in, to give up, to beckon him nearer just to get the endless uncertainty that plagues the aged person over with. Simply by dint of being seventy-three, I knew, of course, that in the natural progression of things he was closer than he'd ever been, and I knew—now, walking down that path and searching for that mental clarity and stillness out of which I write books— that without my noticing it he had been tainting my every thought, desire, activity, or ambition. That I had allowed that; that on some level I was probably thinking I was being mature in accepting my condition, which was old age, but by doing so I was letting him stain and spoil my last years—not *last years* I corrected myself—my *current years*—my life, for what was this, right now, if it wasn't my life?

I will not tell you that I resolved my quandary in the next few minutes, for after all, that is the biggest struggle any old person has to deal with, except for those who deny and deny until the day they are dropped to their knees by a heart attack or a cancer diagnosis, where, in a perfect rage they go their graves still gripping the edges of their coffins with their dead fingernails. Or the opposite: those who give up immediately and spend their last years in a semi-swoon, lying on the sofa with the television set on, being waited on by others, and checking carefully each morning to see if they are still alive; waiting, waiting, waiting for a recalcitrant death to come at last and claim them.

That morning I saw that at root, in my deepest part, I couldn't convince myself that starting another book was worth the effort, not with the Final Spectre breathing down my neck, nudging me now and then with satiric elbow, and making me wonder at the value of any human endeavour if this was always, without exception, what it would come to. This one was indeed too big for me to resolve, and so I returned to platitudes, to the centuries of them, all the ones that I had read and heard and that I knew legions of others my age were repeating to themselves: you're in good health; you'll live to ninety-five as lots of people do; you're only as old as you feel! Etc., etc., etc. But none of that was for me; I loathed the very sound of every one of those banalities; they infuriated me.

I had stopped walking. Now I started again, and slowly, floating or creeping from last year's damp grass and the sun on the trunks of the trees and from something hovering in the air that came from what I couldn't say for sure, but that was nature itself, came the delicate, delicious scent of spring—even here, even in the heart of the city. With this fragrance moving through me, and with it all the springs of my life and all the ones yet to come, my fate—the same as everyone's, after all—seemed of less consequence and much less immediacy; you might say that my fate paled and retreated with gentle steps, wafting away until it dissolved into the fresh spring air. Death will come, but not today. Today I am alive.

Irretrievable

23 — Heavy Weight of Silence

LEE KVERN

WE ARE CLINICAL these final days, pulling back the blue fleece blanket from my mother's atrophied legs, peeling off the white sweat socks to look for signs of purple/black creeping up her skinny ankles. Her pale calves, the edema specific to her right hand that inflates her freckled skin so tight, we're afraid it might burst. The breathing, of course, always the breathing, the telltale sign that we listen for, armed for that moment in our newfound knowledge, the ABCs of death that no one alive is prepared for.

And not just us, but also the nurses, the small wild-haired Pilipino woman who combs my mother's thinning hair, as if that matters, while we await the inevitable. What my mother wants. What she asks for. The Pilipino woman fans my mother's grey hair on the white pillow, as much hair coming off as she combs, then twirls it into a neat, tight bun atop my mother's head; my mother no longer speaking.

Or the slender blonde nurse who comes in later and leans tenderly into my mother as if she is her own.

"Barb," she says, "what can I do for you? What do you need?"

I expect my mother to answer as in past desperate times when she broke her hip and lay in the emergency ward with her right leg impossibly angled. A different nurse leaning, her brown hand on my mother's freckled chest. "Barb, what can I get you?"

My mother's morphine tumble of words.

"What's that, Barb?" the nurse asks again.

The nurse and I bend in closer to my mother.

"A bag of money," my mother says, her grey/green eyes a flutter, a slight smile on her lips.

Or the second time around, hip again, shattered beyond repair, her Humpty Dumpty that cannot be fixed, same emergency ward, similar situation, my mother's morphine high. The young man in the bed next to hers presses the call button every few minutes for the hurried, harassed nurses who rush in and out of the curtained rooms. Until finally one nurse comes and puts the call button out of his reach. My mother and I listen through the cheery yellow plaid curtain after the nurse leaves.

"Help me," the young man says, "help me."

We decide he's confused but not in grave danger, given the seven nurses who have come in to help him in the last thirteen minutes.

"Nurse?" he calls out tentatively at everyone who passes by the station.

My shattered-hip mother lies silent, polite, a model patient in her emergency bed.

He manages to wave down a wayward orderly.

"Can you give me my call button?" the young man asks.

The orderly sifts about the curtained room, we hear the rustle of sheets, plasticized pillows, wood drawers opening, closing until he finds it.

"Where do you want me to put it?" the orderly asks, and before the man can answer: "Stick it up his ass," my mother says in her husky-drug voice.

The weight of stunned silence, then through the cheery yellow curtains, the nurses at the station and I can't breathe from laughing.

⋮ I'm late-night sitting at the kitchen table, working on photographs of my mother, our pictorial pre-eulogy, my last-grasp hold on her while she lies waiting in the long-term care she no longer wants. Instead, the expediency of her final wish, her desired release from her seven-year itch: kidney failure, hooked up to a dialysis machine three days a week like a part-time job that pays her nothing in return.

My young mother captured breathlessly in the black-and-white photographs. In dungarees: my adolescent mother leaning against a summer tree, no doubt waiting and ready for life to roll out before her. Prom: her strapless dress the colour of lemonade, with satin heels, and plaster pearls and a tiny silver bracelet. Leaned against a '53 Ford Fairlane convertible: she smokes Peter Jacksons through a sleek black holder, marvellously like Faye Dunaway or Rita Hayworth, so striking my mother is.

I cut carefully around the beautiful edges of my mother's image, cautious not to clip a finger or a toe, or the stray curl of her lush hair that I will ask the funeral director to clip for me pre-cremation. Her dark hair in each photo meticulously styled, pre-marriage, pre-us. The shine in her eyes that has faded over these last two arduous years. But here and now in this picture, her pretty mouth painted bright red and she's laughing, always laughing. I'm acutely aware of my mother's brilliant life lived out long before any of us girls came along. The only gift I give myself pre-eulogy.

The fact that soon I will no longer be able to call my mother up for her Ukrainian cabbage-roll recipe that I fail to write down because I'd rather talk to her, hear the mother-love lilt in her voice on the telephone when she knows it's me. Or to help me remember what summer, where? When we had a birthday party for my toddler son with lawn chairs and foldout TV trays and cardboard pirate hats in whose backyard? Or where was this house? Or do you remember when? My mother collects memory like immeasurable treasure: hers, mine, ours.

This last photograph I cut out, my seventy-six-year-old mother in her own birthday hat, mouth wide, tears of laughter streaming down her high cheekbones despite the dark hollows beneath her grey eyes. Her lush hair thin. Her years circling, blurring. My mother's ache to be released from this grim mortal coil. When we cannot fathom our existence beyond her. I am suddenly unmoored: what am I going to do without my mother?

"No. More. Dialysis," my mother says. "I'm done."

When we, her daughters, aren't. When we will never be. We need to make sure, ask the doctors, the nurses, our mother, not once but three times over the course of that death-risking week.

"You're done? You're sure? Why now? Why not?"

My mother turns away in her narrow bed; she can't look at us. We can't not look at the unsure set of her quivering jaw as she stares at the beige plaster wall. Until we stop asking. Accept, relent. Relinquish our mother love back to her. Let her go. She knows the score. She's done, and no one needs to ask why.

Post shattered hips. Sunday afternoon. My once-a-week, three-hour visit. We're watching the Rocky Mountains, emerald lakes on her widescreen Sony TV.

"You know what bothers me the most?" my mother says, wistfully, from the airbed that rises and falls mechanically.

The bed she has barely left in two years. No cliff's edge sadness in her voice, only her question. My mother so solid, our mountain rock, our Gibraltar.

"What's that?" I ask.

"That I'll never get to camp at Waterton again. We camped there every summer with my mother and father, even after your dad and I got married and had you girls," she says.

I remember. Our colony of tents. Mountain damp of night, the hard, cold ground, the afternoon sun blistering the familial skin of grandparents, aunts, uncles, us girls, my father, my effervescent mother. Black bears shuffling through the pristine national park. When we girls had to pee late at night, my mother stood guard at the mouth of our room-sized canvas tent, sleeping baby sisters inside, with the heavy, metal flashlight in her hand, a mother-bear weapon if needed, while she illuminated our way to the dark outhouse.

"Mom, you haven't camped in years. When was the last time you slept in a tent, on the mean cold ground?" I laugh, trying to talk her out of it, not understanding what she means.

We pause, both of us listening to the soft hiss of her airbed that prevents her from getting blisters, bedsores that won't heal on her delicate diabetic skin. She doesn't answer, instead watches the images on the television, the unadulterated Rockies, the glacial lakes so ice-cold they turn your shins blue. The wicked hot. The cold night. Day fields of yellow wildflower and white lady slippers and purple prairie crocus. Life lived. Felt. Experienced.

The temperature in my mother's room a uniform 70 degrees Fahrenheit. No wind, no mountain breeze. No heat, no cold, no flowers. This airless artifice filling in for the real deal she is no longer part of. I know she doesn't mean camping.

"Two weeks tops," the doctor says. "Dialysis patients generally don't last more than two weeks. The fluids build up and stop the heart, quick and merciful."

We believe him. So does my mother.

Week one: the slender blonde nurse stopping in to see if my mother has changed her mind and wants to resume her regular dialysis.

"No," my mother says, turning away, away, away.

No one makes eye contact; so difficult is this answer for my rock-solid mother and for us.

Week two: We sit stand sleep roll around her room in long-term care. Sober, somber, solemn, exhausted. Then the schizoid release of our sister-laughter ringing through the quiet hall outside her room. No doubt our laughter registering somewhere deep within our motionless mother who is no longer speaking, yet fully alive despite the doctor's surety that our mother is typical. When she's been anything but over her seventy-six years. No sign of respite for anyone.

Week three: The small, wild-haired Pilipino woman comes in to comb our mother's grey hair, swirls it gently into a bun on top of her head. Then she sponges water on our mother's Vaseline-coated lips to keep her mouth moist while we wait for the mercy the doctor promised all of us, my mother included.

"Is that water keeping her alive?" we ask.

"Possibly," the woman says. "Hard to know, your mother has strong heart."

We nod our heads solemnly. That we know. We can't help her live anymore, but we can help her die.

"No more water," we say, which breaks our hearts.

Week four: The doctor comes in to adjust the morphine that flows like water directly into her veins.

"Can't you give her too much?" we ask.

"No," the doctor says gravely, as if our mother's aim isn't the same as his, and ours.

"We can't do that here," he says.

"What if this was your mother?" we ask.

The doctor doesn't answer. Instead adjusts the needle flywheel in our mother's arm, notes the buildup of fluid inflating her right hand like an overblown glove ready to rupture. He checks her thin ankles, no creeping black.

"Soon," he says. "Hopefully soon."

We bow our heads, not in prayer, but in its place, let the water my mother isn't getting stream down our daughter faces. Want humanity, human decency, the kind expediency of death we reserve for house cats and dogs.

Week five: We are beside ourselves. The heavy wait for our mother's silence. Beside our inert mother on the airbed, water-less, morphine that doesn't quite do the job, and the end is not nigh for her. No one can stand it, we waver, we walk, we pace, we are sleepless, zombies too exhausted to feel anymore.

"Tell your mother it's okay to let go," the slender blonde nurse tells us.

We do, we tell. We tell her a thousand times while we wait beside our mother on her bed that breathes in and out like it's alive.

Week six: Forty-two twenty-four-hour days and nights for our beleaguered mother and us. So far beyond the doctor's promise of *two weeks tops*. We see the signs now, the terrible purple/black bleeding up her ankles, her delicate skin so taut it hurts ours. We know her heart is pressed, pressured beneath her freckled chest. We can barely look at her. We know that she is close. Our fatal yin and yang. What we wait for. What we dread.

But *we* are not present this time; it's only *me* beside my mother in her breathing bed. One sister out in the hall talking to the blonde nurse, the others not arrived yet. We are on shifts now, like death workers in a fickle factory.

I watch my mother: her grey/green eyes shut tight, her freckles no longer bright on her skin, but pallid, her chest rising shallow. Then it comes or goes or stops, I don't know which, and it matters. I lean in to wait for her to exhale but she doesn't. Her strong evanescent heart stops. I wait in the eerie absence of sound, instead hear her airy bed inflating/deflating, no longer of use to either of us.

I am momentarily stunned, not sure if I should run out of the room, alert the slender nurse, the wild-haired woman who kindly cared for my mother right up until this seemingly never-ending end. Alert them to what? For what, I think? That my mother has mercifully gotten what she needed? That she's no longer broken-hipped, bedridden, and on dialysis? That her seven-year itch is finite? That whatever held her here has irreversibly let her go?

I draw a deep breath: grief, sadness, relief, the absence of pain. Hers. The treasure trove of memory I know my mother takes with her, the gift of us. I breathe for my mother, myself, then lean in, press my warm lips against her cool, colourless forehead. Know this is life and this is release. I stand beside her, wait horribly, stoically for my sisters to come so I can tell them, and we can collapse together. Our mother's heavy wait for silence. Done. I want nothing less for her than national parks, icy lakes and pristine mountains, camping on the hard, cold ground. Life after life, I hope.

24 —— Impressions MARGARET MACPHERSON

MY TWENTY-TWO-YEAR-OLD DAUGHTER came home
two weeks ago in the middle of the day. I knew something was
wrong because her boss drove her.

I watched from my office window as the maroon sedan
pulled up beside the house. She was in the passenger seat. Her
head was bowed. She nodded once as they exchanged words.

He put his hand out and touched her shoulder briefly before
she got out of the car. There was tenderness in that touch and
something I couldn't put my finger on.

She walked towards our house. And he sat in the car and
watched her approach. His eyes met mine briefly, through the
double windows, the windscreen of his car, the glass of my
study.

Take charge, his eyes told me. *Take care of her*, he urged. *I have
done what I could.*

He did not drive away until she was safely in the house.
Something had happened. I hurried downstairs, tightness in
my belly.

You want to spare your children everything. It is natural. And
you can't.

As she crossed the threshold and I looked upon my daughter's face I saw that something had changed, hardened, that her
world would never be the same.

All I could do was wait for her to tell me what had happened.

The story came out jagged, punctuated by shuddering breaths. On her lunch hour, she was on her way back to work, walking in front of MacEwan University in downtown Edmonton, when a man, a man she did not know, fell or was pushed or jumped in front of a city bus moving at speed.

She watched his body fly through the air, saw it land, half on the curb, half on the slushy street, right in front of her. A fellow human, mortally wounded, lay broken and bleeding at her feet. And because none of the other shocked pedestrians knew what to do, my daughter, who did, took charge.

It turns out she did all the right things, the ABCs of first aid: Airway, Breathing, Circulation. Amid the streaming blood and the open head wounds, my girl was the first and, as it turned out, the only responder until the efficient ambulance attendants arrived.

It wasn't the accident itself that marked her, however. It was those few moments between the man's falling and the paramedics' taking over.

"There was this guy standing there. Standing. Right. There."

My daughter spat out these words as though they were something foul and repugnant in her mouth.

"I asked him to help me, to hold the man's head, but he wouldn't." Her eyes blazed. "He wouldn't, because he didn't want to get his hands covered in blood. He was wearing a nice suit and he didn't want to mess up his fucking nice suit. The guy on the ground was a homeless guy, an old man. And nobody would help me. Nobody."

Her voice is agony. "Mom, he didn't want to get his fucking hands dirty."

Then she cried. Long and loud, she wept.

What could I say?

⋮ Last weekend my husband and I stole away to our rustic trappers' cabin up north on the banks of the Pembina River. It was after the event, after we'd had time to reflect. My daughter had gone back to work. Things were back to normal. Or so I thought.

But something wasn't right and, again, I couldn't put my finger on it. It was a niggling, a tickle, fingers tap-tap-tapping against the inside of my skull. It wasn't until we were well outside the city that I realized I was waiting for something, the fallout from the bus incident.

We were walking, snowshoeing actually, through the bush and we found a place where a moose had bedded down on the riverbank. You could tell where the animal had slept by the way the snow looked, a concave depression iced over from the heat of the big moose body. The animal was long gone, but a few stray hairs remained frozen in the ice bed. A few spare tufts of moose hair marked the spot where he had taken shelter overnight.

I thought of my daughter, then. How the heat of her large heart and her capable hands melted an indelible impression on that cruel pavement for that particular man in that particular instant. He may never have known she was there, of course, but I am certain she will never forget his pulse, his trembling eyelids, that final thread of exhalation.

Those moments are left for her to hold alone, with the blood and the drama and the adrenalin rush over. She was there, wholly and fully present in a moment of great need. She was a witness to that man's being and, perhaps, his leaving.

⋮ I scanned the papers in the days following her return to work; I searched the obituaries, hoping to learn more about this nameless, possibly homeless man, struck by a bus. I even went as far as to call the hospitals, but they would give me no information. There was no neat closure to this event, no happy wrap-up, no conclusion, no information on whether or not the victim survived.

But something has changed. My daughter's view of the world has shifted, and her eyes now remind me of what I saw on that riverbank. The impression left by the onlooker has iced over. Her eyes are distinguished now by something frozen, those few stray memories, the things that cannot be forgotten.

Perhaps this is what it means to be fully human, to know most won't agree to get their hands dirty, but to act anyway.

I want this chill to leave my daughter's eyes, but as I wait, somehow, I know, I wait in vain.

25 —— Telling

VIVIAN HANSEN

A NOVEMBER SPLASH of cold rain and the first hint of winter on this Sunday morning. Alexis passes me on the Crowsnest Highway that stretches just beyond the Crawford Bay ferry terminal, up toward the winding road to Creston. I can't tell in that moment if I am annoyed or just plain hurt that she has chosen to pass her mother. Why leave me behind? Her tires have hurled a sopping wet force against my sedan, against my windshield. And maybe she just didn't realize she was hurling it against me.

This is the end of a journey that took four days. This is the end of a journey of thirty years, to a family reckoning. This is a story about waiting to hear the words *I am sorry*, like the opening of a door that allows me to enter into forgiveness. Perhaps into echoing those very words myself.

The rain blurs my view ahead. I am trying to keep Alexis in my sight, but she speeds ahead in a bullet of purpose. Or silent fury. It's hard to tell which.

It's all so hard to tell. I had arrived last Thursday morning, after curling into a nest of self in the Ramada hotel in Creston the night before. That winding road is a serpent when you're tired. I know this from years of travelling into this place. How many times I would have given up a few dollars just to get some rest before taking on that road. A whole day travelling straight from Calgary, and by the time I hit Creston, I needed fortification. This time, some forty years after I first entered the Kootenay Lake world, I know the way to make a short entry, and a quick exit.

That first time I entered, in 1977, I was nineteen. I drove a new Volaré—a white, tormented piece of crap, but it had an eight-cylinder engine, and I was out of my element for speed. I had left Calgary at about ten o'clock, south through the Crowsnest Pass. A few detours later, and by nine-thirty in the evening on a hot July day, I found myself at Crawford Bay, dizzy from that last snaking road. At Crawford Bay, I thought I might be in the home-stretch to Proctor. Well, yes, kind of. One large ferry and a cable ferry later, I discovered I was on the right road to my aunt and uncle's place just outside of Proctor.

"Don't move anything in the house," warned Auntie Lise. "Just leave everything to us to unpack." They were off on a trip to Denmark, had just bought the estate right on the hill, and had managed to dump their belongings at the last minute. My uncle had drawn a picture of the winding road that led up to the house. His meandering scrawl on a piece of envelope was etched in my mind. It was that meander that gave me my last wind on that day. I had a key. The whole wretched trip, although scenic-ally lovely, had taken eleven hours. I could have gone to Europe in less time.

I unlocked the pine door just as dusk began to fall, and entered a pine cabin. The fridge wasn't hooked up and I couldn't move it. So much for milk and cereal in the morning. The stove seemed to work but there was no point in cooking anything. I had no place to store leftovers. *Watch out for the bears*, came my aunt's warning voice in my head. That meant I shouldn't throw out any food.

I wandered around through the house and settled on a small basement room with a bed already set up. This would be my den for the next week. I would orient my way around this paradise. Walk some paths. Get to know the neighbours, if there were any. Seek out the bears.

Proctor was the central point of an unseen compass. Wild and fern-dotted, Proctor aligned to the corridor of peace in this valley. I strolled around in the backwoods, helping myself to quiet spots that belonged to others, but no one in particular. The human population around here seemed content to share their space. A small cabin in the woods lay nestled in trees next door, with a manmade pool in the backyard. Snooping around, I discovered a small side cabin that turned out to be a sauna. I looked inside, taking careful inventory: a wood stove, a dirt floor, a smooth pine bench, and a dipper to pour over hot rocks that lay haphazardly on top of the stove.

I closed the door behind me, inspecting the room further. A place to show Jim when he arrived on Saturday. Maybe we could take advantage of the little homemade sauna. There didn't seem to be anyone around to ask permission. I stroked the smooth rocks, examined the clear water that would shout into steam when the stove got hot. If a woman finds a sauna in the woods, and a clear pond to splash in, does anybody hear?

I left the sauna, striding through the forest shadow on the path back to the house. All the paths offered me red berries, somewhat like raspberries, only softer; crushable. I ate them on cereal and warm milk in the morning, just so I could use up the milk I had brought, before it spoiled. I decided that I would buy milk even though I couldn't keep it cool. Just meant I had to drink more than a cereal cup each day.

Savouring my first cup of coffee one morning, and cleaning the berries in the kitchen, I heard a knock. A strange sound in this quiet but bird-filled place. I opened the door to find a handsome middle-aged man. He removed his straw hat, swinging it down to his thigh. "Hi, I'm David Dukoff." I smiled and introduced myself.

"I sold this place to your aunt and uncle. I came by to see if they needed anything."

"They're in Europe by now, I'm sure. I'll be here for a week watching the place."

His eyes opened wider and took me in. "Well, do *you* need anything?"

"No, can't say that I do," I said abruptly, without really thinking it through. "But I wish the fridge was working, or plugged in or something." I opened the door wider, inviting him in. That ownership thing must have been real for him. I didn't feel I could refuse him entry.

"Well, that's something I *can* help you with!" He stepped past me into the hallway and eyed the fridge. "We can both push it into place and plug it in." He tossed his hat onto the kitchen counter and turned back to the fridge. "Okay," he said. "You plug it in and I'll shove." Together we angled the fridge into a corner, then stood there looking at each other. A trickle of sweat appeared on his brow, and he broke my gaze to look for his hat, wiping his forehead.

I guessed that he might like to stay, maybe getting a last look at the house. "I have coffee, David. Don't have any goodies to go with it, but...there's cream and sugar, and...berries."

He nodded. "Love to," he said, and grinned.

We sat down to a pot of coffee, cream, and berries. "What are these called?" I asked.

"They're thimbleberries." He plucked one from his bowl and stuck it on top of an index finger.

"Oh, of course." I laughed and plucked my own thimble from the bowl. There we sat, laughing...with crimson edible thimbles on our index fingers. He plucked out four more berries and placed one on each finger of his right hand, displaying them to me, and to the summer air around us.

"What do you know about this place?" he said, surveying my face again, still holding up his hand, like an odd glove with thimbleberries on top.

"Not a thing. My cousin lives down the road with her partner. I think that's why my aunt and uncle wanted to move here."

"It's Doukhobor territory. My grandfather came here from Russia."

Remembering something I'd heard, I nodded. "Oh, the Doukhobor women...resisters. Didn't they remove their clothes in protest or something?"

David sucked a thimbleberry into his mouth. "Yes, everyone's heard of Doukhobors when it comes to naked old women." He detached berry number two and savoured it. "But no one seems to know that we settled this area, cut the forest back and made homes for ourselves. Raised our families and became keepers and knowers of the forest."

Number-three berry made it into his mouth. He looked at me, then into the forest, fixing his gaze on a cedar branch, maybe. I finished my bowl of berries and leaned back into my chair, and as I waited for his next words, I decided to ask a question. "Where are you living now, if you sold this place?" He yummed back the last berry on his pinky finger, then sucked the one off his thumb. He reminded me of an overgrown child, happy enough to tell a story when he could eat berries.

"Just through that path in the woods...you follow it along for a bit until you come to a small hut."

"The sauna?" I said.

"Yes, you found it." I wasn't sure whether it was a question or a statement. I felt my face grow warm, though.

"Yes, I found it." I thought it best to be straight with him. "I didn't know it was yours."

"You're welcome to use it if you like." He smiled again. Had he been watching me?

"You've done a great job of making that pond. That must've been a lot of work."

"Not so much really. A neat thing to do. Saunas belong with hot springs. This corridor is a place where people and animals intersect. There's a brown bear that likes to amble along the path to my place. He won't pay you any attention if you keep a bit of distance from him."

"Thanks...my boyfriend is coming in on Saturday..."

"Your boyfriend?" He stared at me. I wondered if I had offended him somehow.

"Yes. He's really familiar with the area. He's been to Ainsworth Hot Springs, done some backpacking around here... he spent time on a project called Wilderness Encounter, for teen-agers. He and his group would take them into the backcountry in the summer..."

David shrugged. "Well, he'll fit right in here." And so will I, I thought, lifting my head toward him and staring him down. Not at all sure why I smelled a challenge. "Thanks for helping me move the fridge into place."

"No problem," he said. "Let me know if you need anything. I can always come by each day and check on you."

I nodded, not wanting to display too much of an invitation. He hesitated, then got up and placed his straw hat back on his sweaty head. I walked along behind him to the door. He smiled back at me then ambled toward his forest path, not looking back.

I returned to the picnic table outside. The thimbleberries were all gone. Our two small white bowls gleamed in the warming sun.

Jim arrived the following Saturday. I remember being surprised that he found that furtive dirt road leading up to the estate. I remember asking him how he found it so easily; he seemed surprised by the question. "It was easy. You draw good direc-tions." I knew that he could orient his way around any map.

I showed him around. He followed me into the forest, along the path leading to the sauna. We strolled back to the house. I remember nothing more of his arrival that night. It is possible that we made love. I know I did not sleep. I had waited all week for his arrival, making trips to Nelson, checking out Ainsworth Hot Springs. Picking thimbleberries. I had seen David once; he waved at me as he ambled back to his home by the sauna. Jim's arrival, like a dog marking a tree, had put the run on David, maybe.

It is strange that I remember more about David Dukoff in one scene than I remember about my future husband in the week we spent alone at Proctor. Oh, there was one more thing: the sauna. Jim and I tried it out one night, running naked in the manmade pool, splashing, and giving chase. I imagined a scene in a movie. Yes, that was it. The last time I swam naked through a pool. I can still see myself, in an out-of-body moment. The older me watching from the woods, staring at my younger self splashing wildly in a small pool. Is this what memory grows out of? An older version of yourself, watching a scene and mining it for where you went wrong?

I carry these small snapshots with me, turning their corners as I drive toward Creston forty years later in the now of things, returning home from the funeral. The morning is grey; fog-addled. I choose my CDs carefully: Gregorian chants that offer me no more than the moans of monks who project grief through this fog. I do not understand their Latin any more than I understand the listless motion of grey clouds and fog against this mountain. But the chants are haunting inside these cloud-skirts. I am driving away from the corridor, the place where humans walk through a greenspeak of forest. November offers me endings.

In these past three months, I had waited for Jim to call me. I even imagined that we might hold a ceremony between us that included mutual apologies and kind memories. I imagined that I could distill our history for him, including a small story of myself splashing in that pool with him. As he died slowly of colon cancer, I thought there might be a phone call in there for me. One that talked about our life together for better or for worse.

There was so much I wanted him to say to me, but his voice—if he still had one—grew colder, darker; drifted over the mountains, and became lost in the stone. My waiting for his voice sat like a fog over that mountain—to be lost in the soft light of mourning. A melancholy that rocks itself to sleep.

So on this drive, I am trying instead to focus on our daughter. She drives faster than me now, uninterested in making tracks I can follow. She looks like the me who splashed and danced through the sauna pool forty summers ago. She is like her father, quietly discerning the furtive turn onto the right road. There is no point in my giving her a map, or explaining. She will find her own.

⋮ I had made the ungodly and unhealthy choice to save snapshots of Jim's wrongs done to me; done to his daughter. As I drive along the Crowsnest Highway, my mental catalogue matches the small stories aligned with Jim's, and the moments when his choices hobbled me. His recent widow mentioned on Facebook that Jim had been the love of her life. I am surprised at this; even long after our divorce, I could honestly say that he had never been mine. So what was there to forgive? If two people cannot love one another, there is no colour of life between them. There are only so many tellings.

I remember being at a party with his co-workers, only a month after Alexis was born. I was bone-weary from new motherhood and asked him if we could leave. He turned to me and said, "If you want to leave, get a cab." He said it just loud enough for his co-workers to hear, and a silence fell over the room. He seemed not to notice, and I quietly waited out the evening without interrupting him again. Had he said that equivalent to me in middle age, I would have taken that cab home and cracked his sorry red head into reality the very next day. Does this sway of rage have any place in a marriage? I would never have the stamina to find out. How could any woman say *he was the love of my life*...and actually mean this? Was she lying? Indulging in absurd nostalgia?

The memory clips are relentless, made somehow more ethereal and heavy from the Gregorian chants that have begun to stroke and amplify my forgiveness as I drive. I think the memories will always assault me, but they have also rendered me into the woman I am today.

"I'm taking a backpacking trip in August," he said, tossing his car keys from one hand to another. The motion was one of those things he did when he was quietly angry. Wanting to hit something, smash things against a solid hand.

Alexis was a year old and needed his attention, but he wanted to get away to his beloved mountains. His family was no longer a haven for him. "I need you to drive me to the drop-off point." He didn't even ask whether this was convenient for me or not. He didn't ask whether his little girl might miss him. With only a few weeks of notice, he began to plan his trip. He gathered backpacks, hiking equipment, freeze-dried food, and said little of anything. My purpose, it seemed, was to simply do what I was told. We set off for the mountains, me not knowing where I was driving. Three hours passed with little talk, except my question, "Where are we going?" And his curt response, "I'll let you know when we get there."

"There" was a hiking trail high in the Banff–Radium pass. "Turn right here," was all he said. I did that. He got out of the car and gathered his equipment together. I got Alexis out of the car and took some pictures of her scurrying around, unaware that her father was leaving her for a week. I waited for him to wave goodbye to us, but the gesture did not come. I must have told Alexis to wave bye-bye to Daddy. I watched his back for a long while, until he disappeared, his red hair alive in the mountain wind. His parting comment was an order: "Meet me here in a week, same time, same place." In those days, I got used to following orders. Now, so many years later, I would never have returned to pick him up. If he could survive a high-mountain existence for a week, he could surely find his way back to Calgary. But for Alexis...I had to return.

That week of waiting meant I didn't have to follow orders. I could live a routine that suited me and my little girl. It never even crossed my mind that Jim might get mauled by a bear, break a leg or another limb. I never worried. I didn't care. I knew he would come home. And so, of course he was there a week later. He had not waited long, because of my obedience. For another round of enduring a life with a man I couldn't stand. It perplexes me still that his next wife could so forcefully declare him the love of her life.

⋮ The fog has now become a higher cloud around these mountains; it feels as though they move as I do, in slow motion, as I wind my way home. They remind me that this drive has changed little in forty years. I have been away from Jim long enough to allow some nostalgia, although there is precious little of it. Still, it finds its way toward me. There is something of Annie Dillard's *Pilgrim at Tinker Creek*, which he gave me once when he might have been in love with me, or I with him. There is something of "the love of my life," which I heard from his widow. Certainly, something about Alexis weeping at his funeral. These are not costly tears. He had never supported her. My own eyes may have been the only dry eyes at Proctor Hall at that memorial service.

At his second wedding, Jim and Shirley decided to have a costume party. He and Shirley wore pirate eye patches to the ceremony and the party. A far cry from our church wedding some fifteen years before, when he insisted on a white tuxedo. During his self-imposed exile to Proctor, he had become a "pirate," building a pirate-ship playground in his backyard. Allegedly, he had done this for Alexis. I suppose.

As we walked into Proctor Hall for the memorial, a pile of pirate eye patches lay beside the guest book. We were all to pick one up and wear it through the memorial service. I picked one up, half-hearted. It was decorated with skull and crossbones. I refused to wear it, though; it reminded me way too much of his ridiculous side, the one that couldn't canter up front with responsibility. To her credit, Shirley invited me to be part of the funeral party—to be piped in.

There is something about the skree of bagpipes that wants you to grieve, no matter who died. At the last minute, I declined to join the group. This was her show, not mine. I had relinquished him long ago. My years living in the house in Proctor were a study in quiet desperation, and I did not wish to relive it.

I walked up the aisle alone, past the throng of people who thought they'd known him. When is the one dead ever really the enemy? I sat close to the front, on the side, choosing my own place of honour and memory. I wore an orange beaded shirt, something suitable for a middle-aged woman who doesn't want to blend in with the snow. Or the incessant rain. I wondered if David Dukoff was in the crowd and if I would recognize him, or he me. He would be an old man by now. If I had slept with him that week while I waited for Jim, would the direction of my life have changed? Would I have told Jim to stay in Calgary and not to bother coming out? The inability to text message in 1977 may have carved a decided path in those woods behind Proctor.

The bagpipes skreed, the piper led in the family. Shirley, Alexis, Derek, Jacob, and Shirley's daughter Morgan. I watched them amble in and said a grateful thank you to me for having the good sense to follow my instinct on this one. I was to sit and hear all the pretty good characteristics of my ex-husband, a man whose description at his own funeral I did not recognize. Someone said something about how he'd made Alexis a pirate playground in the backyard in Proctor. He'd always enjoyed banging things together, and I suspected the project had been done more than partly for his own edification.

My grandson Jacob said a few words about his own passion for *Doctor Who* and did not completely comprehend his role in the eulogy. But, dressed cutely as a miniature Doctor Who, and sporting a pirate patch, Jacob wore a camel hair jacket that was too long for him, and scarlet running shoes that Alexis had painted with red nail polish. At one point the MC said, "You should all see what I see, a room full of one-eyed pirates!" She never looked in my direction.

Everyone leaned forward when Alexis came to the front to talk about her father. I had to grant her a classiness that I didn't possess; a love for her father, and grief I couldn't comprehend. She ended her eulogy in a shocking breach of confidence that I could only admire. As her father lay dying, I had sought to console her by trying to remember the best of him. A shaft of light had come to me, as though I had joined them on their walk that day so long ago, and I had sent her this email:

> *I've been going through papers, trying to decide what to throw out. I found a letter I wrote to you on your 18th birthday. In that letter was a memory—when we got home from the hospital after you were born, your dad wrapped you up in his baby-walking pack. It was a breezy day in August. He grabbed you and went for a walk. It was like he wanted to have you in the place just under his heart, where I'd had you for all this time. It was his turn. You spent the walk looking around at this new world, so full of light and beauty. He said you looked at the leaves, how they blew in the wind, your eyes following the movement. He probably talked to you, explained about the leaves and what they could be expected to do. When he came home, I saw that he was in love—head over heels—with his little girl.*

I had given her this message because I wanted to let her know that her father had actually loved her in his own unique patterns. I had never intended for her to share the story, but she did not know this.

I sat staring at her as she read from my email message. She was so composed—the papers did not shake in her hands. So perfect; her red taffeta dress spilling over her womanly curves. So complete in her self—the daughter who Jim and I had created together. And I wanted her to stop talking, stop sharing the perfection of her father—I wanted...to remember only the worst of him. But my memory of her birth and early years were full of him—I could not keep him out of the equation after all.

I slipped outside Proctor Hall alone after the funeral and found my grandson Jacob weeping on the cold concrete stairs. The rain had softened, but the grey stairs slopped with tiny pools. Jacob held a funeral card picture of his grandpa in one small hand. I sat down beside him, telling myself that I could endure awhile in the wet, for the sake of a sad little boy. I plucked the funeral card from his hand and put it safely in my purse, noticing that the wet of Jacob's tears and the rain were draining the watercolour picture of Jim. Jacob seemed not to notice the thin lack of it as I plucked it from his fingers. I wrapped my arms around his Dr. Who jacket and his heaving shoulders. He cried loudly.

He still wore that stupid eye patch, which must have been filling with tears. I didn't remove it. All these people had worn it in honour of Jim. I searched for mine in my purse, and without taking my arm from Jacob's shoulder, I placed the pirate patch over my right eye. If everyone around me chose to see Jim with only one good eye, I guessed that I could do the same. Masking myself, just this once.

26 —— Tom Petty Just Isn't There for You

Riffs on Waiting

AS A WRITER, you know how to wait. For acceptance. For rejection. For those promised edits that fail to appear, week after week, in your inbox, substituted instead with a series of increasingly thin, gruel-like promises. And the soundtrack of your life includes the perfect backdrop for this. When you post a link on social media to a YouTube clip of Tom Petty singing "The Waiting," it's a universally recognized shorthand among your writer friends, who respond without needing to know the specifics, their "likes" acknowledging those moments when your writing has been placed in the hands of others, when you're powerless. When there's no longer a single damn thing you can do or have any control over.

Tom Petty's irresistible 80s classic is about the heaven and the agony of waiting for the woman he loves, not about the writing life, but he nails it: waiting really is the hardest part. Tom provides you with a measure of catharsis—you are not alone in your artistic suffering. It's a song the non-writers in your world recognize, too. Everyone ends up humming, connected for a moment, the despair of waiting temporarily averted.

That's what Tom Petty does, right? He's there for the times that everyone knows will ultimately resolve themselves shortly after the last guitar chords fade away. The easy stuff that we proclaim to be the hard stuff.

But where's Tom Petty when it comes to all those non-catchy waitings that you rarely talk about: the complicated forms that shun speech? The ones that summon spirits and dreams of revenge. The black waitings: the bitter, and the bleak.

In the good times, Tom gets it completely right. In the opening lines of "The Waiting," for example, when he describes his new love with a delighted, giddy anticipation. He compares the feeling to heaven, or to a wonderful dream—one of those times when the waiting can be the most delicious part. You get that. When you were a kid, you never wanted to open Christmas gifts early. Your sisters and brother would beg your parents on Christmas Eve, just one, just a little one, please. Your parents were democratic—if the majority wanted to open one gift, they'd allow it. You were the annoying kid, the one who pissed off your siblings with your reluctance.

What you loved most were the moments before opening the gifts. You loved looking at them—the shiny paper, the hand-curled ribbons, the bows re-used from year to year and held on with tape. The possibilities were endless and sparkly in the multicoloured tree lights—there could be anything in there! Anything at all! You protested the 5:30 a.m. awakening. You staggered out slow and groggy in the morning in your pyjamas, hair sticking out everywhere, happy to heed your parents' insistence that you wait until they'd tossed breakfast meat pies into the oven before joining you on the floor to begin the ritual handing out of the gifts. You never tried to guess, even accidentally, what was underneath that paper. You loved your gifts more before you knew what they were. Part of you wouldn't have minded leaving them wrapped forever while you sat on the floor suspended in the moment, the boxes before you a constant reminder of unknown beauty and potential.

Even now, you continue to actively avoid guessing your gifts. The box tucked near the back of the tree that is clearly the new printer you need? You avert your eyes, look to the white fairy lights of the tree, follow their trajectory as they bounce off the gold and purple and green and silver and red papers and ribbons, refusing to trace the shapes beneath the sparkle for fear of revealing a secret before its time.

You are still slow to open gifts—you run your finger under the tape, try not to tear the paper. You remove the bows and set them aside. You read the card or the sticker. You examine the way the corners were folded: the unknowing signatures people leave on the gifts they wrap. You want to take longer than you do, but some people find it annoying—worse, weird. And so, occasionally, when you understand you've been taking too long, when too many eyes have settled on you, you rip at the paper carelessly, to blend in.

And what about that first kiss? Oh, god, and then the second? The torture of waiting for the next sighting, as you throw yourself cautiously but headlong into love? That's part of the heaven Tom Petty talks about—the conflation of the delicious anticipation with the agony of waiting for it. Enduring the workday, the phone calls that aren't him, when you tell yourself, as Tom does in the first verse, that you've never known anything like this before.

And you indulge in the rituals that accompany this luxurious desire-waiting—you shave yourself silky smooth in the first bubble bath you've drawn in years, you stroke fragrant lotions into your skin and check the time again and again and add a little more eyeliner to your already smoky eyelids, and you know these moments of waiting are perfect in and of themselves. You pause and pay attention to your stomach and loins and heart and mouth and skin as they jiggle and stir and flip and purse and crawl, curl, shiver, and clench, etc., exactly as the romance writers describe—and you've never felt so physical, so in love with yourself as you prepare to lower yourself into the dark and brilliant agony of new love.

Tom Petty really does get it when he calls it heaven, but he still wants to race straight to the prize. In the second verse he sings about the women he wasted his time chasing before his love helped him to discover what his life could be, and by the third verse he has plunged into reassurances mixed with despair—will they manage to come together despite the world's attempts to keep them apart? You, on the other hand, don't mind a few obstacles or delays—you like to flirt around the prize, never letting it out of your sight but prolonging your approach for as long as you can bear. This delicious man, like your Christmas gifts, can only be unwrapped for the first time once; but, unlike your Christmas gifts, the delay here is about torture, about building the anticipation to fever pitch.

Ultimately, though, Tom's a rocker, not a romantic. He has three stanzas in which to set up the conflict and then resolve it—all while remaining appropriate for Top 40 radio. And so the parallel with your experience fades in a couple of ways—his rush to resolve, and his resolve to remain PG. That's fine, because when you post a YouTube link to "The Waiting" on social media, you're not alluding to all that brilliant hot-sex-waiting—you're talking about the writer-waiting, the sort that will resolve itself soon—the type of waiting that begins to feel better the minute you publicly whine about how agonizing it is. You save the hot-sex-waiting conversations for drinks with your girlfriends, where you all laugh knowingly and shiver with your own memories. Tom filled a lot of holes in the 80s and 90s, but he can't replace your girlfriends.

But poor Tom. Your insistence on deviating, after the first verse, from previously agreed-upon topics, such as the delicious agony of waiting to reunite with a new lover, is obviously another case of your overthinking things—a crime you've been accused of a number of times. Be that as it may, if you couldn't make it to verse two with Tom during the good times, it was clearly too much to ask that he be there while you were waiting to be haunted.

Like those times when your dog was alive but not in the house—staying overnight at the vet's after surgery to remove the fuzzy yellow chunk of the neighbour kid's tennis ball from his large intestine—the chunk the vet then presented to you in a pill bottle and that you still have in a box in the basement. Or the times you got home from your vacation or weekend away too late, and had to wait until the next day to pick him up from the dog sitter. On those nights, when he sat on the other side of town, nose and ears pointed southeast toward your house, and you sat on the empty couch in your living room, face tilted to the northwest window, you felt his presence. The air in the house would move; you'd almost catch a swish of tail, a millisecond too late, from the corner of your eye. You'd feel the warmth of his body on the floor beside the couch, just beyond the reach of your fingers, as you lay reading. Once the lights were out, you'd feel the bottom right corner of the bed shift slightly as he retucked his black nose under his frondy white tail the way spitz breeds do.

After he died, you waited for this presence—this haunting that had comforted and connected you for seventeen years—you expected, despite his absence, that some ethereal version of him would show up again, as he always had. Even after that first month—the one that took a year to endure—when the air was entirely still and the house was entirely vacant even as you sat in it, you folded over on yourself and continued to wait without hope.

Tom doesn't cover hauntings, real or elusive—he's waiting for a girl, waiting for society to leave them alone or something like that. Nowhere in his massive litany of catchy tunes does he cover the hopeless day-by-day heart-grinding required to wait for a ghost that doesn't show up. You know this for a truth because you have listened to a lot of Tom Petty.

Nor does Tom cover revenge-waiting, which you've been doing for years but didn't fully understand the purpose of until you hit your forties. Waiting to run into certain people. Plotting what you'd say or do when faced with them again, once you were prepared, finally, to no longer be nice—once you were willing to make a scene, had learned that sometimes a scene is necessary. You suspect many women your age bear scars from sexual humiliations or violations, and so you suspect most women have revenge fantasies about those episodes. Undiscussable fantasies.

What would you do if you saw the man today who, more than twenty-five years ago, in the parking lot of a bar, removed your bra while a group of people watched, then handed it back to you with a triumphant magician's flourish because it was all just a big fucking party trick? That's right, he removed your bra without removing your jacket or your shirt: he twirled you around and around, eventually pulled it out through your sleeve.

And his hands were huge, and you were off balance and you couldn't get a grip on his arms with your fingernails, and when he let you go you had to clutch at those big arms for a minute so you didn't fall down. And you staggered away in shock, stuffing your bra into your jacket pocket.

You spent years thinking about what you would say or do the next time you saw Bra Guy. You thought a lot about what you would do the next time someone tried to do something like that to you. A distressingly long time later, you began to think about what you should have said to those acquaintances who watched. And you began waiting to run into them again, as well, so that you could say it, even though you now lived in a different city.

These waitings are both power fantasies and revenge ones. Now you know you were reliving these moments in order to hone your survival skills and rewrite the ending—the one you are always waiting to rewrite in real life the next time someone tries to violate you. Your fantasies ranged from eloquent denunciations of those who watched to physical violence to Bra Guy—and let's not pretend that's not still your dark preference. You've never put your knee into anyone's testicles, but in your heart you've ripped them off his body with your fingernails. You've left him bleeding and curled in the fetal position. No longer able to father children. And eyeless.

These waitings are hellishly hard. Waiting to come face to face with an enemy, to shake off the self-loathing sexual violation breeds in so many women—to replace it with a sense of power you didn't understand you needed until Bra Guy unsnapped it and pulled it out of your sleeve. These waitings are what led you on another night several years later to grab a man by the hair at the nape of his neck and smash his face into a wall. You'd warned him three times to stop touching you and he wouldn't stop touching you.

Tom tells you not to let them get to you, whoever "they" are. He tells you not to let it kill you. That's good advice, and there are some parallels here, because you're both facing bastards—it's verse three now, and Tom Petty is railing at the villains who are keeping his love apart from him. You're railing at the villains who threaten your personal autonomy and physical safety. Love and bra thefts: you cannot let either one kill you.

Ah, Tom. He's such a rocker; such a bass-driven optimist. Even when everything seems hopeless, he still expects a good outcome—if waiting is the hardest thing to endure, that implies resolution will bring relief. And that makes him utterly useless when it comes to death-waiting. Like when you're waiting for your father to die—watching it happen while your suddenly too-large, embarrassingly solid feet and hands smack up against the metal legs of hospital beds and the delicate skin of your father's wrists, and all the corresponding too-large and exceedingly slippery feelings alternately repel and smack up against all the non-dying world around you. You give Tom this, the waiting does feel like the hardest part—at least until you're through it and beyond and looking around in bewilderment at a landscape that is jarringly unchanged. No, for you the death-waiting is painful but also filled with joy, as your father gives you one last handful of stories you hadn't heard yet, as you say and hear everything a daughter could ever need to say and hear, as you watch him move away from you toward a light-filled level of forgiveness you aren't sure you'll ever achieve.

The hardest part of death-waiting is afterward, when you've returned home to wander your house, unable to focus, waiting for the sense of confusion and rootlessness to pass. When, despite all the cruel and pointed moments of clarity, some part of your heart stubbornly waits for this stupid rite of passage to be over—once you've put in the time, lost the sleep, learned the lesson, laid the flowers or scattered the ashes, earned those stripes, whatever the fuck it is you're supposed to be doing—so that you can just get back to reality and talk to your father on the phone again, because it's not even possible, even after all these months, that you're never going to be able to make that call. It's really about patience—wait out this shitty time and maybe it will be like the despised 1986 season opener of the TV show *Dallas*, where they nullified all of season nine in order to bring Bobby back from the dead—just a stupid, pointless dream.

What about all those baby memories you didn't retain, the ones your father held for you, of your first steps and then your third and nineteenth steps? All the times your infant self vomited on him without apology and he kissed your stinky, sticky face? He owns a piece of your physical being in this world that you don't have access to. How does a chunk of your life vanish without causing some sort of temporal rift? And how do half the genes that created you disappear? Your body would fall apart, wouldn't it?

In verse three, Tom Petty offers to take on his love's pain by being her crying fool, but that doesn't cut it for this death-waiting. Because this one isn't going to resolve itself, despite your restless waiting. Guitar chords may fade and true love may triumph in the end on YouTube, but the inexplicable absence of your father will continue to be a hole in the space-time continuum. You're told you'll get used to the hole—that you'll learn to function around the hole. And perhaps you will, but you're not at that point yet. Right now, you're not even waiting to get there.

Guts

27 —— Wait Training   Samantha Albert

I'M A PROFESSIONAL WAITER. If Michelin were to do a guide to hospital waiting rooms in Toronto and beyond, I could be their agent on the ground. My life with a serious, chronic bone marrow illness means that I sometimes clock up to three hundred hours a year in waiting rooms. I see eight specialists and have cards for five different hospitals.

I'm not looking for sympathy or special treatment; I simply want to establish my credentials in this matter. I know the squishy farting noise that the ubiquitous vinyl-covered chairs make as I shift in my seat. I know that the televisions will be forever tuned to the local sensational news station (except for the one blood clinic where they play *I Love Lucy* reruns). I know that the more modern variety of waiting rooms will be decorated in dusty rose, blue, or beige. I crave vivid, dangerous colours after a day spent in these sanitary, pastel paradises.

I can provide you with the insider details that a casual visitor would miss. For example, the plushest waiting area and cleanest washrooms are in the breast clinic at Mount Sinai Hospital. That receptionist at the Princess Margaret chemo unit who always appears to be in a bad mood is actually kind and funny, in a slow, sardonic way, when you get to know her. It helps if you bring chocolate at Christmas. Someone at the kidney clinic at Toronto General likes to post signs such as *Please put your garbage in the can and not on the floor.* I have been tempted to post one that reads *Please pee into the toilet and not into the sink.*

I understand the way people shift around in waiting spaces and elevators like molecules in a beaker of water, claiming their full territory. I can spot the good waiters, those who calmly observe the world around them. Like the lean, aging cowboy who click-clacked into a waiting room one day with his cane and sharp boots, a long grey ponytail snaking out from under his cowboy hat. He looked absolutely at ease, as if there were nowhere else he'd rather be.

And I've witnessed those whose struggles to wait have resulted in tantrums. Like the woman in the glasses that made her eyes look like a bug's. She appeared to be just one big angry mouth while she yelled over and over again to the poor receptionist, "I've been coming here ten years and I've never had to wait this long before," as all of the rest of us in the waiting room stared, happily horrified by this outrageous behaviour.

Central Command for me is the Hematology North waiting room on the second floor of Princess Margaret. Doctors, nurses, and receptionists come and go, retire and change jobs, but I continue to show up every six weeks to sit in my usual waiting spot in the atrium, where the air is less tense. I will likely be tethered to this room to the end of my days.

I'm based out of Hematology North, but since I have a systemic illness, many additional specialists fill slots on my dance card. Each appointment with a doctor is accompanied by at least one test or procedure with its own waiting room. Add in visits to specialists peripheral to my illness, visits to my family doc, drug infusions, and the occasional trip to emerg, and we easily arrive at three hundred hours a year, which averages out to about six hours a week. Like a part-time occasional job, except I can't call in sick.

I try not to bring anyone along with me to my appointments. After years of cultivating my waiting-room stamina, I can be patient with the longest wait times, the dingiest waiting rooms, or the most inefficient clinic managers. I can do the long haul. But when I bring others, they fidget and sigh in exasperation. "How can you stand it?"

⋮ I engaged in some serious wait training in 2008, eight years after my diagnosis, when I began to visit the chemo unit at Princess Margaret every week for a new medication. The treatment itself was mild—a non-chemo drug that took less than a minute to administer. But each week I faced a mountain of a wait before I even made it to a chair.

When I first started going to the chemo unit, I saw waiting as a black hole of time. The world was going on without me, while I was trapped like a beetle suspended in amber. My real, vibrant, and important life was held hostage to the time in this inefficient jail and would only begin moving again once the waiting was over. I ranted to anyone who would listen about the soul-sucking nature of waiting rooms and allowed myself to feel tortured by the wait of indeterminate time.

Flipping through an abandoned newspaper one day in my usual chair in the atrium, I spotted a picture with a long line of people. I zeroed in on the caption. The people were lined up for food in a relief camp in Pakistan. Most of the people in the photo looked at ease with their body and at ease with the wait, despite their probable anxiety about receiving those supplies.

With that picture in mind, my radar was set to spot other images of waiting people. Women queuing up in long lines for water in the Central African Republic; long lines of voters clutching their ballots in rural India. And in every picture, I saw patience and calm in the faces and bodies of the waiting people.

I reflected on my own frustrations with waiting. It occurred to me that in the West, we feel that we have a right to be protected from waiting. We "tsk, tsk" the customer service in an establishment if we have to wait more than a nanosecond to be served.

We demand our proper turn. We get snippy with service staff. We devote an entire academic discipline, queuing theory, to exploring how mathematical models might reduce our wait times, or at least distract us from them.

My impatience implied that my time was too important to be spent on this mundane act of waiting. But was it really? Perhaps if I were in the midst of developing a life-saving vaccine or negotiating the end of hostilities in the Middle East, I could say that. But really, I just wanted out of that hospital.

Maybe where I saw a black hole, other people, other cultures, saw an opportunity for quiet, stillness, and a readiness to engage with the world. Perhaps if I were to view waiting as my occupation rather than as something to endure, I might resist it less.

Most Tuesdays saw me staggering under a backpack full of supplies, as if I were heading off on an extended expedition. I carried lunch, extra snacks, books, knitting, and technology to insulate me against the wait. I was the Girl Guide of the waiting room.

As my perspective on waiting shifted, I considered how I approached my long waits. I decided that I would challenge myself by showing up one Tuesday with nothing but the essentials. I still had my smartphone, but it was confined to my purse, under strict orders to stay put. I found a nook away from the crowds and sat down with a feeling of anxiety, wondering if I was ready for such an extreme action. How would I wait that long? I felt naked and unprotected without my bag of tricks.

At first I felt squirrely and fidgety. My fingers reached automatically for my smartphone and I had to smack them back. I bounced and jiggled to calm my legs. Then I fell asleep until my appointment, which felt like a cheat. So the next week, I repeated the experiment. It took some time, but finally I was able to settle into a wait and lose some of the anxious energy. And the longer I sat, the easier it became. So easy, that when I went in for my appointment, my blood pressure was lower than usual.

Although I eventually returned to my old waiting room habits, I wasn't the same waiter that I had been. I stopped my complaining about the waiting room, realizing that maybe the problem wasn't the waiting room, but my ability to wait. Of course, after so many weeks, I simply acclimatized to the wait and stopped resisting it. In fact, there were times when the waiting room time was a welcome, forced vacation from the world—a little bubble of protected time.

Most importantly, however, I began to realize that it was a waste of energy to fret over the minor inconvenience of the waiting room when my illness was challenging me with more complex and profound waits than I had ever experienced before. The waiting room of the chemo unit at Princess Margaret turned out to be just the warm-up.

⋮ One Tuesday before my clinic, I poked my head into the waiting room of the blood lab at Princess Margaret. I felt as if I had been transported to a crowded market bazaar. Nurses and volunteers called names and numbers like street hawkers. There was a steady buzz of conversation in at least four different languages. Patients and their loved ones were squeezed into every available seat, juggling coats, bags, and coffee mugs. The ones left standing leaned against walls and poles and looked longingly at the chairs, or milled about in the lobby. The long registration line, in its cramped space, was scattered every so often by a speeding wheelchair, only to form again in the chair's wake.

In the early days of being sick, I would have sighed at my lot in having to spend so much time in this crowded waiting room. But on this day, I felt more reflective and aware of the other patients. Where would all these people be and what would they be doing if illness had not sideswiped them? Surely every one of them had sat in a doctor's office hearing some version of, "I'm sorry to tell you..." and been thrown off whatever life trajectory they were following.

Each of them would have their own tales of waiting. I counted on my fingers all the kinds of waiting I'd experienced with this illness. There were the tense months where I waited for a diagnosis. There was the panic-filled wait for a life-altering procedure. There were, and continue to be, years of waiting and watching the course of this illness for signs of progression, punctuated by moments of drama when those signs would appear.

By far the most arduous of these was the wait to get back to the life I had planned; to get back to what I thought was my real life.

⋮ The garbage bag of give-away clothes was filling up as I culled down to the essentials. I wanted more space and less stuff. Everything had to be tried on and I was ruthless in my pronouncements.

"Doesn't fit." Into the bag.

"Colour is terrible!" Into the bag.

"Mutton dressed as lamb!" Into the bag.

And then as I worked my way to the back of the closet I spotted my suit—my one beautiful suit—and my determination flagged. I pulled it out of the closet and sat down on the bed, clutching it to me. I didn't need to try it on. I knew I was long past fitting into it. The disease had transformed my body in numerous ways that now made wearing the suit impossible.

Years earlier, after recovering from the initial, dramatic treatment for my illness, I had gone back to my consulting work, believing the worst was behind me. My mother had taken me to buy this suit as part of my coming out again into the world. Its sleek, iron-grey look had made my gaunt, post-chemo face and hair stubble look hip and professional.

I wore that suit to every important meeting and conference, feeling sharp and confident. I was back and I was hot, making new contacts, soliciting new contracts, growing my career. After being off for so long, I liked having something to say at parties when people asked,

"What do you do?"

"Ah," I would drop casually. "I'm a community development consultant."

And perhaps they wouldn't know what that meant, but it sounded substantial and useful.

Less than a year after I started back at work, however, crushing fatigue returned. The disease was active again and it was soon clear that I needed to give up my contracts and refocus on my health. I exchanged the suit for my rubber-ducky flannel pyjamas and my world shrank to the dimensions of my bedroom. Once again, my life was suspended and I lay in bed, adjusting to new medication, awaiting my second coming.

I kept the suit, believing it would not be long before I was up and about and back at work. At the occasional social gathering I attended, I would say, "Well, I'm a community development consultant. I was working on some exciting projects, but right now I'm on health leave."

As the years passed, the possibility of going back to work seemed increasingly remote. My energy waxed and waned and could not be counted upon.

I still kept the suit. Even though my time away from work became greater than the time I had spent working, even though the suit no longer fit. I would stroke it every so often, saying to myself, "When I am better, I will need that suit."

When asked what it was I did, I wasn't sure how to answer.

"Well, I have a serious illness and that takes up much of my time." And there would be a dull silence as the other person considered what to say next.

"But I used to work in community development," I would add and the other person would brighten and we would be off and running. I started avoiding social gatherings with strangers.

In my bedroom now, surrounded by discarded clothes, I sat holding the suit, rocking myself, remembering the person I had been before, that person who had energy, who could get up for work in the morning and drive places and work a conference. Who was I fooling by keeping this suit? I was no longer that person and I didn't know if I ever would be again. There was no point in waiting any longer. This life that I had, this life of illness, *this* was my life.

I sat until daylight disappeared and I was in darkness. I could hear my family downstairs making dinner. Finally, I folded the suit and put it in the bag, trying not to cry. In the closet there was a yawning pit where the suit had been. It threatened to pull me into its blackness. I pulled a string of other clothes over to fill the hole and closed the door.

After giving up the suit, I felt as if a black hole had opened up in my world. This wait to return to what I thought was a normal life had infused every part of me, it was the filter through which I had viewed the world. Without that wait, I lay in my bed, staring at the trees outside my window, believing that without that "real" life to look forward to, there wasn't much point in anything.

Then I read a story about an imprisoned Syrian man who spent his days reciting all the literature and poetry he could remember to help both himself and his fellow inmates. I was awed by the strength of character this man possessed. Considering how I was handling the prison of my illness, I was ashamed to admit that I would likely have been one of the other prisoners curled up in the fetal position in despair. Once again, as in the waiting room, I was challenged to rethink my ideas of waiting. Could I follow his example? Yes, I was imprisoned by my disease, but I didn't have to wait for, to yearn for, a different life.

What would be the equivalent of reciting poetry in my life? Perhaps it was simply taking notice of the things that were right in front of me that had meaning and beauty—a slash of light illuminating a bright red painting, the joy of my son when he wore a goofy costume, the taste of a perfect apple. Perhaps it was attending to my relationships with friends and family. Perhaps it was rising to my best self—to reach beyond myself—to help those immediately around me. For isn't that what the man trapped in prison did? He remembered the beauty of the poetry and was generous enough to share it with those around him. Even if he were to die the next day, those moments of reciting would have had meaning and purpose.

As time passed, and the grief became less acute, I challenged myself to look for opportunities to make meaning of any given moment. How could I be kinder to those around me? How could I help to quiet the worry of my loved ones? How could I be more generous?

I was not transformed into a saint (as my husband would be happy to tell you), but somehow things became easier. I could more fully embrace the life I had.

Recently my health issues have come to the forefront again, shrinking my physical world even further and blaring in my head like heavy-metal music. I thought I had figured out how to live with this, I thought my wait training was complete, but I was unprepared for this latest change. The last few months have seen me grieving and cursing my luck—wallowing. But as my head starts to clear, I can begin to look beyond myself again. It will take some work and patience, but I am optimistic that the poetry will return.

28 —— Waiting for a Hero   JANE HARRIS

I HAVE SPENT most of my life waiting, but I am no peaceful, patient, saintly Mother Teresa look-alike who lets the universe unfold on its own. Mine has been a terrified waiting, praying to be rescued, but believing that all hell would and should break loose on top of me, even if I had to force the avalanche myself.

Despite a dozen years of fundamentalist Sunday school classes that taught me that "consulting with mediums and wizards" was a sure ticket to hell, I once went to a psychic fair. I was newly divorced and nearly friendless—sick, battered, desperate, and broken—when I paid a middle-aged woman, who looked more like a farmer's wife than the Witch of Endor, twenty dollars to give me answers—any answers at all—that could help me navigate myself out of my hopelessness.

She said she sensed I was waiting for someone to rescue me but that the spirits told her no help was coming. I was going to be isolated and friendless for a long, long time. There would be no escape. Besides, she said, waiting was making me sick. She told me to stop waiting.

I don't know whether she thought she was a genuine psychic, but I do know that anyone with one eye open could see I was waiting helplessly for a rescue, and losing hope that it would come. I wore terror on my bloodless, frozen face, and a timid, wide-eyed gaze that made strangers stop to ask me if I was okay. It was in every glass of water I spilled, every twisted ankle I got when I tripped on pavement, and in the endless hours I spent deciding what to wear, what book to read, or what food to put into my grocery cart. A wrong choice could leave me with no money to pay the rent, and I did not trust myself to make the right choices.

You didn't need to be a psychic to figure out that my waiting was partly fuelled by my strained, desperate, faint hope that a hero would appear to guide me past circumstances I could not navigate myself out of. Or perhaps my rescuer would transform the monsters in my life into benevolent wizards and fairy godmothers, while he pulled me out of the witch's oven, along with Hansel and Gretel.

I filled my mind with made-up fairy stories, wild scenarios of sudden wealth or success, instead of focusing on what I needed to do each day, because I felt as doomed and friendless as Hans Christian Andersen's little match girl. At my core, I believed that no one would hire me, the bottom would fall out of my finances, I would always be abused, I would become a homeless person, and I would die alone, outside, shivering in the mud, under the railway bridge as the snow fell over me. End of story.

What the purported psychic did not understand was that I could not stop waiting any more than I could stop breathing, and there were times I thought of that. I was frozen in waiting—waiting for a reason to hope, waiting for a "why" and "how" to move forward, waiting for some magical rescuer to show up, but convinced deep down that I had no future.

This waiting hounded me like a pack of hungry wolves. It seemed more terrifying than giving up and letting the wolves eat me. As dread encircled me, my skin prickled, every tiny hair of my naked body stood upright. I froze like a fawn waiting for the wolf to eat it; my terror locked my joints, clenched my jaws, and froze my fists. Sometimes I slumped like a broken porcelain doll; sometimes I pulled myself upright as my body turned as stiff as steel to hide the terror.

When the terror got to be too much I hurtled myself into the clearest, quickest path toward destruction, just to ease the fear. Even if that meant doing the opposite of what I believed, or what I knew was the best for me. Even if it meant consorting with the Witch of Endor and falling for her delusion-filled prophecies.

It occurred to me a couple of days ago, when I was walking the dog along Whoop-Up Drive, that waiting no longer terror-izes me as often as it used to. That I no longer feel possessed to throw myself into the fire, or collaborate with people who want to pull me way from my own power into poverty and marginal-ization. As I watched the dusk suck colour from the horizon, and the downtown lights fill the sky on the other side of the river, it dawned on me. I am living in my happy ending. My hero has come, and my rescuer turned out to be me.

Terror began to tire of stalking me three years ago, on the day I decided not to die. It was the day when my grey-faced monster held me down on the bed with his claws around my neck, when I shouted, "God," inside my brain without making a sound or moving my lips, and felt the softness of grace surround me like a blanket, when in a flash I knew that no everlasting hellfire would drown me if I decided I was too tired to go on one more day. That it was other people, not God, who forced suffering on me, and that even if this monster charmed the world into thinking he was my fairy godfather, even if he killed me and buried me under the cherry tree we'd planted, I was forever free from his devilish enchantment.

In that moment, I knew I could choose not to fight anymore, and I need not fear punishment for making the wrong choice. In that split second, when I felt free to choose life or death, I chose to live. And as I chose, I realized I had enough power to overcome the monster on top of me, pressing his fingers into my throat. I knew I could overcome all the other monsters that stretched their arms out to strangle me, and that the ghosts who kept me poor and voiceless were dead things that drew their power from my fear.

I knew what to do. I pushed the monster off me. I ran, and I kept on running.

I have been pushing off ghouls for over three years now. Listening again and again to the internal voice that tells me how to lock fiends behind doors and where to run for safety.

⋮ My feet are tired and I have missed the bus from downtown. So here I sit, in Esquires Coffee House, drinking my third cup of tea from a paper cup—wasting more time, money, and trees. I am waiting again, when I want to be moving on.

I sit in the same chair, at the same table where I waited in 1998, watching the man who became my second husband park and get out of his truck, with his blond curls flying behind him, on his way to our first date. I tell myself I have chosen this seat again because I can watch the time on the post-office clock from this spot.

The clock ticks down its second century, with the generation that lifted it six storeys above the city nowhere in sight. My eyes are fixed on its minute hand, but I am in the arms of the monster again.

No one else seems to feel it, but the terror breeze wafts over me as I appear to watch the clock. As the first warm sip of tea hits the inside of my throat, I am dug back into the carpet of my bedroom floor, while a monster aims his club at my skull.

The beast tells me I should have died that day. It tells me I am a fool to think I have escaped, that it will always find me, that my aging parents and grown-up children are in great danger, and it is all my fault because I am downtown drinking tea in a coffee house at 5:00 p.m. instead of waiting by the phone at home to hear their calls for help.

I have learned many names for this slow wafting breeze of doom that still slips itself over me each evening like puffs of wind before a hailstorm: Post-Traumatic Stress Disorder, Hypervigilance, Doom, Hopelessness, Frozen Terror, Night Terrors, Panic, Waiting to be Eaten—the husband who jumps up from a candlelit table in my dreams to chase me with a butcher's axe.

This beast still chases me, but I have spent three years learning how to cast away its spell. Now, as the frost nips at my joints, before I am frozen like a mouse under a barn cat's paw, before its fangs break my neck, I call the beast by its name and kick it way. As the first bus arrives at the hub across the street, I remove its mask, pull off its cloak, and see its puny nakedness.

I stuff my phone into my purse and pull on my coat. Before the beast can claw its way back onto the window seat of Esquires, I rush myself through the glass door, onto the street. Running to my bus, I glimpse my reflection in a shop window, a pudgy middle-aged woman's reflection, my mother's reflection. Few would guess what monsters chase me, or that I've just kicked another one to the floor.

29 —— Bones, Honey

ROBERTA REES

"WE'RE BORN TO DIE," my mother says. "It's what we do in between, how we treat each other, that counts."

She yanks the oxygen cannula out of her nostrils, "Fuck, I hate these things, my nose is full of sores," shoves them back in askew, "but I need them, I need the tanks, they're part of my life. I have to make them part of my life or I'll give up, lie around waiting for death."

She leans back on her couch—skeletal beneath her fragile bruised skin. "I'm not dead yet."

Watching her—jutting bone beneath purple, black, and blue bruises, little muscle or fat between her skin and skull—I try not to think corpse, try not to think future, look up at the black-and-white photos of her family when she was a child. Death already waiting in her mother's oxygen-starved face. Poverty and worry and spunk in my mother's child face. The child who sold ice the rail workers at the train yard across the street gave her. Watermelon they gave her. Loaded ice and watermelon on her wooden wagon, hauled around to sell for medicine for her mother, ran errands for residents of the brick apartment buildings among the warehouses in her inner-city district. Learned how to load the syringe beside her mother's bed with adrenalin, her suffocating mother too weak to lift the syringe, learned to load the syringe, slide it into her mother's bony thigh, waited for adrenalin to hit her mother's heart, held the pan for her mother to vomit in. Waited—vigilant, alert—for the next attack.

"I loved my mother, sick as she was, she made sure we had food, clothing, talked to us about life. I think she knew she was dying, the week she died she sewed all us kids new shirts, pants, used Robin Hood flour sacks, whatever she could find. Called us to her sick bed, gave them to us. When they took her out in the ambulance, I knew in my bones she wouldn't come back, but I waited up all night for her. My sister came in the morning, told me Mom died, she won't be coming home."

Spark of my mother's deep green eyes, and I try not to imagine what the world will be like when that spark is gone, when she can't see us, when I won't be able to sit on her couch, talk with her about life, politics, the state of the world, religion, war. She rolls her head against the back of the couch. "I wanted to die, I was screaming and screaming, thrashing. My brother wrapped me in a blanket, held me. They were worried I'd hurt myself, sent me to a farm the day before her funeral. I woke up with a dead snake around my neck, an iodine needle stuck through its temple, got up and walked all the way into the city to the funeral home. A man came out, said, 'The funeral's over.' I sat on the sidewalk outside the funeral home all day, waiting for her to come out, walk me home."

She sighs—rattly, phlegmy. "I knew my mom was dead, but I kept waiting for her to come back. One day walking by the Bay on 8th Avenue I thought I saw her ahead of me in one of her jaunty coats and hats, striding along the way she did when she could breathe. 'Wait,' I yelled, 'Mommy, wait,' ran, threw myself into her arms."

My mother sits still, rattle of her wheeze, her eyes far away. "That woman hugged me, cried, 'I'm sorry, honey, I'm sorry I'm not your mother, but right now I wish I was, I wish I was.'"

My mother sits forward, props her fragile arms on a pillow across her knees. "We had a fight just before she died. I got up in the night, stole the cheese she was saving for the family—took a lot to feed eight kids—ate it all, woke up puking, diarrhea. She said, 'That's what you get for stealing.' I said, 'I hate you.'"

My mother's laboured breath. Heartbeat whoosh of her oxygen machine.

"You were a child," I say, "children say that. I said it to you."

She tries to smile—hollowed cheeks, curve of her red lipsticked lips. "But I never got to say I didn't mean it."

"She knew you didn't."

"I guess." She plucks at the pillow, cocks her head. "Bones," she drawls, "that's what I am—a bag of bones with a thatch of hair on top, red lips." She looks at me spunky-eyed, "Just call me Bones, honey."

"Okay, Bones honey," I say, and she laughs.

"I'm waiting until the kids are done university," she looks up at the photos of her grandkids on the wall. "If I die when they're away it'll be too hard for them."

"Do you think you can wait?" I say in the matter-of-fact way we've learned to talk.

She rolls her shoulders, the jazz dance defiance still there in her fragile body. "I'm doing my best." She leans forward, points at me, her hand cadaver thin, "Don't feel sorry for me, I hate pity. Pity robs a person of who they are. This is my life, I've had a good life."

"Okay, but don't you feel sorry for me either."

She laughs her gutsy laugh, "That's easier to say than do."

"I know." I lean back on her couch and she leans back beside me, puts her head on my shoulder. "But I'll try," I say.

"Tanks," her head a small hard nugget and she waves toward the oxygen canisters lined up by her door, "Tanks a lot."

She was eleven.

He was waiting for her. A stranger. In the shadows of Lowney's warehouse two warehouses down from her house, her mother in bed fighting for air.

Stepped out of the shadows, "Hey little girl, anyone ever tell you that you look just like Shirley Temple? Know how Shirley Temple got famous?" Grabbed her as she turned to run back to her house, to her mother waiting for her to go fetch her dad from the bar. "I'll make you famous." Dragged her past warehouses, clapboard houses, no one she knew on the streets. Dragged her along the river out of the city.

Beat her, bit her, raped her. Over and over.

Went to get a rock to kill her.

Semi-conscious, she heard her mother call her name, staggered up from the ground, staggered to the river. Threw herself in. Unable to swim, not knowing where she was, where he was, she thrashed to the other side. Started banging on the doors of the houses along the river.

Four people opened their doors, looked at her—tiny, bloody, battered, torn, half-naked, trembling child—slammed their doors shut.

The fifth—an elderly woman—pulled her inside, wrapped her in a quilt, phoned the police, "Send the woman officer." Held my mother, rocked her, "You did nothing wrong, this was not your fault," while they waited.

The woman officer held my mother in the quilt while her partner drove, "You did nothing wrong, what happened was not your fault."

They got my mother's mother up from her sick bed. Her mother held her, rocked her in the woman's quilt, "This is not your fault, this is not your fault." At the hospital the doctor told her, "Your daughter's insides are so damaged she'll never have children."

Her mother held her, rocked her—at the police station when my mother testified, at home where my mother couldn't stop shaking, couldn't bear her brothers she loved or her father who was violent when he drank. Only her mother or her oldest sister—her speed-skating, barrel-jumping, archer sister who worked at the biscuit factory across the alley. Mostly her mother, while her sisters worked and her brothers worked or went to school. Her mother held her in bed, fed her, told her over and over, "You are not to blame."

Three weeks later her mother died. My mother thought it was her fault.

A grief-stricken, traumatized child, she had to go to court with her grief-stricken father to testify. The man who'd raped and tortured her stood up in the prisoner's box, pointed at her. "You wait, kid, when I'm out in five, I'll find you and I'll finish what I started."

Her oldest sister, Edna, held her in the long nights, "When Lester and I get married, you'll come live with us," died a year later after three days of vicious headache, vomiting, slurred speech. Three days of waiting for a doctor—five doctors my mother phoned from the neighbours' house, begged to come and they kept saying give her an aspirin and wait, she'll be okay. Even when her sister couldn't stand, couldn't use her legs, her arms, and my mother and her other sister had to make a diaper for her and their sick sister cried in the night, "Help me, help me," until she couldn't talk at all, could only moan and roll her head, and my mother phoned and they waited for an ambulance and my mother waited at home, sick and shaking, for her sister who never came home. Later heard a woman tell another woman that a girl died hard on her unit in the isolation hospital, a hard death that didn't need to happen if she'd gotten penicillin.

"Did you wait in fear," I ask my mother.

"Fear of what," she says, her voice tough and strong out of her frail body, her body that until the last five years was muscled, powerful, sometimes plump. Her boxing, softball-pitching, homerun-batting, power-tool-using, four-babies-birthing, twenty-year-painting-business body. I look up at the photo of the scrawny little girl, her face more like my mother's now than in the years of raising children and grandchildren, working as a cleaner, painter, waitress, cook. A scrawny little girl.

"The man who raped you," I say. "Did you wait in fear?"

She looks out the window at the magpie in the mountain ash. "I couldn't afford to wait—we had to move, my dad was beating the shit out of me. I ran, got a job picking berries in BC—Mom and Pop Simons—they treated me so good. Then I got work at the hospital in Banff, lied about my age, thought I might become a nun, but saw too much there. Then I got a job in laundry in the basement of Brewster's Hotel in Banff. I loved that job—the upper-class women always asked for me to iron their pleated skirts; I could do it perfect. Auntie Taylor, the woman who ran the laundry, she was a caring woman, made sure I got the extra jobs, wouldn't take the money I offered her."

My mother's profile—delicate curve of her full lips, clear tube around her ear, across her cheek, up her flared nostril, bruises where the hose rubs her skin. "I wasn't giving him another second of my life."

"Who were you running from?"

She gives me her lip-curled disgust look. "The police. They wanted to put me in a home for incorrigible kids, for running away from my father. I knew I wouldn't survive one of those places, so I kept running. Friends would warn me if the police had been around asking about me."

"Didn't you end up in jail?"

She curls her lip again, bares her teeth. "Yuh, my brother Norm turned me in, I went into a café to meet him and they were waiting for me. Put me in a cell for a couple weeks with another girl. She was fifteen, I was thirteen. We talked about everything— what we'd been through, what we were going to do when we got out. The police released me into the custody of my dad—a drunk. He tried to trade me for booze, beat the shit out of me. I waited until he was drunk, crawled to the road. Bus driver picked me up, drove past people waiting at the stops, took me downtown. I phoned a friend who said the police are looking for you, found a job on another farm. I loved the mother—she treated me well, but I hated the son—he was always coming out where I was working, watching me, waiting to touch me. So I ran again— came to the city, lied about my age, got a job waitressing at the Stampede Grill across from the race track."

She smiles. "I loved that job. Johnny Robinson was good to me. The jockeys, the truckers—they treated me good. Some of the high-class guys thought all waitresses were sluts, but I knew how to put them in their place."

"How old were you then?"

She points up to a black-and-white photo of her in an elegant off-the-shoulder black dress, black-and-white choker necklace, earrings, lipstick on her full smiling lips. A kid trying to look adult. "Fifteen. That was taken on my birthday."

My head swims. I close my eyes. See images of another fifteen-year-old girl looking into a camera. "Mom, do you remember the news about the girl they pulled from the Red River a couple years ago?"

My mother pulls her knees up to her chest. "Of course I do."

"Tina Fontaine," I say.

My mother's face goes slack, she starts to cough, gasp, hands shaking, reaches for her inhaler. I turn my head, keep it turned, wait as she gasps, chokes, coughs, spits into a wad of toilet paper, waits for her meds to kick in.

"She was a kid, for Christ's sake, a kid with a whole life ahead of her," she pants. Leans her elbows on the cushion across her knees. "At least I got to live my life."

"She was wrapped in a quilt cover," I say.

Suddenly erect, fierce, my mother slices her hand through the air, "I'd like to go carve that guy's penis."

"I watched her great-aunt on the news, she lived with her great-aunt," I say, point to the photos of my nieces and nephew on the walls. Chubby-cheeked babies. Missing-toothed little kids.

Serious-eyed teenagers. "Her walls are covered with pictures like these," I say, "pictures of Tina."

We sit silent, and I wait to tell her how Tina's great-aunt described the agony of waiting for news of her disappeared girl, the grief when her girl's body was pulled from the river, the agonizing eighteen months while the police tracked down the owner of the quilt cover. I don't tell my mom how someday Tina's great-aunt hopes to forgive the man who murdered her niece so she won't carry hatred, but she's not ready yet.

"I would," my mother says, her eyes dark, furious, "I'd like to make him suffer the way he made her suffer."

I take a deep breath, wait for the violent revenge fantasy surging through me to subside. "Do you think things have changed?" I ask her.

She leans back against the couch, pulls her knees up. "Yes and no. We're talking more about violence against women, but it's still happening. Especially to First Nations women."

"Do you think it'll change, with the inquiry into murdered and missing Aboriginal girls and women?"

She shakes her head, "I hope so. They've been working and waiting a long time."

⋮ "Why did she wait so long to tell me?" my mother asks about my sister, "I would have believed her. Dad would have believed her."

"I know you would have," I say, "but look what happened to the women in the Ghomeshi trial. Look what that judge said to that woman in court testifying against the guy who raped her—why don't you just keep your knees together."

My mother takes the cannula out of her nose, the clear plastic cord from around her neck, straightens the twisted cord, plugs herself back in. "They still blame the victim. You have to wait until you're beaten to death or murdered before they listen."

They—a group of boys—waited for my sister on main street where she'd have to walk by on her way to the school bus stop. In front of the lockers at school where she'd have to pass them on her way to class. In the arena where she'd hear them when she went to curl or play hockey.

"Slut. Fuck her, slut. Give her what she wants."

She was thirteen when it started, the summer she developed large breasts. I was sixteen, small-breasted. Even though we shared a small bedroom, sometimes a bed, I was unaware at first of how my sister's dignity, her sense of self, were being assaulted, violated on a daily basis.

"Slut, fucking slut. You know you want it."

A grown man in town called her a slut in the arena and our father—small, shy—shoved him up against the wall, "You ever speak to my daughter that way again and I'll kill you."

By the time she was fourteen my witty, playful sister became broody, walked with her head drooped, hair shielding her face, shoulders hunched, started wearing layers of loose clothing. Self-absorbed, I assumed she was suffering the normal stresses of becoming a teen.

She tells me that I was her ally, that when I left home at seventeen, she felt abandoned, but I don't remember offering much understanding or comfort until she started visiting me in the city and I saw how she always wore a coat, how she'd ask me to walk her to the bathroom in public places, walk between her and men on the street, turn to me when guys at parties or on the street came up to her with some version of, "Hey, you have beautiful mammaries (or breasts or tits), can I touch one." Their vitriol when she turned away—shaking, or told them to go away, keep their hands to themselves. "Bitch—I was giving you a compliment. You need to learn to take compliments."

And years later, after she moved to the city to escape the assault of eyes, hands, insults—"slut, fucking slut." She'd phone me from her work at a hospital in Calgary, "I don't know what to do—he waits until I'm coming across the foyer, waits for me every day, walks toward me staring at my breasts the whole time. He never looks in my eyes, he's never looked me in the eye. I don't know what to do."

"You should report him."

"I can't. He's a doctor. I'm a dietary tech. No one's going to believe me."

"You don't know that."

"I do know that." Her voice broke, "Sorry," and she started to sob.

"You're not the one who needs to apologize," I said, the familiar mixture of anger and sorrow making my heart hammer. "Here's how I see it. You have two options—teach your breasts ventriloquism and have them say 'What the fuck you looking at, asshole' or wait until he starts walking and stare at his crotch the whole way."

"I did it," she mimics herself dropping her gaze, "Waited until he came around the corner, stared at his crotch, didn't look away once."

"What happened?"

She straightens her shoulders. "By the time he got to me, he was shuffling sideways, couldn't get by me fast enough."

"So he didn't do it again?"

She throws her head back, laughs, "He never came through the foyer again after shift—must have found another way out. Maybe the garbage chute."

"Why do victims of assault, bullying, harassment, wait?" so many of us ask, sometimes even those of us who have waited.

How disclosure rhymes with exposure.

That dirty, sinking shame in the gut.

In my sister's case he was a handsome boy a couple of years older than her, a friend of the boys mercilessly bullying her, a bit arrogant. She had a crush on him.

He'd been a friend of mine when we were younger. A fishing, horseback-riding, garden-raiding, snorkeling-mountain-streams friend. We hung around until I hit puberty and turned to friends my own age.

My sister was fifteen, in high school, where the boys lined up along the lockers, hissed at her as she passed, "Slut, fuck her, you want it, you know you want it."

The boy—my friend, son of a man our father knew since childhood—was waiting outside the arena two blocks from our house.

When she came out, he stepped toward her and she hoped he might offer to walk her home.

Which he did. Roughly.

Behind the garage at the back of our yard, the handsome boy we knew threw her to the ground, dropped on top of her, crushed her windpipe with his arm, gagged her mouth with his hand, "You want this, you know you want this, tell and no one'll believe you, tell and I'll fucking kill you."

Why? Why do we wait?

She tells me she was shaking when she went into the house. I was away at university. Our mother was at the arena. Our father was home.

She sat beside him on the couch. He put his arm around her, "What's wrong, what happened," felt the pack of cigarettes in her sleeve pocket, "Jesus Christ, what the hell, how can you be so stupid."

She went up to our bedroom without telling, waited for our mother to come home, waited for night to pass, for morning to come, for the nausea to pass, the shame, the fear of pregnancy, dread of seeing him, the other boys, the shock, the disbelief, to die down.

But of course they don't. Not for victims of sexual assault, rape, bullying. They fester. Along with the confusion and self-doubt.

The next day he was one of the ringleaders of the laughing, hissing, jeering boys she had to pass on her way to the school bus stop, the lockers on the way to class. "Slut, fucking slut, you want it, you're asking for it."

The woman she had to walk by on her way into the arena, wife of the man who'd called her a slut, was on the phone behind the concession stand, "Yeah, C. Rees is down in the dressing room, gang banging the boys," her mean little eyes, little brain somehow not registering the impossibility of her hateful lie, even with my traumatized sister right in front of her.

⋮ Hate speech. Rape culture. Relentless bullying, shaming. Three more years. Until she left home, still waiting to tell, waiting to feel safe enough, confident enough. Waiting for a culture that routinely blames, ridicules, exposes, undermines victims of sexual assault, to change.

The abusive men she went out with. The two breast reduction surgeries, the first at nineteen. The paralyzing fear of doing anything that exposed her—a woman with a haunting voice afraid to sing.

In hindsight, I know that these are ways of telling.

Why did she/he wait thirty years, people ask of sexual assault victims, as we watch victims who do lay charges go through a system that "whacks," shames, discredits, exposes every aspect of their lives, publicly picks over, pulls apart, judges, maligns them.

Or—but she waited so long to disclose. As if that somehow erases the assault, the long-term damage, as if consent can be given retroactively.

Or—she's just saying this now to get attention, as if the predictable onslaught of public blaming, shaming, doubt, are the kind of attention victims seek.

"Have you been following the Ghomeshi trial," my sister asks.

"Yes," I say, "he'll get off—even if he did it, he'll get off. They'll run the complainants through the grinder."

She starts to cry, "My rape was forty-two years ago, why are we still using an archaic system?"

⋮ I turn on CBC Radio, catch a comedian, Heather Jordan Ross, talk about the show she and six other comedians who've been raped put together and performed in Vancouver—"Rape is real and everywhere."

"What's so funny," she says, "is that since I reported it I've been calling it in my head, because I used to be a journalist, I've been calling it my *alleged* sexual assault. In my head I was correcting myself—*alleged* sexual assault? I was like, no, I was there—I know it happened."

⋮ "Why can't I get over it?" my sister asks. "Sometimes I wonder if it really happened, if I just had sex with him. But I know he raped me. How can I know and not know?"

"That's how trauma works," I say, "I was listening to a neurologist on CBC talk about this—victims remember some details, not others. The legal system wants narrative, but that's not how the brain works."

"Do you believe me?"

"Of course I do."

"I remember him pushing me down," my sister says, "I remember him on top of me, his knees between my legs, his arm crushing my windpipe, his hand choking me, his words—'You want this as much as I do, cunt, you tell and I'll kill you.' But I don't remember the zipper, my pants being pulled down, being penetrated."

"Whether you were penetrated or not, it was sexual assault."

"But I know I was penetrated, I worried sick about being pregnant."

"So you know you were assaulted and you were raped."

"It wasn't anything I wore or said or did, it was my body—they thought they had the right to my body."

"You didn't do anything wrong—he did it, he raped you." I wait for her to stop crying. "If we go to the high-school reunion I'm going to make conversation with him, like, 'Do you remember when we rode your horse together up the mountains'; 'Do you remember how we went snorkeling in Gold Creek'; 'Do you remember how you raped my sister?'"

My sister snorts, my nieces burst out laughing.

A sheen swims over my sister's eyes, she crosses her arms over her chest. "I don't know if I can go. He probably doesn't think he raped me. He's gone on to have a normal life—got married, has kids, works in the hospital. When I went home to Bellevue to live with Mom when the girls were little, I felt sick the whole time, that's why we came back to the city."

Waiting. Passive. Active.

For apologies, death, change, love, healing, liberation, food, shelter, justice, birth, humanity.

Time being the essence—integral to "waiting."

How long is a moment, a present moment, as in we only have the present moment? Three seconds? Ninety seconds? A fraction of a second?

And how about the Oxford physicists with their theory of time that I am simultaneously attracted to and horrified by—time is not linear, as in past/present/future, but exists all at once? More like a loaf of bread than a river, they say, though I prefer the metaphor of a lake.

Whenever I think of that conception of time I think of what Primo Levi said about the Holocaust, "It happened, therefore it can happen again: this is the core of what we have to say. It can happen, and it can happen everywhere."

This is the root of my ambiguous response to the Oxford physicists' theory of time—it leaves the victims of abuse and injustice, the suffering ill and injured, the sad and sorrowing, trapped in events that they cannot leave behind. At the same time, it echoes Primo Levi's warning, a warning increasingly pertinent as climate change, poverty, war drive people from their homes in search of refuge.

"The good things, too," my husband says, "in that theory of time, good things would exist forever as well." An environmental scientist with huge heart and brain, he makes a statement that I find particularly profound: "If there were a god and that god were just, eternity would be every being that has ever lived or ever will live living the life of every being that has ever lived or ever will live."

"Animals and insects?"

"Every being."

⋮ On CBC Radio the interviewer asks the man who started the Death Cafés, where strangers come together to talk about death, "What have you learned after talking so much about death?"

"I've learned about life," he says, "about how important relationships are with people in my life."

⋮ My mother and I have a pact—make each other laugh every day that we talk.

"What do you call someone like you when you get more than one migraine a week," she asks me.

"I don't know."

"Multigrain." I laugh and she pops salad that she made into my mouth, every dying cell in her lungs straining for air, keeps feeding me like a baby bird until we've finished the salad, go sit together on her couch.

Home during their breaks from university and immediately after their last classes, my twin nieces come every second day to her apartment to do her laundry, cook, clean, vacuum, visit their beloved grandma who flew to Australia when they were born three months early—tiny, thin, transparent as featherless baby birds—and she helped my sister feed, love, care for them. Their grandma they have lived with off and on since my sister moved back to Canada when they were nine months old. Strong, capable, big-hearted grandma teaching them, us, how choosing to wait on people has nothing to do with subservience or waiting to die—it has to do with living until death, with creating relationships and memories and values that endure beyond death.

"You'll probably die standing up," I say, "cooking for someone."

"Maybe," she says. These days standing at the counter exhausts her to trembling and panting. "I like cooking for people."

My husband and I do her grocery shopping—more meat and chocolate bars and fruits and vegetables than she can eat. When we're not there to witness how hard it is for her, she cooks food that she shares with people in her building—the woman who immigrated to escape political tyranny and is dying of cancer, the old boned-down man who used to rage at my mother and call her a bitch for how she parked her car. "He's lonely," she says, preparing a plate of food one of her grandchildren will deliver to his apartment, "he has no one."

"My mom fed people during the Depression," she says, "we were poor and she had eight kids to feed and was always sick, but she'd bake a pie and leave it out for people to take. Then the Radulskys took me in when I was on my own—taught me to cook and bank. They were refugees themselves, and they took me in until they had another baby." She sighs, "I loved my mom, I still miss her. I miss your dad, too—he's been dead longer than we were together."

⋮ She was sixteen. Five years since she was brutally assaulted, since her mother died, four since her beloved sister died.

New Year's Eve, almost closing time. Tickets to a dance her boss gave her, "Make sure you go and have some fun," in her apron pocket.

Scrubbing down the salt and sugar containers, the tables. She looked out the plate glass window of the Stampede Grill.

A man, a boy really. Watching her.

Heart hammering, she marched out the door through the blowing snow, toward him weaving on his feet, snow piling in his black curls. The apprentice jockey she liked for his gentle shyness, his haunting singing voice.

"She dumped me," he slurred, and my mother marched him into the café, closed up, walked him to his rooming house, climbed into the window of his room, put him in a tub of water, cleaned him up, just as she will do thirty years in the future when he is dying of cancer and though she was preparing to leave him because of his increasing disrespect toward her, changes her mind when he is diagnosed, "I couldn't abandon him, how could I do that," looks after him at home until he dies, lies in bed with him during the day when he asks, "I don't deserve your time, but would you have time for me," holds him up in the shower when he can no longer stand on his own, "I forgive you, you're a good person, you have to forgive yourself."

Cleaned him up when he was eighteen, drunk, lonely and suffering a deep sense of inferiority. "When you were little I made an appointment with a psychiatrist for him to go talk about his inferiority complex," she tells me, "but he got sick whenever he was supposed to go."

"You're a good person, you treat people fair," she tells him as she cleans him up when he's eighteen, just as she'll remind him, when he's dying at fifty, of the man's life he saved on the mine bus when the others thought the man was drunk, said wait, let him sleep it off, but my father pushed a candy into the man's mouth, brought him out of a diabetic coma. She'll remind him of his running back to the bus when it crashed to pull another man with a broken leg away from the bus before it burned. At sixteen she helps him out of the tub, dries him, dresses him in his blue suit, takes him dancing.

"Pregnant," her boss Ping told her at the downtown café where she waitressed after the Stampede Grill. "A wonderful boss," she tells me, "always made sure I had enough to eat, sent me home in a taxi when I worked late."

"Can't be," she told Ping, "I can't have kids. Must be stomach flu."

Five months of throwing up and she went to see a doctor. "Pregnant," he said.

"Can't be, my insides were too damaged when I was raped."

She's told me this story many times, and I often ask, "How did you feel when you found out you were pregnant?"

"Thrilled," she always says, "you were a new life, someone I could pour my love on."

"What about when you told Dad?" I often ask, and she tells me how she told him in the morning, in their apartment where their new plates exploded in the cupboards at night and they couldn't stop laughing, how she told him early in the morning before he went down to the rail yard to load the horses for the races in Toronto, races he was supposed to go ride in.

"I told him I was pregnant, but I didn't expect him to stay."

She tells me how he left and she watched him walk away down the street toward the track, how she finished breakfast, cleaned up the apartment, got ready for work.

"Were you waiting for him?" I always ask.

"No, I didn't expect him to come back."

"But he did," I always say of the young man who I already know became the father who took me everywhere with him— target practice, horseback riding, music practices with his band, to "shoot the shit" with his friends—and she tells me how he helped load the horses, then came back to the apartment, told her a new life was more important, and his words are filtered through her, as hers are through me, in this narrative of waiting for the baby who was me to enter the lives of the teenagers who were my parents, that thrill of waiting that makes a future out of the past, despite or maybe because of the body.

"We can't time travel until we figure out how to keep from destroying the person," says another physicist I listen to. "In order to move a person through time, we'd have to destroy him or her, then put them back together." She goes on to explain how due to the laws of time and space, we can only go forward in time, the only person who has accomplished that is a Russian astronaut, and the future he moved into was ninety-eight one-hundredths of a second.

At the Ottawa Literary Festival I go to a talk by physicist Leonard Susskind on black holes and the question of whether they destroy matter that enters them. I go with a Polish-born mathematician and her husband. She doesn't know yet that a tumour, of the kind that has recently killed my husband's youngest sister, is growing in her brain, of the sorrow that will haunt her gentle poet husband and autistic son when she is no longer alive, sorrow she has witnessed in my husband and heard about in my nephews, three and six, when their mother died.

On the ride back to their house and at their dining table surrounded by orchids, we talk about Susskind's theory that matter is both destroyed and not destroyed, depending where the observer is, discuss his example of how a person entering a black hole would be seen to be completely destroyed if we were witnessing from outside the black hole, yet if we were inside the black hole we would witness the person cross unscathed through the event horizon into the black hole, and if we happened to be holding the hand of the person as they/we crossed, we would see them simultaneously destroyed and not destroyed.

"I don't believe in life after death," my mother says, "I believe that heaven and hell are here on earth."

⦙ When she was in her sixties my mother went back to Australia where she'd worked at fifty-five on a cattle ranch in the Outback, as a horseback tour guide through the rain forest, to visit a friend. I hadn't heard from her in a couple of weeks.

I was upstairs lying down. "Roberta." I turned my head, but she wasn't there. "Roberta, Roberta."

I went downstairs. "My mother's in trouble," I said to my husband, phoned my brothers, "Mom's in trouble."

"She's having fun," they said.

"I heard her say my name," I said, "I don't believe in the paranormal or god or ghosts, but when she's in trouble I hear her say my name."

The tiny Outback hospital phoned me two days later to tell us she'd arrived there with the flu that was killing people worldwide, her systems had almost entirely shut down, but she's a tough bird, looks like she might make it. She didn't want them to phone us until she was better.

⦙ She was seventeen when I was born. "You couldn't wait," she says, "they'd just sent Dad home, you started coming bum first, Dr. Sinclair told me to wait, don't push, cut me, put his hand in, slid it between the umbilical cord and your throat or you would have choked to death."

She tells how she nursed other babies after each of her four babies' births, wept when she breastfed the baby boy the nurse tucked into her arms, said his mom died on the way to the hospital.

She died once, my mother, the kind of death she will die again—drowning, struggling for air. She was eighteen, I was ten months old.

My paternal grandmother kidnapped me while my mother was in hospital with a severe asthma attack triggered by the damp air on the West Coast where we lived at the time. When my mother came to get me, my grandmother, who my mother will take in when my grandmother is old and ill, wouldn't let my mother in the house, waited until my mother collapsed before she phoned the ambulance.

In the hospital my mother's heart stopped. She was at the bottom of a hill. Her dead mother was on top of the hill, waving her up, "Come on, you can make it."

She regained consciousness to a young intern banging on her chest, "Come on, you can make it," though her doctor feared she wouldn't, had her bed moved to the window so she could get natural light, told my father, "Bring the baby."

According to my mother, they put me on her hospital bed and I crawled all over her, kissed her, pulled her hair, her lips.

"You pulled me back," she says on her couch, her big green eyes intense.

She takes my hand, squeezes hard.

Pulse of her oxygen machine, phlegmy wheezing.

"What do you think of the idea that if there were a god and that god was just, every living being would live the life of every being that's ever lived," I ask.

"I think that it's a good idea—it would make people happier in themselves and accept others for who they are. What do you think?"

30 — Undeterred   JOHN GRAHAM-POLE

I MET LEAH for the first time one Monday morning three days after a surgical biopsy had confirmed that the mushrooming growth eroding most of her left hip bone was cancer. The eighteen-year-old had already suffered through her first round of chemotherapy, which had left the lining of her mouth and throat raw and painful. This dreadful side effect of our drugs, coupled with gnawing pain from the mass in her hip, had put her in an extremely cranky mood towards the whole medical profession. And as I was soon to find out, Leah never shrank from making her feelings known. As I approached her bedside to introduce myself, she grabbed the end of my tie, yanked it hard, and held on.

"Give me morphine," she croaked through cracked lips.

A quick look told me her mucositis was already severe, so I ordered the stat dose of narcotic that was clearly indicated. The next day, when I visited her bedside once more (*sans* tie), she presented me with a cartoon drawing that captured both of us to perfection: her face caught in a tantrum, mine in astonishment at being greeted by her physical assault. That twenty-four-hour intervention between my two visits had been long enough for Leah to reassert her feisty sense of humour—and to put her artistic talent to work.

Soon after her discharge from hospital, she was sitting in my office while I bemoaned the fact that I'd changed offices half a dozen times during my twenty-year tenure, and never once secured a window. A few days later, she reappeared with a two-by-three-foot image of a gorgeous stained-glass window to grace the wall in front of my desk. No depiction of a religious icon, though—this was a lifelike rendition of Kermit and Miss Piggy, hand in hand and gazing soulfully into each other's eyes.

Undeterred by the catastrophe of developing cancer on the threshold of adult life, Leah went on to hone her artistic talents at Stetson University, and it was no surprise when she earned a full scholarship to the University of Chicago to study for an MFA. But two months before she was due to start graduate work, the deep throbbing in her hip reared up once more, and a CT scan confirmed the cancer had recurred. We achieved a partial remission with more radiation and new chemotherapy drugs, only for the disease to reappear, this time in both her lower spine and her lungs. I knew now, as I'm sure she did, that it was just a matter of time.

Leah had become seriously involved with her boyfriend Josh, and she took to making her hospital visits with him rather than with her parents. "They always want to come," she told me, as she struggled to make herself halfway comfy on the clinic's unyielding exam table, "and they only cave in when I promise I'll report back in full. The thing is, Doc, I can take whatever it is you're going to dish out when it's just Josh and me. But when Mom loses it, I start in too. Then Dad, he gets to *disputing* every word you say. It's too much, I just stop thinking."

"I get the picture, Leah."

"So I want the straight poop, okay?"

"You know me, aren't I always the up-front shooter?"

But it's never easy to tell the unvarnished truth to a person, however brave and forthright you know her to be, when that truth is that she has only a few months left on earth. I laid my hand on her arm and left it lying, trying to offer some silent solace. Josh squeezed up tighter on the edge of the gurney, and

Leah rolled her head over for a kiss before bringing her eyes back to mine.

"Leah, this isn't going to come as a bombshell. Your scans show fresh cancer—in both your spine and your lungs. It's no wonder your pain's a whole lot worse."

Her response to my news was a typically spunky attempt at humour: "It's not dying I mind, Doc—just not in diapers, okay? I'm starting to have these accidents already, can't always get my pants down. Josh will be wiping my butt soon!" She took refuge in anger. "Doc, you know that Barlow, he saw me for you last week—gave me a diddlysquat three-day supply of Oxy. What, is he—worried I'll get hooked?"

"Hon, I'm real sorry. They check on us a good bit nowadays over these sorts of prescriptions."

"Yeah, I know it. I just get mad is all. So how long have I got?"

She had clearly anticipated what I was going to tell her. The only sign of distress was the whitening of her knuckles as she gripped Josh's hand.

"How long do *you* think?"

"Hey, you're the doctor. *You're* supposed to tell *me!*"

"Leah, people in your situation, they often have a lot of say about the *how long*. Oldies keep trucking long after you'd expect, just so their grandkids can visit one last time. Maybe there's a few things *you* want to do..."

"Well, you bet, now you come to mention it—like me and Josh getting hitched! Yeah, for real! We want to honeymoon in Atlanta—Taylor Swift's playing Chastain Park."

I managed to bounce back fast. "Wow! Congratulations to you both, that's just wonderful. So, Josh, you've been consulted on this, have you?"

"You kidding? We got together with our minister last week. Took some talking, though—I guess he wondered if I knew what I was getting into. But he's doing the formalities at Leah's, just our parents for witnesses, and my bro as best man. We'd sure love *you* to be there, Doc, though I guess that'd be hard—the distance and all?"

"I'll be there in spirit, you can count on that. But you'd best fix an early date..."

"All set for next weekend," Leah cut in. "And we do want to make that trip—just a couple of nights."

"I think we can pull that one off, Leah. I'll be sure to load you up with pain pills. Best you talk to the airline, though—you'll be needing a wheelchair."

"So you're not going to push any more of your poisons on me?"

"No, hon, no more chemo. Radiation might help your pain some, and slow things down a bit. But you would need to stay in hospital for it—and I've heard your views on that loud and clear. Far better we just get you on the right morphine dose, and set you up with hospice."

"Yeah, I know all about hospice—from when my gran was dying." Then she swiveled towards Josh: "Well, babe, I just hope you find another girl as good as me. Even if my body is in its urn, I'll be watching you, so you'd better treat her right! But right now, we're going to set up house, you and me. Wedding pictures on the mantel, you bringing me breakfast in bed, all that stuff married people do."

They looked intently at each other, the love between them a palpable thing. I felt a pricking behind my own eyelids.

The last time she made it to clinic, I was delayed by an emergency in the hospital.

"I'm very sorry to have kept you hanging, Leah."

"Hey, Doc, I'm used to it by now. I've been checking out the new ceiling tiles."

We both gazed up at the plasterboard tiles in the false ceiling, each one awash with colour. Leah had dreamed up her *Healing Ceilings* project one long-off clinic day. Soon there were tiles in every exam room bearing patients' handiwork—violet moonbeams, fire-red sunflowers, multi-hued rainbows, gold-dusted angels. Myriad twelve-by-twelve-inch tempera-painted panels holding vigil over each person lying on a gurney or an exam table, counting the minutes, or hours, until a nurse came to start their iv. Or until a doctor arrived to bring the latest news. News that might mean there was only one thing left to look forward to.

"I've got something else for you, Doc. But someone else will have to finish it up—I just get started and I find myself catching a zizz."

She presented me with the colouring book that she had been working on. Thirty pages in all, each one depicting a cartoon self-portrait of the life of an adolescent with cancer. She had drawn the pictures all in broad outlines, leaving space for colouring—an activity no longer off limits to teens. The first image depicted a nurse checking her temperature as she sat upright in bed clutching a tattered teddy bear; there were pictures of her boohooing when she was first losing her curls to chemo; of a cheery doc prodding her tummy, sheets drawn halfway down and nightie halfway up; of a nurse drawing a sample of blood from her infusaport; then, of Leah curled up in front of a large machine as it delivered her first dose of radiation. The final portrait showed her leaving the hospital, arm in arm with her dad. On the back cover, a mock prescription in calligraphic script: *Rx: A hug a day keeps the doctor away!*

"Leah, this is beautiful. Whatever the future holds, this is going to be some kind of legacy—this and *Healing Ceilings*!"

The American Cancer Society underwrote the publication and distribution of Leah's colouring book to cancer centres throughout the US, and Leah and Josh did get married, but they never made it to Atlanta. Instead, they spent their weekend honeymoon at nearby Disney World. By that time, she was indeed in diapers, with Josh changing them whenever the need arose. I never found out if they used the Women's or the Men's facilities.

31 —— Sa Ta Na Ma

KATHY SEIFERT

THE SCENERY on this grey-sky January morning is as bleak as the day itself. I look out the car window at a grey garbage bin with "Clean Sweep" painted on the side and a discarded pink mattress leaned up against it. Next to that, an orange Shop-Vac shares a weathered blue couch with a discarded fax machine and some sort of grey-green industrial machinery with an acned face of buttons and dials. All is silent except for the occasional sound of a semi-trailer passing nearby on the Trans-Canada Highway.

My husband and I are stuck in a snowbank in the industrial part of town. We had taken a turn down a back alley hoping it would take us somewhere, but instead it has led us to a dead end. In our attempt to back out, we have hit a deep shelf of drifted snow. The car's engine is throaty and hard at work, the rear wheels fly, but the car refuses to move.

"It's high-centred," my husband says as he tries to dig us out with a two-by-four, pilfered from a pile of industrial junk. I haven't a clue what this means, but I do know that we've tried everything from rocking the car—one person pushing while the other gives it the gas—to placing a discarded carpet under the wheels to provide traction. But the car, like a turtle stranded on a rock, is supported under its sternum and underbelly by a thick patch of compacted snow, which lifts the vehicle just enough that the wheels flail helplessly.

Having given up, we are now waiting for a tow truck to arrive and even though I have everything I need—water, warmth, a fully charged cell phone—I feel anxious. Why is that? We can walk to a nearby business, if need be. It's not a busy morning, there have been no major storms and so the tow truck should arrive in twenty or thirty minutes. I keep telling myself to find the humour in the situation. How, for our friends Doug and Debra, this would become a hilarious story they would recount over a beer after a curling game. But I don't view life that way, it seems. I view it as a worrisome, serious business, and no matter how I try to get off that grid, I can't. Even in a situation like this. Especially in a situation like this.

As small pellets of snow hit the windshield, I text my husband, who has left the vehicle and gone to the other side of the building to direct the tow truck when it arrives. I am all a-frazzle trying to keep it together. What if the truck doesn't come? What if it takes too long? What if we need food?

"You know this place," I remind myself. "Get out of your head. Get out of yourself."

Calm. Yoga breath.

Fast forward three months later to April, and to a similar scene. My sister and I are driving home from visiting my mother, where we had spent our time together knitting and watching curling on TV. The drive is forty-five minutes from my mom's extended care centre to my sister's home, mainly on secondary highways—the kind with a yellow stripe down the centre and thin gravel shoulders. About halfway through the drive we hear a heavy *boof*. My sister, turns to me, her face lined in irritation and says, "Shit, did we just get a flat?"

After she pulls over to the side of the highway, I get out and confirm that the front passenger-side tire is, indeed, flat. So flat it is squared off at the bottom—sharp angles appear where the tire should be soft and round.

We sit pondering as the emergency flashers tick reliably in the background.

"Maybe I should call Andrew," she says, "or Dan." Son. Partner. Guys who can help change the tire. I nod, thinking that it would be nice to have someone we know near us for comfort, for another vehicle, for familiarity. But when the logistics become too difficult she reconsiders and then says, "Or maybe we should just phone the automobile association."

We wait on hold. Between bursts of formless music, we are assured by the mechanical voice on the other end of the line that they are experiencing higher than normal call volumes and to stay on the line for the next available agent. We could be on hold with Visa, or WestJet, or Sears, for all we know. The wait makes me feel anxious, and I can feel the familiar gears whirring and clicking away inside. What if we never get through? What if the call gets dropped and we have to start all over again? How long will we be here? I remind myself we are safe. We are okay. I look down the road to an intersection where a few houses are grouped together, and I see the red and white sign of a convenience store. It's about half a kilometre away—we could walk there if we needed to.

But I am not comforted by all this Rational Thinking because its sparring partner, Emotion, steps into the ring, gloves raised, and delivers a solid punch to the gut. "What if we have to wait so long that I have a hypoglycemic attack?" Emotion says.

"You're being ridiculous," Rational replies, "you just ate two hours ago."

Emotion doesn't back down. "A salad at Boston Pizza...no protein, mainly greens...a definite cause for concern—"

"You could simply *walk* to the convenience store," Rational interrupts. "Get something to eat there if you get desperate."

"Okay. Let's see how that plays out," Emotion says as it unpacks an old movie projector from a hard-shell case. It threads

249

a strip of film through a maze of cogs and rollers until the film is attached reel-to-reel and ready to roll.

The movie opens with an image of me walking down the gravel shoulder, cars zooming by. I feel the push of slipstream wind as they pass. Next, a close-up of my face, complete with a tight jaw and a worry-lined forehead...then, cue the background sound effects of my heart thumping in a rapid, uneven pulse. It's the sign of a hypoglycemic attack combined with anxiety. The movie ends with a wide angle of me, stranded halfway between the car and the convenience store, uncertain about whether to go on or turn back.

After the last few frames have wound their way through the machine, Rational stands with its arms folded across its chest in a "decision made" stance, while Emotion waves its hands maniacally as if trying to stop a train that is barrelling down the tracks. Both come to the same conclusion, "stay in the car and wait." I sit and feel the familiar burn of anxiety, bordering on panic, and I wonder why? Why do I react this way and where does it come from? I take a deep breath and focus on a mantra I once learned in meditation class. "Sa Ta Na Ma...Sa Ta Na Ma." Birth, life, death, rebirth. "Sa Ta Na Ma." Maybe it's not the best thing to be repeating in this situation, especially with the death bit in there, but it's the only mantra I can remember. And it does help.

⋮ Here's the thing about anxiety. What pushes my anxiety level to red alert may seem irrational to someone else. And the opposite is equally true. What others may perceive as a threat may not produce an anxiety response in me. Case in point. Today my husband and I have gone on a hike. We have packed our lunches and are eating them somewhere trailside. It is springtime in the Rockies and the bears are just waking up, hungry after a winter of hibernation.

"What would you do if a bear came out of the woods right now?" my husband asks, taking a bite of his sandwich.

"I'd leave all this stuff for the bear," I say, pointing to our packs and unwrapped sandwiches, "then, I'd leash up Toby and lead him away." I search for all the usual places that anxiety hides, mostly my stomach, often my shoulders, definitely my chest. There is none. I don't feel any fear or anxiety about this prospect. Perhaps it's because I've seen several bears in my time. The one last summer, strolling past our camper; the one on a bike trip a couple of years ago; the one on the golf course eating berries next to the tee box. I don't take these incidents lightly, but for some reason, calm, Rational Thinking kicks in on these instances, rather than a rush of anxiety or fear.

I know many people who are just the opposite. I've heard the in-suck of breath when I tell them these stories. The look of fear, bordering on panic as they bring their hands to their mouths and utter, "oh god, so scary." These same people would probably have no concern about the last time they ate while they were waiting for a tow truck, or much else for that matter. Or would they?

Here's the other thing about anxiety. It all happens below the surface, in the darkness of your innards. Most times, you'd hardly know when I, or someone else, is having an attack. We could still be talking, and smiling, and eating, or doing whatever it is that we are doing, while our insides are one big electrified mess of nerve wires, firing chaotically, sparking and shorting out.

So, suppose you were to go back to the car where my sister and I are waiting for the tow truck to arrive, and suppose you were to look in at us from the outside. Imagine your nose squashed up on the glass, your hands like visors blocking the light, your eyes squinting for a good view. When you see us, you might believe you are witnessing the very picture of content-ment. My sister would be in the driver's seat watching curling on her smart phone and occasionally calling out the play-by-play to me. I would have pulled out my knitting and resumed work on a scarf. Seeing this, you would have no idea of the anxiety I feel churning on the inside. I'm pretty sure even my sister, who has been sitting right next to me the whole time, has no idea either. Like many things in life, we all get good at hiding our inner truth. I think back to our friends Doug and Debra who would probably turn all these incidents into another funny story, but who I also know have suffered their fair share of personal heartaches and regrets. We all have our "things." Who really knows what's going on inside of anyone, anyway?

Recently I was in a writing group where we wrote freely— words floating from heads to hands, without censor, starting with this prompt: "Sometimes I wonder..." After five minutes were up, we each read out loud to the group. *Sometimes I wonder if I will ever be able to...Sometimes I wonder if people think that I... Sometimes I wonder why I didn't tell her...Sometimes I wonder why I can't admit...* People writing about their personal fears, anxieties, and doubts through the words of loss, regret and guilt— all of this going on beneath those happy, put-together faces.

Speed rewind to the beginning where I am back with my husband in our stranded vehicle. Help has arrived. I watch as the tow-truck driver expertly backs his flatbed trailer down the back alley, stopping just short of our car. The driver, middle-aged, grey-haired, and unhurried, gets out to assess the situation. I wonder if I am seeing a hint of a *how do people get themselves into this?* smile curl at the corner of his mouth. But he doesn't ask. He sets about hooking the chains to the underside of our car and with a quick-and-easy pull we are free, and my anxieties fade to memory...for this moment at least. If only all of life were that simple. A short tug and you are unstuck. A quick release and you are on your way. A deep breath and all is calm.

Sa Ta Na Ma.

32 —— We Come and We Go

I PICTURE HIM as he appears in the 3x3 photo I treasure, eyes seemingly unworried, standing on the open bed of a white UN Jeep as though he doesn't have a care in the world. As though he isn't in a war zone disguised as a peacekeeping mission. He wears a faded olive-green uniform, the same one I would wear thirty years later, and he is laughing, teeth exposed and a dusting of facial hair forming a semblance of moustache on his twenty-year-old face, because everyone had a moustache in the 70s. In my idealized vision, there are no bullets whizzing by my father's head, no angry Egyptians screaming, no Rules of Engagement being broken by officer order. In my head, he does not mind fighting an impossible war because he is surrounded by friends and comrades; people he trusts. He is happy to be there, helping. That is what I dream of when I hold this photo from 1974.

At my desk as a thirty-three-year-old veteran, staring at this picture, dog-eared and faded, I know I am kidding myself.

There was no way of knowing that National Peacekeepers' Day, August 9 of each year, would be a special date of solemnity in our house. The day commemorates the date in 1974, when, in the single greatest loss of UN Peacekeepers, a plane of nine Canadian soldiers was shot down over Syria, killing everyone on board the Buffalo. I did not know that my dad was meant to be on this plane, returning to his position in Egypt. Overcrowding and his generalized fear of flying saved his life. I never knew how close he came to dying, how my father spent hours collecting the body parts of his friends when the missile scattered remains across the desert. I also didn't know, until many years later, how he'd been ordered to collect the destroyed plane remnants in search of the serial number, as proof that Syria had been the country that pressed the big red launch button that would change the course of our family's future. Of course, I'd have no idea of the danger this would have placed Dad in, Dad barely a man—how he would be shot at and how he would have shot back and how the whole thing would damage him forever. And above all, no one could have known that when he came home he would be permanently changed, angry with everyone, from bank tellers to grocery cashiers. Death had become an entrenched aspect of his existence.

Mom was waiting at home, planning their wedding. She sent Dad letters about how the flowers were going to match the napkins, how the church ladies would make the meal to be served at the reception in the church basement, how they would take photos in Simcoe's Wellington Park and the goose shit wouldn't matter, since a dress train could hide a multitude of sins. She would have been crossing days off the calendar, sending letters in loopy cursive as she tried to express bridal excitement combined with the unsaid words, *Life continues on without you here.*

Back then, I wouldn't have appeared on the radar of life, Mom having never wanted children. My parents couldn't have imagined that coming together would result in another generation to carry on the family business, the fourth generation, in fact. They wouldn't have guessed that I would be a soldier. Above all, no one could have predicted that I'd be that military wife too, the one waiting at home, checking the calendar with a red Sharpie, questioning the safety of her spouse in the sandy heat of Egypt.

My own military career lasted just eight years, punctuated by a medical release after a serious leg break that never healed properly. But I'd met my husband in basic training and fell in love when he carried me for three kilometres after said leg break. So I turned my attention to employment that was easily uprooted with Joe's postings and promotions: the nomadic life of a writer.

What I've learned in half a decade of being a military spouse is that sharing life with a soldier is as good as being in the Forces yourself, minus the push-ups and saluting. Posting season, between January and April of each year, remained an arduous time, fraught with anticipation, assumptions, and guesses about which random new location would be called home. Both raised army brats, Joe and I had been through the months of apprehension more often than we cared to.

December was usually safe, questions of future moves not yet considered thanks to the distraction of holidays. Joe and I walked through our Trenton subdivision, mid-December eerily mild for Ontario. Our bull terrier, Pot Roast, skipped between us, triangle eyes pointed upwards, vacillating his adoration between us. Me. Joe. Me. Joe. He chased our shadows highlighted on the pavement and barrelled towards Joe's silhouetted head, barking and scampering.

"Our dog is demented."

"Tell me about it."

"So," Joe said with a nervous laugh. He swung our entwined hands back and forth, frosty air circulating between our gloved fingers. "Career manager called me today."

I stopped walking. Pot Roast took the opportunity to sniff at a lamppost and drizzle a line of pale urine down the side. "I take it we're posted," I said, tugging my cap lower on my ears. We'd been in Trenton for six months. Our brand-new house—the backsplash installed, the carpet selected—all pointless. Again.

"Don't. It's not that bad." Joe's smile said otherwise. I didn't move. Didn't speak. *Tell me.*

"So, good news is I'm promoted. Major Shorrocks. Sounds nice, eh?"

"That's great news, hon," I said, not at all congratulatory, waiting for the other shoe to drop. The driveway asphalt was still curing. I'd planted lavender that would only start to bloom in the spring. My home office had only just been completed with the framing of a piece of art. "Now what's the bad news?"

"Egypt."

"Pardon?"

"They want to send me on a tour to Egypt. One year. Unaccompanied."

Unaccompanied postings were relatively unusual in the Canadian Armed Forces, the administrative bureaucrats having recognized that long separations weren't exactly conducive to happy families. Although prying for information about Dad's tour would have been akin to an interrogation, I'd learned enough to know that Egypt had almost been the end of Mom and Dad before they'd walked down the aisle. Absence makes the heart grow fonder until the heart shrinks with the lack of a life shared. The intrinsic value of relationships was held in grocery shopping together and lazy nights in front of the television. Above all, having seen what deployments had done to Dad, I feared welcoming home a stranger after more than a decade spent with Joe, who was more familiar to me than the smell of my own hair or the line of moles across my cheek.

Since hearing Dad's limited tales of Egyptian life, I'd dreamed of a trip to see the pyramids and King Tut's tomb for myself. When I was growing up, our house was laden with Egyptian trinkets, Cleopatra busts carved into ivory and wooden jewellery boxes inlaid with hieroglyphic symbols. When I tried to ask Dad about what Egypt was like, his only comment was "hot," and so the rest had to be conjured from my imagination. Of course, the images that swirled in my head were akin to something from *Aladdin*, with starry nights like God had tossed crystals into the sky, and hand-woven carpets that sprang to life and mimed conversations. But ISIS and the devastation in Syria were making Egypt a scarier place, no longer encouraged for camel expeditions or floating in coastal waters off Sharm el-Sheikh. Travel Canada said to avoid all unnecessary travel, and yet the military wanted my husband there. Without me. For a year.

"It wouldn't be that bad," Joe said, as though it wasn't inevitable. As though we had a choice. As though we could say, *But we really wanted to start a family. But my wife works from home and I'm her only social life.* As though any of those statements would make a difference. "We'd get two two-week breaks in that year, and we could meet up in Europe somewhere and make a trip out of it. You've always wanted to go to Greece. We could see the Mediterranean, eat too much souvlaki." Joe stared straight ahead, both of our eyes watering from what we would assure each other was only the wind. Not sadness or longing. Not the foreshadowing of separation. Not the imagined dog walks alone.

Ahead of us, hot on the trail of an errant tennis ball in the storm gutter, Pot Roast snatched the ball between his teeth and hurried to take his place between us again. Eyes to me. Joe. Me. Joe. We trudged forward, a depressing trio, spring robbed from everyone's step except the dog's.

"When do you leave?"

"It's not for sure yet. They're giving me the option of saying no."

I scoffed and walked faster. Perhaps the ridiculous concept of turning down a tour was a lie easily told to another spouse, but not to a veteran. Denying a posting, promotion or tour was professional suicide, which, we joked, resulted in "revenge postings" to sparsely populated postings in the middle of nowhere.

"We signed up for this, remember?" Joe nudged my hand back into his. "Military life. We come and we go."

I let my silence serve as acquiescence, tightened my collar around my neck as an excuse to free my hand from his, pointlessly angry with Joe for a situation he couldn't control. "So, when are you leaving?"

"Early July sometime." He hung his head. "No" was not in the cards.

"Well, you haven't had to spend too much time apart before," said Dad over the phone, serious as anything.

"In three years of marriage, we've been apart at least four or five months out of every year," I said. Whether it was courses, operations, exercises or work trips, I'd grown used to counting down days, taking selfies with Pot Roast to show Joe he was still a part of our stunted little family, no matter where he was.

"Well, it's not as hard as when I was there. We didn't have Skype and email and all that."

"It doesn't mean it won't be hard."

"You know, when I was in the Golan..."

I stopped listening. Tuned into some Netflix show that I wasn't really watching, comforted by the fact it could be rewound, fast-forwarded. I never had to miss a beat.

Joe came home from work with brown Pelican cases stuffed full of new gear in desert camouflage pattern to replace the green relish of his everyday uniform. There were rucksacks and socks, pants and tunics, scarves and T-shirts, everything in varying shades of computer-generated tan, pixelated and sharp.

"You're so white, if someone puts you in this getup, you'll disappear into the Sinai." I held up a sock as evidence, the colour deeper than his face that always looked permanently dusted in flour.

"No kidding. I'm going to need so much sunscreen, the military might not be able to afford to send me."

We snickered to hide the anxiety that bubbled under our skin. The calendar in my office indicated three months, two days until deployment. Our personal family D-Day. I watched the event approach with anticipation, desperate for ignorance. Why couldn't he just leave so that I could get on with my planned pining, accompanied by tubs of ice cream, lovelorn letters (did emails count?), and moping in shared loneliness with the dog? Waiting for the waiting was exhausting.

"Want me to throw this all in the wash?"

"Yeah, that would be great," Joe said, picking up a ballistic vest that was still missing its Kevlar protection plates. "Because then I have to take everything in to be dipped. Chemical dip," he said when I raised my eyebrows. "Wards off mosquitoes for six months, apparently."

"And gives you some kind of cancer, no doubt." Joe shrugged, both of us accepting the reality that military protection measures were often just as dangerous as the alternative. Dig a shell scrape but risk being shot in the process. Dip clothes in chemicals that we don't know the impact of. We'd even heard our helmets did nothing in the wake of gunfire, sharp exit tracks from bullets potentially releasing Kevlar shrapnel more dangerous than a rifle. Maybe this was a rumour, but I suspected it was evidence gathered by some unsuspecting soldier who witnessed the account firsthand. "Maybe you should ask for some mefloquine too, see if we can't make you crazy and cancerous." He kissed me on the cheek in passing as I loaded the washer, somewhat horrified with my newfound domesticity. He smelled of army; mod tent and summery skin combined with the tinge of asbestos-filled buildings built in the 1930s. I used to smell like that. I used to like it.

"I need everything washed and ready to go, since I have to get my photo done too."

"Photo?" I bent and snuggled Pot Roast, who was anxious at the appearance of luggage that didn't seem to include dog treats and poop bags, hinting at a trip he wouldn't be on.

"Yeah, you know. My hero shot. Canada flag and all that shit."

Yes, the hero shot: the portrait of a soldier before deployment that would play on the newsreel if he were killed overseas. I had to swallow twice, the tan uniform pattern blurring in my tight grip while I poured in too much liquid soap. If Joe were killed, I'd ensure his picture was one of him on top a snowy mountain, after he had conquered it with his ice axe and crampons. I would show a photo of him laughing, on vacation, playing squash, doing something other than wearing that damn desert uniform with a solemn expression that gave away nothing.

"You better be here when I get back," Joe said playfully, following me to the washing machine with an armful of kit. "You're my greatest adventure."

"Are you kidding?" I laughed as he put his stubbly cheek into the crook of my neck and nibbled on my exposed clavicle. "After basic training I waited for ten years before you loved me back. You think I can't handle one more?"

⋮ Joe is away, gone, in another part of the world, while I hammer out stories and books in my home office, Pot Roast snoring on the couch. The dog and I prepare for Joe's return by maintaining routine. Wake. Eat. Work. Sleep. My new uniform is one of comfort, stretchy pants and a T-shirt. I heed article deadlines too, have a stack of invoices to file for words I wrote.

Meanwhile, Joe will sleep in dry desert heat with a mosquito net draped over his bed, the sound of gunfire his own cacophonic lullaby. Near his pillow there will be a picture of me sitting on a wall during a trip to Ireland, bum balanced on the edge of a castle old beyond our recognition. I'm smiling wide in the photo, a loch glimmering light reflections behind my head.

For a year, I'll go to sleep alone in our king-size bed in Ontario. Each morning I will feed the dog, make coffee, settle onto the couch for an hour of television before work. But I cannot start the day without holding my breath, checking the news for updates on Egypt, any detail that hints at the potential threat of a new Arab Spring. Then and only then, I will take out the Sharpie, approach the stark whiteness of my calendar and cross off another day with long, red streaks of blood-coloured marker. Three hundred twenty days. Two hundred seventy-eight days. Two hundred one days. One hundred nineteen days. Five more days. Mom says it is the lot in life of military spouses; the anticipation, the lack of answers. We are professional patience minders, husbands, wives, daughters and sons. We are all the space in between.

Joe will return home safe, in all likelihood. Until then, I will cross my fingers, drum nails on my desk, distract myself with work. I will pick him up from the airport with my hair done, bikini line waxed, makeup carefully applied like it were a first date, because it might as well be, and that night I will nervously peel back the sheets to welcome my husband, the man who will be a stranger until once again we warm up to the temperature of one another.

After a few weeks, maybe months, we will revert to our bastardized sense of normalcy, until posting season arrives again, and together we will hold our breath until the answers come.

— Notes

"Saturday" by Anne Lévesque

An earlier version of this essay was published under a different title in the May 2016 issue of *Gravel* magazine (www.gravelmag.com).

"Waiting for Now: Four Stories" by Steven Ross Smith

The words of Steve Reich are taken from a 1996 interview conducted by Jonathan Cott and can be found in the "Articles, Interviews" section at http://www.stevereich.com. The idea of "being [t]here" can be explored further in Baba Ram Dass (Richard Alpert), *Be Here Now* (San Cristobal, NM: Lama Foundation, 1971). The author's memory of Reunion as performed in Toronto was aided by the event description and background written by Lowell Cross, found at http://johncage.org/reunion/cross_reunion_ revised.pdf.

"The Escape" by Edythe Anstey Hanen

An earlier version of this essay appeared in the Canadian Authors Association's 2012 anthology *National Voices*.

"The Past Was a Small Notebook, Much Scribbled-Upon" by Cora Siré

This essay's title and headings are quotes from *Zama*, the novel by Antonio Di Benedetto, translated by Esther Allen, *New York Review of Books*, 2016.

"Beyond the Horizon" by Julie Sedivy

Václav Havel later expanded his thoughts on hope in a series of recorded interviews with Karel Hvížd'ala, which were published in English in 1990 (translated from Czech by Paul Wilson) under the title *Disturbing the Peace*. His remarks on hope appear as chapter 5, "The Politics of Hope."

"The Next Minute" by Jane Cawthorne

An earlier version of this essay appeared under a different title in the *Globe and Mail*.

"Undeterred" by John Graham-Pole

The names of the people in this essay are not their actual names.

___ Contributors

Although she never fulfilled her dreams of being on the stage, **Samantha Albert** takes vicarious pleasure in living in Stratford, Ontario, the home of the famed Shakespearean theatre festival. Her essay, "Wait Training," will be included in her forthcoming book, *The Girl with the Backpack*, a memoir about living with long-term critical illness. Pained by the writing struggles of many of the young people in her life, she is developing a series of innovative workshops to help students engage in and enjoy the writing process. By day she is a writing coach.

Rona Altrows writes fiction, essays, and plays, and has an editing practice. She is the author of two books of short fiction, *A Run on Hose* and *Key in Lock*, and with Naomi K. Lewis she co-edited *Shy: An Anthology* (University of Alberta Press). For her essay in *Waiting*, "Letter of Intent," she won the Jon Whyte Memorial Essay Award. Her work has also earned her the W.O. Mitchell Book Prize and, with Lewis, an IPPY silver medal. Her latest book, *At this Juncture: A Book of Letters*, was released in spring 2018.

Sharon Butala has published eighteen books of fiction and nonfiction. Her most recent, the memoir *Where I Live Now* (Simon & Schuster Canada), was shortlisted for the Governor General's Award (her third nomination for the award). Her mystery, *Zara's Dead*, was published in 2018 by Coteau Books, and a collection of short stories will be released in 2019, also by Coteau. Born, raised, and educated in Saskatchewan, she has lived in Calgary since 2008. She has won numerous awards and prizes, has had several books on the bestseller list, and is an Officer of the Order of Canada.

Jane Cawthorne's work has appeared in literary and academic journals, newspapers, magazines, and anthologies. She is the co-editor of *Writing Menopause: An Anthology of Fiction, Poetry and Creative Nonfiction* with E.D. Morin (Inanna, 2017), and her play, *The Abortion Monologues*, has been produced many times in the United States and Canada. She earned her MFA from the Solstice Creative Writing Program at Pine Manor College in Boston and currently lives, writes, waits, and bakes pies in Toronto.

Finalist for the 2008 Governor General's Award for his second book of poetry, *Noise from the Laundry*, **Weyman Chan** divides his time between writing, family, electron micrographs, and nonsequitor fluxes in spacetime, brought on by insomnia... Catfish. As poetry editor of Calgary's experimental literary magazine *filling Station*, he's convinced that alien intelligence has already nested and fledged in every uttered branch of our language tree. His latest poetry book, *Human Tissue: a primer for Not Knowing*, examines rage and the quest for origin.

Rebecca Danos is an emerging author and PHD physicist. She is an alumna of McGill University, UCLA, and Wellesley College and was a CITA National Fellow. She has published a dozen refereed physics articles in high-impact journals and dozens of interviews and essays in *Wellesley Underground* where she served as senior editor. Her credit highlights include a TV appearance reading a poem excerpt for the CTV Winnipeg news, a poem in the *Kaaterskill Basin Literary Journal*, and over sixty blog entries.

She is a dreamer, a pianist, a singer, a mathematician, dances ballet, and is in perpetual reinvention. @RebeccaDanos

Patti Edgar is an Alberta writer. Her words have appeared in *Grain*, CBC, the *Ottawa Citizen*, and several other newspapers and magazines. She teaches journalism at Mount Royal University and holds an MFA in Creative Writing from the University of British Columbia. *Patti Edgar es una escritora de Alberta. Sus palabras han aparecido en Grain, CBC, Ottawa Citizen y muchos otros periódicos y revistas. Es profesora de periodismo en la Universidad de Mount Royal y posee un MFA en Escritura Creativa de la Universidad de la Columbia Británica.*

John Graham-Pole lives blissfully with his wife, Dorothy, and Asia, their cat, in sunny Nova Scotia. He's emeritus professor, pediatric oncology/palliative care, from University of Florida, where he co-founded the Center for Arts Medicine (www.arts. ufl.edu.cam). He's published six books (arts & health and poetry), including *Illness and the Art of Creative Self-Expression*, plus stories and essays (*Ars Medica*, CMA *Journal*, *Friends Journal*, *Hektoen*, *Hospital Drive*, *Medical Humanities*, *Yale Journal of Humanities*). His memoir, *Journeys with a Thousand Heroes: A Child Oncologist's Story*, was published by Wising Up Press in 2018. He's still busy selling his first novel. www.johngrahampole. com; www.facebook.com/johngrahampoleauthor/; @GpPole

Leslie Greentree is the author of three books: *A Minor Planet for You* (University of Alberta Press), winner of the 2007 Howard O'Hagan Prize for Short Fiction; and two poetry books, *go-go dancing for Elvis*, shortlisted for the 2004 Griffin Prize for Poetry, and *guys named Bill*. Leslie has won CBC literary competitions for short fiction and poetry, and the 2013 Little Bird short fiction competition for a story that appears in her forthcoming book, *This Is Not the Apocalypse I Was Hoping For*. She co-wrote the play *Oral Fixations* with Blaine Newton; it was professionally produced in 2014 by Ignition Theatre.

Edythe Anstey Hanen is a writer living on Bowen Island, British Columbia. She studied at the Creative Writing program at the University of British Columbia and was a writer and editor for the *Bowen Island Undercurrent* community newspaper for seventeen years. She has published articles, short stories, and poetry in literary magazines, in *The Globe and Mail*, *National Post*, and *The Bay Observer* (Hamilton). She is a regular contributor to *Mexconnect*, an online travel magazine, and has published prize-winning stories in several literary magazines and four anthologies. Her novel *Nine Birds Singing* was published in 2017 with New Arcadia Publishing.

Vivian Hansen's books of poetry include *A Tincture of Sunlight*, *A Bitter Mood of Clouds*, and *Leylines of My Flesh*. She is the author of two chapbooks: *Angel Alley: The Victims of Jack the Ripper* and *Never Call It Bird: The Melodies of AIDS*. "Hundedagene and the Foxtail Phenomena" appears in *Coming Here, Being Here*. Vivian teaches in the Creative Writing Certificate program with the University of Calgary, Mount Royal University, and Alexandra Writers' Centre. She holds an MFA in Creative Writing from the University of British Columbia.

Jane Harris's books include *Finding Home in the Promised Land* (J. Gordon Shillingford Publishing, 2015; Signature Editions, 2016) and *Eugenics and the Firewall: Canada's Nasty Little Secret* (J. Gordon Shillingford, 2010). She's contributed to three Canadian anthologies and has 100+ bylines in more than a dozen publications including *Write*, *Alberta Views*, *Winnipeg Free Press*, *Canadian Capital*, and *The Anglican Journal*. In 2016 Jane won the James H. Gray Award for Short Nonfiction at the Alberta Literary Awards and was a finalist in the AMPA Showcase

Awards for "The Unheard Patient." She's currently writing an essay series and a novel.

Richard Harrison's *On Not Losing My Father's Ashes in the Flood* won the 2017 Governor General's and Stephan G. Stephansson awards for poetry. Among his five other books of poetry is *Hero of the Play*, the first book of poetry launched at the Hockey Hall of Fame. Richard's work has been published worldwide in French, Spanish, Portuguese, Italian, and Arabic. In 2001 Richard founded the Thursday Group Workshop, whose members, many award-finalists or winners themselves, have published over a dozen books. Richard teaches comics, graphic novels, and creative, essay, and life writing at Calgary's Mount Royal University.

Elizabeth Haynes's fiction and nonfiction have appeared in magazines including *Alberta Views*, *The New Quarterly*, *The Malahat Review*, *Prism*, *Room*, and in anthologies, most recently *Walk Myself Home: An Anthology to End Violence Against Women* (Caitlin Press) and *Shy: An Anthology* (University of Alberta Press). Her collection of short fiction, *Speak Mandarin Not Dialect* (Thistledown Press) was a finalist for the Alberta Book Awards. She works as a speech-language pathologist in Calgary.

Lee Kvern is a Canadian award-winning author of short stories and novels. Her short stories in *7 Ways to Sunday* have garnered the national CBC Literary Award, the Western Magazine Award, the Hazel Hilles Memorial Short Fiction Prize, and the Howard O'Hagan Award. Her novel *Afterall* was selected for Canada Reads (regional) and nominated for the Alberta Book Awards. *The Matter of Sylvie* was nominated for the Alberta Book Awards and the Ottawa Relit Award. Her work has been produced for CBC Radio, and published in *Event, Descant, Air Canada* *enRoute*, *Tishman Review*, *subTerrain*, and online at Joyland.ca, Foundpress.com, and LittleFiction.com.

Anne Lévesque is a Cape Breton writer of poetry, fiction, and creative nonfiction whose work has appeared in Canadian and international journals and anthologies. She has a BSW (Laurentian) and an MED Counselling (Acadia), and worked as a social worker and employment counsellor. She lives with her husband in the old farmhouse where they raised their four sons. Her novel *Lucy Cloud*, which is set in Cape Breton, was published by Pottersfield Press in spring 2018.

Margaret Macpherson is an award-winning fiction writer, essayist, poet, and storyteller from the Northwest Territories. Her first short-story collection *Perilous Departures* (2004) and first novel *Released* (2007) were both nominated for Manitoba Book Awards. A nonfiction biography, *Nellie McClung: Voice for the Voiceless*, won the Canadian Authors Association (CAA) Exporting Alberta Award, and her third novel *Body Trade* (2011), won the De Beers NorthWords Prize. Margaret represented Edmonton in the National CBC Poetry Face-Off and regularly competes in Story Slam. An expressive art practitioner, Margaret writes and paints from her home studio in Edmonton.

Alice Major's eleventh poetry collection is *Welcome to the Anthropocene* (University of Alberta Press). She is also the author of the essay collection *Intersecting Sets: A Poet Looks at Science* (University of Alberta Press). Her awards include a National Magazine Award gold medal for essay writing and the Pat Lowther prize, awarded for a book of poetry by a Canadian woman. Alice served as first poet laureate of Edmonton and founder of the Edmonton Poetry Festival and received the 2017 Lieutenant Governor of Alberta Distinguished Artist Award.

Wendy McGrath's most recent project is BOX—an adaptation of her eponymous long poem. BOX is a genre-blurring combination of jazz, experimental music, and voice with the group Quarto & Sound. McGrath has written three novels and two books of poetry. Her most recent poetry collection, *A Revision of Forward* (NeWest Press), is the culmination of a collaboration with print-maker Walter Jule. She recently completed the final novel in her *Santa Rosa* trilogy, and is working on a collection of ekphrastic poetry inspired by bird photographs taken by Danny Miles, drummer in the band July Talk.

Stuart Ian McKay is a Calgary poet. His second book of poetry *a cognate of prayer* was published in 2013. His poetry has been published in journals and anthologies throughout Canada. Stuart is one of the first artists in the country awarded the Cultivate: Professional Development Grant by the Canada Council for the Arts. He serves on the editorial board of *filling Station* magazine. Stuart has recently completed his third book of poetry, *voicing corona over devonian*, and he is at work on his fourth book, *Bohemia, with a twist of lemon, please*.

Lorri Neilsen Glenn's most recent book is *Following the River: Traces of Red River Women* (Wolsak & Wynn, 2017). Lorri is the author and editor of fourteen acclaimed books of poetry, creative nonfiction, and scholarly work. Former Halifax poet laureate, Lorri is currently professor emerita at Mount Saint Vincent University and a mentor in the MFA program in Creative Nonfiction at the University of King's College. She has won awards for her innovative teaching, research, poetry, and essays. @neilsenglenn

Susan Olding is the author of *Pathologies: A Life in Essays*. Her writing has won a National Magazine Award and the Edna Staebler Award for the Personal Essay, and has appeared in *The Bellingham Review*, *The Los Angeles Review of Books*,

Maisonneuve, *The Malahat Review*, *The New Quarterly*, and the *Utne Reader*, and in anthologies including *Best Canadian Essays, 2016* and *In Fine Form, 2nd Edition*. She lives in Kingston, Ontario, where she is currently pursuing a PHD in Cultural Studies at Queen's University.

Roberta Rees's writing is described as musical and moving. Her publications include three award-winning books—*Long After Fathers*, *Beneath the Faceless Mountain*, and *Eyes Like Pigeons*—as well as many essays, poems, stories, and a thirty-minute film, *Ethyl Mermaid*. Writing awards include: the ReLit Award for Short Fiction, the Canadian Literary Award for Personal Essay, the Canadian Literary Award for Poetry, the Writers Guild of Alberta Novel Award, and the League of Canadian Poets Gerald Lampert Award. In 2018 her essay "Evie's Massage Parlour" was nominated for the James H. Gray Award for Short Nonfiction.

Julie Sedivy is a language scientist and writer of nonfiction. She has written for publications such as *Swerve*, *Literary Review of Canada*, *Nautilus*, *Discover*, *Scientific American*, and *Politico*. She is the lead author of *Sold on Language: How Advertisers Talk to You and What This Says About You* and has published a textbook about psycholinguistics. She is currently writing a scientific memoir about losing and reclaiming a native tongue, to be published by Harvard University Press. She has taught at Brown University and the University of Calgary, and now makes her home on the heart-achingly beautiful lands of Treaty 7.

Kathryn Seifert is a writer and former yarn shop owner whose work has appeared in publications including *Grain*, *Enterprise*, the *Calgary Herald*, and *Sunday Magazine*. She was a finalist for the Western Magazine Awards for her piece entitled, "Sedimentary My Dear Watson." She holds a master's in Continuing Education from the University of Calgary, with a specialty in workplace learning. Her final project focused on the use of storytelling in organizations. Kathy lives in Canmore, Alberta, where she is currently working on a novel and trying to knit her way through her epic-sized yarn stash.

Cora Siré is the author of three books. Her latest novel, *Behold Things Beautiful*, was a finalist for the Quebec Writers' Federation Paragraphe Hugh MacLennan Prize for Fiction in 2017. Her essays, short stories, and poetry have appeared in magazines such as the *Literary Review of Canada*, *Geist*, *Arc Poetry*, *The Puritan*, *Montreal Review of Books*, *carte blanche*, *Montreal Serai*, and *The Ekphrastic Review*, as well as in numerous anthologies. Based in Montreal, she often writes of elsewheres, drawing on her encounters in faraway places. For details, please visit her website, www.quena.ca.

Steven Ross Smith is a poet, prose writer, and arts journalist. His recent work appears in *GalleriesWest*, *Poets & Writers*, and *Grain*. His latest poetry book is *Emanations: Fluttertongue 6* (BookThug, Toronto). He has received the Saskatchewan Book of the Year Award (2005) and the bpNichol Chapbook Award (2006). He appears in journals, and audio and video recordings in Canada, USA, and abroad. Smith was the director of Literary Arts, Banff Centre (2008–2014) and the director of Sage Hill Writing Experience (1990–2008). He writes in Banff and on Galiano Island. Find him at: fluttertongue.ca; stevenrosssmith.com; and on Twitter @SonnyBoySmith.

Anne Sorbie holds an MA in Creative Writing from the University of Calgary. Her work has appeared in anthologies and publications such as *Nuvo*, *Alberta Views*, *Geist*, and *FreeFall* magazines and online at Brick Books, CBC Books, and Blue Skies Poetry. Anne has published two books including the novel *Memoir of a Good Death*, which was a semi-finalist for the 2012 Alberta Readers' Choice Award. In 2013 a short piece, "Thomas Horne," placed in the top 20 in the CBC Canada Writes, BloodLines competition. Her first collection of poetry, *Falling Backwards Into Mirrors*, is forthcoming with Inanna Publications (2019).

Glen Sorestad is a Saskatoon writer, best known as a widely published poet, with well over twenty poetry books and chapbooks. He was appointed Saskatchewan's first poet laureate and became Canada's first provincial poet laureate. His poetry has been published widely in many countries, has appeared in over seventy anthologies and textbooks, and has been translated into eight languages. Sorestad also writes short fiction and essays. He is a life member of both the League of Canadian Poets and the Saskatchewan Writers' Guild; in 2010, he was appointed a Member of the Order of Canada.

Kelly S. Thompson is a writer, editor, and former military officer with a master's in Creative Writing from the University of British Columbia. She won the 2014 and 2017 Barbara Novak Award for Personal Essay and the House of Anansi Press Golden Anniversary Award for fiction, and she was shortlisted for *Room* magazine's 2013 and 2014 creative nonfiction awards. Her essays have appeared in anthologies with Heritage House Press, Caitlin Press, and Simon & Schuster Canada, and her work has appeared in *Chatelaine*, *Maisonneuve*, and *Maclean's*, and is forthcoming in *carte blanche*. McClelland & Stewart will release Kelly's military memoir in 2019.

Robin van Eck's writing has appeared in *Prairie Journal*, the *Freshwater Pearls* anthology, *FreeFall Magazine*, *Alberta Views*, and other anthologies and online publications. She has several 2018 and forthcoming publications: two short stories, "Unspooled" in a crime anthology (Coffin Hop Press) and "Nicky

Nicky Nine Doors" (Woven Tale Press), and an essay, "Chasing Home," in an anthology edited by Naomi Lewis and Aaron Giovannone. She shares her world with, in no particular order, her husband, daughter, two cats, her love of words, and the Alexandra Writers' Centre, where she teaches and works.

Aritha van Herk is the author of five novels, *Judith*, *The Tent Peg*, *No Fixed Address*, *Places Far from Ellesmere*, and *Restlessness*. Her irreverent but relevant history of Alberta *Mavericks: An Incorrigible History of Alberta* frames the Alberta history exhibition at the Glenbow Museum in Calgary. With photographer George Webber she has published *In This Place: Calgary 2004–2011* and *Prairie Gothic*. Her most recent work of prose-poetry, *Stampede and the Westness of West*, appeared in 2016. She is a member of the Alberta Order of Excellence and has been honoured as one of the twenty-five most influential artists in Alberta.